Gregg Speed Building

Shorthand written
by Jerome P. Edelman

Speed Building

John Robert Gregg

Louis A. Leslie
Coauthor, Gregg Shorthand, Series 90

Charles E. Zoubek
Coauthor, Gregg Shorthand, Series 90

Kay Mendenhall
Instructor, Orem High School, Utah

Gregg Division
McGraw-Hill Book Company
New York / Atlanta / Dallas / St. Louis / San Francisco
Auckland / Bogotá / Düsseldorf / Johannesburg / London / Madrid
Mexico / Montreal / New Delhi / Panama / Paris
São Paulo / Singapore / Sydney / Tokyo / Toronto

Photo acknowledgments

Chapter openers 1, 13: Kenneth Karp. 2: Shelton/Monkmeyer. 3, 15: Jane Hamilton-Merritt. 4: Kinne/Photo Researchers, Inc. 5: Grimes/Black Star. 6: Photo Researchers, Inc. 7: Grunzweig/Photo Researchers, Inc. 8, 10: Brack/Black Star. 9: Higgins/Photo Researchers, Inc. 11: Choplin/Black Star. 12: Fann/Black Star. 14: Spain/Black Star. 16: *St. Louis Post Dispatch*/Black Star. Page 137: Bucher/Photo Researchers, Inc. 162: Courtesy Pfizer, Inc. 251: Love/Black Star. 292: Wolff/Black Star. 323: Kelly/Black Star. 353: Gillette/Photo Researchers, Inc.

Library of Congress Cataloging in Publication Data
Main entry under title:

Gregg speed building, series 90.

Includes index.
1. Shorthand—Gregg. I. Gregg, John Robert, date
Z56.G8316 1979 653'.427042'5 77-10798
ISBN 0-07-024476-6

Gregg Speed Building,
Series 90

3 4 5 6 7 8 9 0 DODO 7 8 7 6 5 4 3 2

Preface

Gregg Speed Building, Series 90, is an advanced shorthand text that has two major objectives:

1 To develop the students' ability to take dictation rapidly on a constantly expanding vocabulary.

2 To develop the students' ability to transcribe letters rapidly and accurately, letters that contain no errors in spelling and punctuation and that are attractively placed on letterheads.

Like the other volumes in Series 90, *Gregg Speed Building* is lesson planned. It is organized in 4 parts consisting of 16 chapters, which in turn are divided into 80 lessons. Each lesson contains practice material for a homework assignment of approximately 40 minutes.

Shorthand Skill Development

The students' ability to construct outlines under the stress of dictation is developed through the following carefully planned features:

CYCLE OF REVIEW DRILLS

Each of the 16 chapters contains a five-drill review cycle that covers all the major principles of Gregg Shorthand in this sequence:

First lesson **Outline Construction** These drills enable the students to take advantage of a very helpful principle for building shorthand vocabulary—analogy.

Second lesson **Recall Drill** These drills review the situations in which the alphabetic characters of Gregg Shorthand are used.

Third lesson **Word Families** These drills are another effective device for increasing the students' ability to construct outlines for unfamiliar words. The words in each family contain a common word-building problem.

Frequently Used Names These drills teach the students fluent outlines for common surnames and for first names of men and women.

Fourth lesson **Frequently Used Phrases** These drills review the most frequently used business-letter phrases.

Fifth lesson **Word Beginnings and Endings** These drills review all the word beginnings and endings of Gregg Shorthand.

BRIEF-FORM CHARTS

At the end of each of the first four chapters there is a chart of brief forms and derivatives. Near the back of the text is a complete chart of the brief forms given in alphabetic order.

CONNECTED PRACTICE MATERIAL

Each lesson in *Gregg Speed Building, Series 90,* contains a wealth of connected practice material. The material consists of modern, representative business letters and articles that have been selected not only for their shorthand value but for their informative content as well. The connected practice material within each chapter is devoted to a specific line of business or to a specific industry and is presented in three forms:

1 **Reading and Writing Practice** Each of the 80 lessons has a Reading and Writing Practice in shorthand.

2 **Writing Practice** Each second, third, and fourth lesson contains a Writing Practice consisting of several letters in type. The letters are counted in such a way that the teacher may dictate them either separately, to develop speed by short spurts, or consecutively, to develop endurance. Each Writing Practice is preceded by a shorthand preview.

3 **Progressive Speed Builder** The fifth lesson of each chapter contains a Progressive Speed Builder designed to force the students' speed. The Progressive Speed Builder consists of five 1-minute letters (preceded by a shorthand preview) counted at progressively increasing speeds.

The letters within each Progressive Speed Builder relate to the same transaction and contain substantially the same vocabulary. Consequently, after the students have taken the first letter from dictation, their problem in taking the succeeding letters at faster speeds is simplified.

Transcription Skill Development

The students' ability to handle the nonshorthand factors of transcription is developed through the following features:

Punctuation and Typing Style In Chapters 1 through 4 the punctuation and typing style pointers presented earlier in the students' stenographic course are reviewed. In Chapter 5 more advanced points are presented. In every Reading and Writing Practice, punctuation marks are circled and a brief explanation of the reason for the use of each mark is indicated directly above the mark.

Spelling Words that often cause transcription difficulty have been selected from the Reading and Writing Practice exercises and appear in type in the margins of the shorthand.

Vocabulary Building Many of the lessons contain a Business Vocabulary Builder, which gives words or expressions from the connected practice material that may be unfamiliar to the students. These words and expressions are defined briefly as they are used in the practice material.

The first lesson of each chapter, beginning with Chapter 6, contains a Similar-Words Drill, which alerts the students to pairs of words that stenographers often mistranscribe because of similarity of sound.

Accuracy Practice The second lesson of each chapter, beginning with Chapter 6, contains an Accuracy Practice, which stresses the importance of proper proportion.

Secretarial Tips Throughout the book the students will find secretarial tips that provide information that will be helpful to them when they become secretaries.

Other Features

Model Letters The student is supplied with several letter models that show the most common letter styles used in business.

Part Openings Each of the parts opens with a discussion of some phase of shorthand speed development or transcription and gives the student helpful suggestions on such topics as self-dictation, devising shortcuts, and so on.

Photographs That Teach Many photographs of "office workers in action" appear throughout the book. The photographs not only brighten the appearance of the book but also teach the students something about office work.

Supplementary Letters

In the *Instructor's Handbook for Gregg Speed Building,* there are supplementary letters for each of the 80 lessons in the text. The letters for each lesson in the handbook are replies to or are related to the letters in the corresponding text lesson. Addresses to be used by the students when transcribing these letters are provided on pages 442-446 of the text.

The authors are confident that *Gregg Speed Building, Series 90,* will enable teachers to do an even more effective job of developing rapid and efficient transcribers.

The Publishers

Contents

PART

Practice in Self-Dictation

A major factor in your shorthand speed development is large quantities of the right kind of dictation. The more dictation practice you get, the more rapidly will your shorthand speed increase.

Of course, you will receive a great deal of dictation practice in class, and it is there that your greatest growth will take place.

However, you can supplement that class dictation with additional practice at home. There are a number of ways in which you can obtain this additional dictation practice:

1 **Ask a member of your family to act as dictator.** This, however, has some disadvantages. A member of the family may not be available when you want to practice, and an inexperienced dictator may retard rather than increase your shorthand speed.

2 **Use the television or the radio.** In general, people on television and radio speak too rapidly, with the result that your efforts in trying to keep up with them may be discouraging. However, you may occasionally be able to tune in someone who speaks approximately at your dictation speed.

3 **Use records and tapes.** This is by far the most satisfactory way to obtain home dictation practice. There is available today a large selection of dictation records and tapes. Their use has definite advantages. You can choose records and tapes that contain dictation within the range of speed that you are writing, and the material on them is read by experienced dictators. Ask your teacher about the dictation records and tapes that are available.

4 **Use the "self-dictation" method that will enable you to practice by yourself.** Here are the steps you should follow:

a Select a magazine or other reading matter that is printed in a fairly large-size type. (Full-page advertisements in some of the leading national magazines are ideal for this purpose.) Select material that deals with many different types of subject matter—cars, radios, books, airplanes, and so on—so that you will get the widest possible vocabulary.

b Read through the material quickly to be sure that you can write the outlines for all the words. If you find you do not know the outlines for some of the words, look up those words in the *Gregg Shorthand Dictionary* or construct an outline of your own. By eliminating the stumbling blocks, you will be able to write continuously as you dictate to yourself.

c Read the material aloud at the fastest rate that you can write fairly good notes, and write on the copy itself, slightly below the words that you read. The exact point at which you write each outline is not important.

This type of self-dictation may seem a little strange to you during the first few attempts, but you will soon be able to adjust your self-dictation to the speed that you can write.

d After you have self-dictated the material once, re-dictate it a second time, faster. Write over the outlines that you originally wrote.

e Occasionally dictate a piece of material slowly, striving for perfection of outline rather than for increase of speed.

Occasionally when you want to practice at home, try this method of self-dictation; you will be pleased with the effect it will have on your shorthand writing speed.

Both newspapers and the weekly or monthly magazines are so often taken for granted. Many people have little idea of the work that goes into any printed page.

The first job in getting together a printed page belongs to the editors. The editors must decide what articles and pictures they want to go into their particular magazine and then get the articles written and the pictures taken. Then the typist must prepare the manuscript, being careful that the length of each article is appropriate. Then an array of people discuss the way each article is to be presented and the sequence the articles will take.

The copy is then marked up and the pictures engraved. The next phase of the job is the printer's. The printer carefully checks all the markings the editor has made on the copy. Then the typesetting machine is set accordingly.

Some type is set by a machine that is similar to a typewriter; however, much of the typesetting today is done by computer. The computer actually gauges the length of the line and divides words correctly by means of an extensive vocabulary in its memory bank. When the job of typesetting is completed, the proof is carefully read by the editors before it is prepared for final publication.

Illustration of self-dictation

Home Furnishings and Maintenance

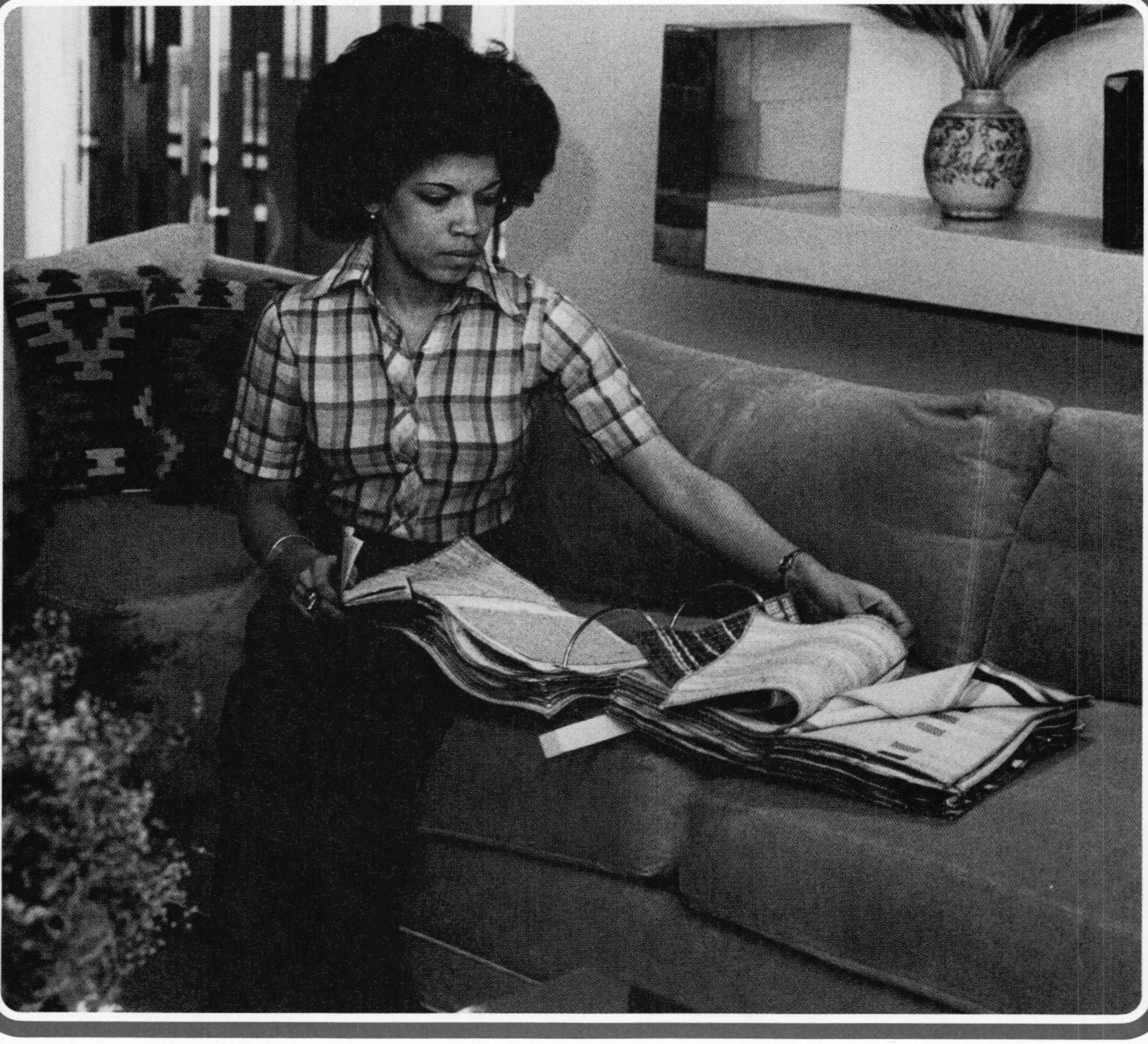

Punctuation Brushup

The objective of *Gregg Speed Building, Series 90,* is to build your shorthand and transcription speed while continuing to improve your ability to spell and punctuate. Chapters 1 through 5 will review the points of punctuation and typing style that you studied in earlier volumes of Series 90 to be sure that you have not forgotten them. Chapter 6 will introduce you to more advanced points of punctuation and typing style that you have not previously studied.

Punctuation marks will be identified for you in each Reading and Writing Practice exercise in *Gregg Speed Building.* They will be circled and printed in a second color with the reason for their use indicated above the circles. Spelling words will also appear in a second color both in the margins and in the shorthand.

HOW TO PRACTICE PUNCTUATION

1 Read each punctuation rule that follows to make sure you understand it. Then, study the examples.

2 As you come to punctuation in the Reading and Writing Practice, stop long enough to ensure that you understand why the mark is used. Note any you do not understand so that you can ask your teacher about them the next day.

3 Make a shorthand copy of the Reading and Writing Practice. As you copy, insert the punctuation marks in your notes.

SPELLING

1 In the Reading and Writing Practice you will occasionally find shorthand outlines printed in a second color. These outlines represent words that secretaries often misspell. When you encounter one of these outlines, finish reading the sentence in which it occurs; then glance at the margin, where you will find the word in type, properly syllabicated.

2 Spell the word, aloud if possible, pausing slightly after each word division. This helps to impress the correct spelling on your mind.

The lessons of Chapter 1 will review the following 11 common uses of the comma:

par ,

, parenthetical

A word, phrase, or clause that is not necessary to the grammatical completeness of the thought of the sentence should be set off by commas. If the expression occurs at the end of a sentence, only one comma is needed.

We think, however, that we should finish the course first.
We are not in a position to help you, Ms. James.

ap ,

, apposition

Expressions that identify or explain other expressions should be set off by commas. If the expression occurs at the end of a sentence, only one comma is needed.

Mr. Agronski, my assistant, will attend the meeting.
Miss Tatum will be home on Thursday, June 2.

ser ,

, series

When the last member of a series of three or more items is preceded by a coordinating conjunction (*and, or,* or *nor*), place a comma before the conjunction as well as between the other items.

We need to purchase paper, pencils, and other office supplies.
We will not be in town January 1, 2, or 3.

conj ,

, conjunction

A comma is used to separate two independent clauses that are joined by a coordinating conjunction.

Our manufacturing department tells us that the product is poorly designed, and we need suggestions on how to improve it.
I think I can attend the game with you, but I will not be sure until tomorrow.

and o ,

, and omitted

When two or more consecutive adjectives modify the same noun, separate the adjectives by commas.

Lee is a quiet, efficient person.

The comma is not used, however, if the first adjective modifies the combined idea of the second adjective plus the noun.

The package was wrapped in beautiful blue paper.

nonr

, nonrestrictive

A nonrestrictive, or nonessential, clause or phrase—one that can be omitted without changing the meaning of a sentence—should be set off by commas.

Allison Mason, who has been with the organization several years, will head the committee.

, when clause when

, if clause if

, as clause as

, introductory intro

A comma is used to separate a dependent clause from a following main clause.
A comma is also used after such introductory expressions as *frankly, consequently, in addition.*

When I have the information, I will send you a note.
As you know, Friday is a holiday.
If you need more time, you may have it.
Before I leave on vacation, I will finish the report.
Frankly, I think we made several mistakes.
In addition, you added the column of figures incorrectly.

geo

, geographical expressions

Place a comma between the name of a city and state.

Janice moved to Alexandria, Virginia.

If the name of the state does not end the sentence, place a comma after it also.

Next week I will travel to our Salem, Massachusetts, office.

Developing Shorthand Writing Power

1 OUTLINE CONSTRUCTION

In each chapter the first lesson contains a number of principles of outline construction. Your ability to construct outlines will depend in large part on your ability to apply these principles.

Use the following procedure when you practice the lists of words below and those in succeeding lessons:

- 1 Cover the type key and read the shorthand outlines.
- 2 When you encounter an outline you cannot read, spell it.
- 3 If the spelling does not give you the meaning of the outline within a few seconds, refer to the type key. It should take you no more than a minute or two to read any word or phrase list in *Gregg Speed Building.*

Vowel Written In -ance, -ence The vowel is written in the word endings *-ance, -ence* when those endings follow *i, n, r,* or *l.*

I

1

N

2

R

3

L

4

1. *Appliance, reliance, self-reliance, compliance, science.*
2. *Maintenance, dominance, finance, prominence.*
3. *Insurance, appearance, assurance, clearance, reference, conference.*
4. *Resemblance, balance, violence, silence, excellence.*

Vowel Omitted In -ance, -ence The vowel in the word endings *-ance, -ence* is omitted in the following words because its omission gives much more fluent, legible outlines.

-ance

1

-ence

2

1. *Allowance, accordance, acquaintance, annoyance, disturbance.*
2. *Intelligence, absence, influence, independence, essence, negligence.*

Building Transcription Skills

2 BUSINESS VOCABULARY BUILDER The Business Vocabulary Builders improve your command of business terminology. The more familiar you become with business words, the easier it will be to take dictation and to transcribe. Study each Business Vocabulary Builder so that you understand the meanings of the words and expressions used in the Reading and Writing Practice.

Business Vocabulary Builder

precautions Safeguards.

reprint Something printed again; a copy.

concealed *(adjective)* Hidden.

● Reading and Writing Practice

Reading and writing a great deal of well-written shorthand, such as that in the Reading and Writing Practice exercises, will help your shorthand skill grow quickly because it impresses in your mind the correct joinings of alphabetic strokes in many different combinations.

3 Modern Home Appliances

Be sure

[202]

4 LETTERS

50

ap·pli·ance

of·fer·ing

intro

vac·u·um

ad·di·tion

par

al·low·ance

ex·cel·lence

main·ten·ance

quiet

and o

ser

san·i·tary

if

[161]

5

as

ap

geo

ap

as·sur·ance

sat·is·fied

intro

re·ar·ranged

conj

bal·ance

par

ap·pre·ci·ate

conj

con·tin·u·a·tion

[136]

6

as

de·stroys

in·sur·ance pol·i·cies

ser

if

can·celed

nonr

con·cealed

conj

210

tax-de·duct·ible

when

if

prompt·ly

[135]

LESSON 2

Developing Shorthand Writing Power

7 RECALL DRILL s

This drill illustrates various situations in which the *s* stroke is used in Gregg Shorthand. Read from the shorthand, referring to the key whenever you cannot immediately read an outline.

Self-, Circum-

1 

Super-

2 

Sub-

3 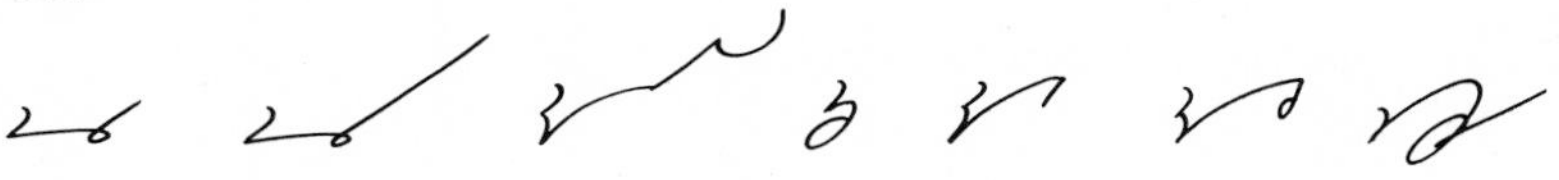

-ings

4 

Percent

5 

---

1. *Self-assurance, self-reliance, self-made, selfish, circumstances, circumstantial.*
2. *Superintendent, supervise, supervision, supersede, superhuman, superior.*
3. *Submit, submitted, substandard, subway, substantial, substantially, subdivide.*
4. *Hearings, workings, holdings, makings, feelings, proceedings, sayings.*
5. *10 percent, 25 percent, 100 percent, 80 percent, 90 percent, 78 percent.*

Building Transcription Skills

8 Business Vocabulary Builder

initially At the beginning.

dispute *(noun)* Problem; trouble.

indestructible Impossible to destroy.

Writing Practice

The second, third, and fourth lessons of each chapter include business letters in type. To make it easier for you to take the letters from dictation, previews in shorthand of the more difficult words and phrases that occur in those letters are provided.

Follow the procedures for practice given in paragraph 1 of Lesson 1 to obtain the greatest benefit from the previews. In addition, make one shorthand copy of the entire list.

9 PREVIEW

The numbers before each line in the preview refer to the letters that follow. Before you take the dictation from letter 10 , for example, practice the words and phrases in the preview line which starts with the number 10 .

☐ 10

☐ 11

☐ 12

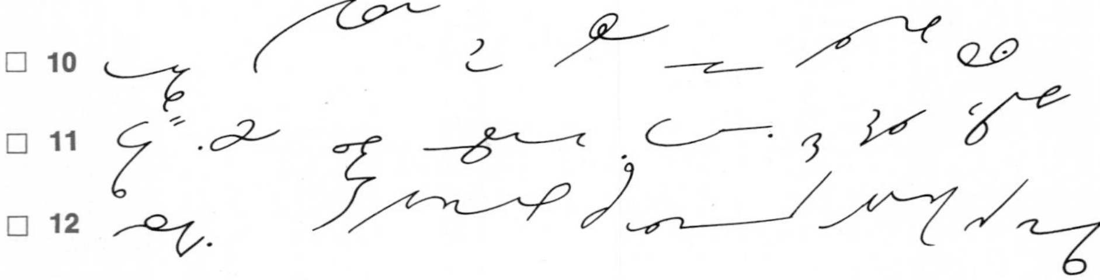

10 *Lopez, temperature, superior, dial, moment, degrees, area.*
11 *Probably, aware, inexpensive, materials, plumbing, yourself, substitute, self-addressed.*
12 *Carpeting, discoloration, heavily, recommend, indestructible, your order, you will be able.*

LETTERS

Note: Each small raised number represents 20 standard words.

10

Dear Ms. Lopez: Would you like to have the same convenient temperature control in your car that you have in your home?[1] You can have this control if you install a Superior air-conditioning unit.

Here is the way the unit[2] works. You set the dial to the temperature you desire and press a button. From that moment on, the temperature[3] level in your car will never vary more than a few degrees.

The Superior air-conditioning unit[4] is easy to install and is priced substantially lower than competing models.

Stop by our showroom when you[5] are in the area. We will be happy to give you a demonstration of the Superior. Sincerely,[6]

11

Dear Miss Billings: If you are building a new home, you are probably aware of the many inexpensive plumbing[7] materials that are being advertised. These materials may save you 10 to 15 percent initially,[8] but they could cost you a great deal more in the long run. You owe it to yourself, Miss Billings, to install copper[9] plumbing in your new home.

Over the years, copper plumbing will actually save you money. Because it is[10] substantially stronger and lasts longer than the cheaper substitute materials, your plumbing bills will be kept to[11] a minimum.

If you would like to have more information about the benefits of copper plumbing, just fill[12] out the enclosed form and return it to us in the stamped, self-addressed envelope that is provided. Yours truly,[13]

12

Dear Mr. Hastings: Take just a moment to look at the carpeting in your home. Are there places where your carpeting[14] shows discoloration and wear? Are there spots in heavily traveled areas? Have you often wished these[15] particular areas were not carpeted? If the answer to these questions is yes, we recommend that you[16] consider the installation of General tile.

General tile is beautiful, easy to clean, and practically[17] indestructible. Under normal circumstances, it will last as long as your home does.

We are now having a[18] special sale on General tile at the Home Center. If you place your order with us before the end of February,[19] you will be able to save up to 25 percent of the regular cost.

Miss Mary Jennings, who[20] is our representative in your area, will be happy to bring a sample of General tile to your[21] home. To arrange for an appointment, just fill out and mail the self-addressed card that is enclosed. Very truly yours,[22]

[440]

Reading and Writing Practice

13

plumb·ing

par

cus·tom·ers

al·le·vi·ate

intro

sit·u·a·tion

buy·ers

ap

for·eign

fa·vor·ably

mer·chan·dise

if

[150]

14

man·u·fac·tur·ing

ad·vance

prom·i·nent

when

loss

nonr

of·fer·ing

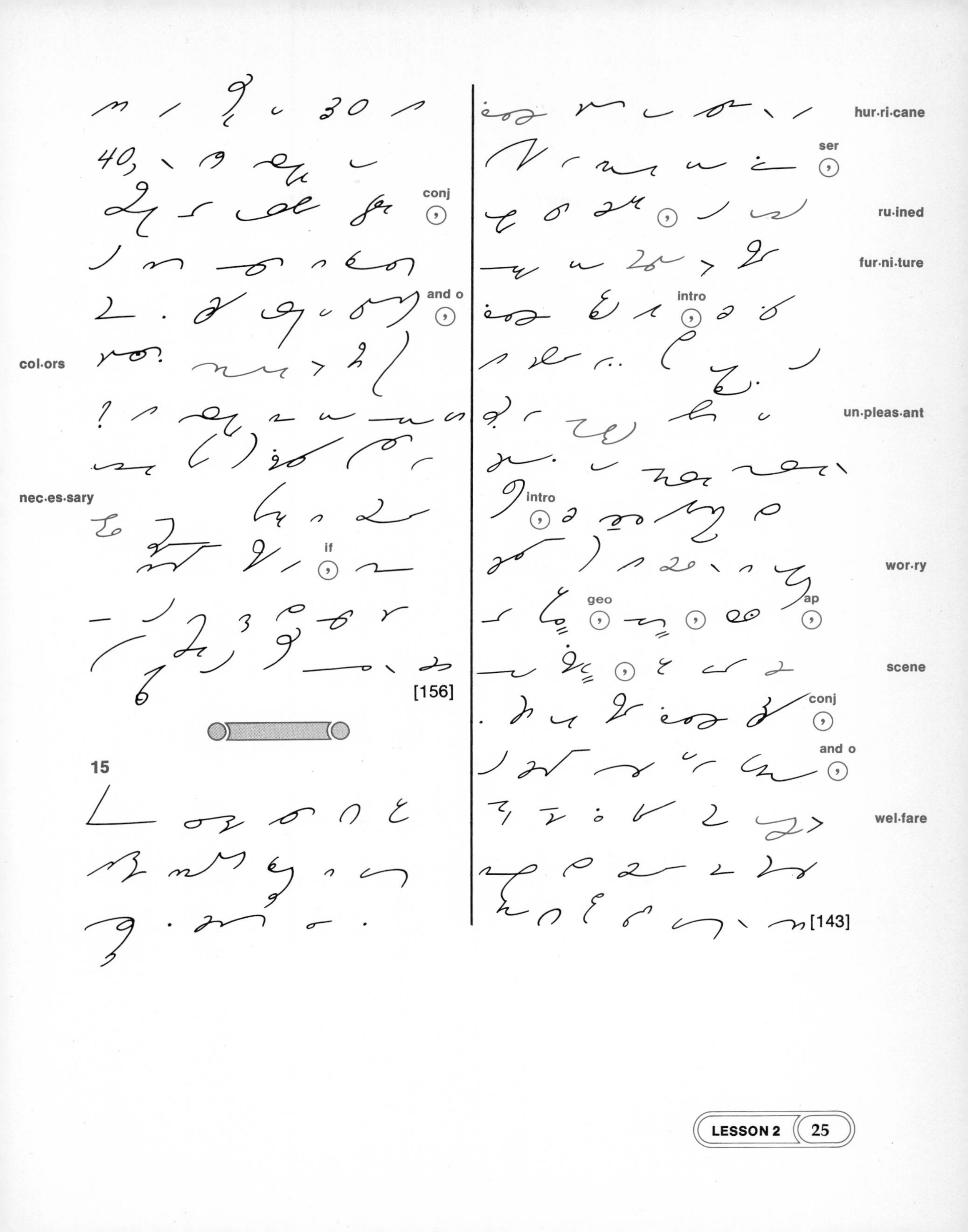

conj

and o

col·ors

nec·es·sary

if

[156]

15

hur·ri·cane

ser

ru·ined

fur·ni·ture

intro

un·pleas·ant

intro

wor·ry

geo

ap

scene

conj

and o

wel·fare

[143]

Developing Shorthand Writing Power

16 WORD FAMILIES

Notice that the words in each family below have a common element. You can take advantage of analogy in constructing shorthand outlines for new words.

In the third lesson of each chapter you will find a number of word families. Read the shorthand words in each family, referring to the key if you cannot read a word.

1. *Amount, count, account, accountant, discount, paramount.*
2. *Sure, assure, treasure, pleasure, reassure, leisure, pressure.*

17 FREQUENTLY USED NAMES

In the third lesson of each chapter you will also find a number of frequently used last names and frequently used women's or men's first names.

Read through the list, referring to the key whenever you cannot immediately read a name. You will find some of these names used in the practice material of this lesson.

Last Names

1

Women's First Names

2

1. *Baker, Armstrong, Smith, Brown, Tucker, Anderson.*
2. *Ann, Mary, Jane, Sally, Marilyn, Barbara.*

Building Transcription Skills

18 Business Vocabulary Builder

ensure To make certain or safe.

arduous Difficult; strenuous.

Writing Practice

19 PREVIEW

☐ 20

☐ 21

☐ 22

20 *Modern, techniques, alter, patterns, efficient, yes, everything, return, to us.*
21 *Custom, draperies, personalized, employs, next time, to give you.*
22 *Forget, furniture, families, relocation, to survey, gathered, paramount.*

LETTERS

20

Dear Miss Tucker: Would you like to learn to sew using the most modern techniques? Would you like to learn how to alter[1] patterns to make garments that fit perfectly? Would you like to learn to use the most efficient sewing machines on[2] the market today?

If your answer is yes, you should enroll in our new sewing course that covers everything from[3] choosing the proper pattern size to finishing the hem. You will learn many tricks of the trade that will make sewing[4] a real pleasure.

The first class will be held at our store on Saturday, February 27. To enroll,[5] fill out the enclosed form and return it to us with your check in the amount of $20. Sincerely yours,[6]

21

Dear Mrs. Brown: Fifteen years ago Mary's Custom Draperies opened its doors for business in a tiny shop.[7] Business was slow in those days, but Mary did everything possible to ensure that all customers could count on[8] receiving the personalized service they deserved.

Today, Mary's Custom Draperies employs 23 tailors,[9] 5 full-time sales representatives, and 6 installers. Mary is still at the helm of the business, and she[10] still firmly believes that the customer deserves only the best.

The next time you need new draperies for your home,[11] call Mary. You can count on her to give you the personalized service you want and deserve. Very truly yours,[12]

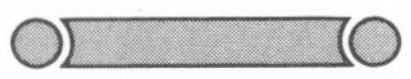

22

Dear Mr. Smith: Some movers forget something when they move furniture. They forget about the people who own the[13] furniture. We at National Vans believe your family is more important than anything we move.

Last year[14] we made it our business to learn even more about families that move and their needs during the period of[15] relocation. In cooperation with a major research organization, we corresponded with many[16] people to survey the effects of moving on their families. Thanks to excellent responses, we gathered[17] a great deal of important data that we try to apply to every family we move.

The next time you move,[18] call us. Families are of paramount importance to us. We move people, not just furniture. Cordially yours,[19] [380]

Reading and Writing Practice

23

re·al·ize

out·doors

ser

intro

bu·sy

suf·fi·cient

fam·i·lies

as

ma·jor

oc·cu·pies

ar·ea

ar·du·ous

rea·son·able

conj

555-1851 if

en·joy·able

and o

[186]

24

Mas·sa·chu·setts

geo

dec·o·rat·ing

when

spe·cial·ize

intro

nonr

416

ware·house

con·ve·nience

if

par

[118]

Model Letters

1 Short letter—double spaced, semiblocked style, standard punctuation.

2 Short letter—single spaced, blocked style, standard punctuation with postscript.

3 Average-length letter, blocked style with attention line, standard punctuation.

4 Long letter, blocked style, standard punctuation.

5 Interoffice memorandum.

6 Two-page letter, simplified style.

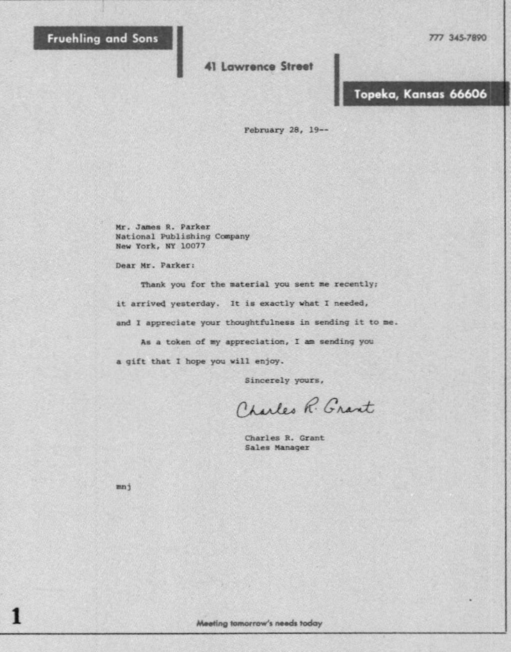

Fruehling and Sons

41 Lawrence Street

Topeka, Kansas 66606

777 345-7890

February 28, 19--

Mr. James R. Parker
National Publishing Company
New York, NY 10077

Dear Mr. Parker:

Thank you for the material you sent me recently; it arrived yesterday. It is exactly what I needed, and I appreciate your thoughtfulness in sending it to me.

As a token of my appreciation, I am sending you a gift that I hope you will enjoy.

Sincerely yours,

Charles R. Grant

Charles R. Grant
Sales Manager

mnj

Meeting tomorrow's needs today

1

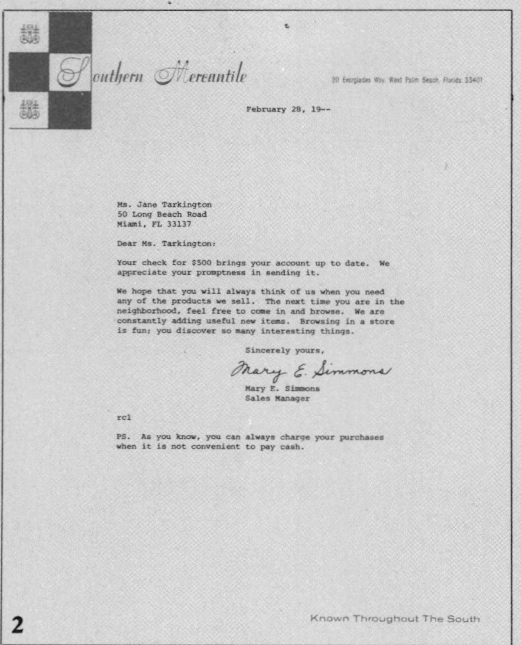

Southern Mercantile

20 Everglades Way, West Palm Beach, Florida 33401

February 28, 19--

Ms. Jane Tarkington
50 Long Beach Road
Miami, FL 33137

Dear Ms. Tarkington:

Your check for $500 brings your account up to date. We appreciate your promptness in sending it.

We hope that you will always think of us when you need any of the products we sell. The next time you are in the neighborhood, feel free to come in and browse. We are constantly adding useful new items. Browsing in a store is fun; you discover so many interesting things.

Sincerely yours,

Mary E. Simmons

Mary E. Simmons
Sales Manager

rcl

PS. As you know, you can always charge your purchases when it is not convenient to pay cash.

Known Throughout The South

2

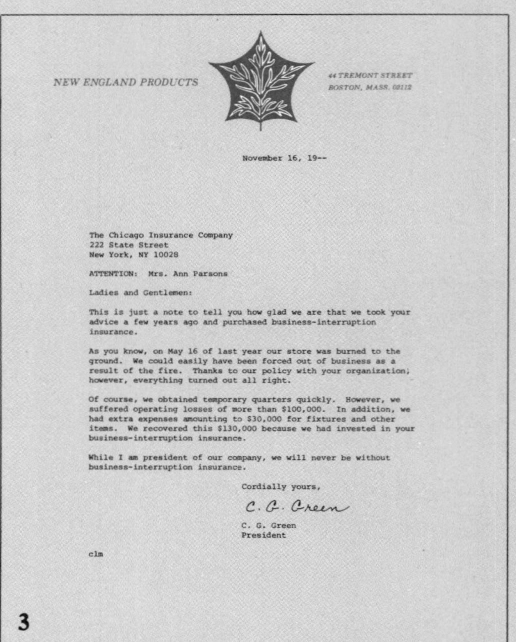

NEW ENGLAND PRODUCTS

44 TREMONT STREET
BOSTON, MASS. 02112

November 16, 19--

The Chicago Insurance Company
222 State Street
New York, NY 10028

ATTENTION: Mrs. Ann Parsons

Ladies and Gentlemen:

This is just a note to tell you how glad we are that we took your advice a few years ago and purchased business-interruption insurance.

As you know, on May 16 of last year our store was burned to the ground. We could easily have been forced out of business as a result of the fire. Thanks to our policy with your organization, however, everything turned out all right.

Of course, we obtained temporary quarters quickly. However, we suffered operating losses of more than $100,000. In addition, we had extra expenses amounting to $30,000 for fixtures and other items. We recovered this $130,000 because we had invested in your business-interruption insurance.

While I am president of our company, we will never be without business-interruption insurance.

Cordially yours,

C. G. Green

C. G. Green
President

clm

3

29 EAST CANYON AVENUE, SANTA FE, NEW MEXICO 87501

Cable: SPLAGAR

SPLANE & GARDNER, INC.

TEL. 445-7890

April 14, 19--

Mrs. Charles R. Gray
3313 Western Parkway
Santa Fe, NM 87501

Dear Mrs. Gray:

I must make a confession. When I came here last fall to take over the Santa Fe branch of Johnson and Company, I was sure that it would be easy to sell a great deal of furniture in a short time. The sight of the homes here in Santa Fe must have caused me to be overoptimistic.

In anticipation of the sales that I expected, I bought large quantities of fine furniture. In spite of the quality of the furniture and the appeal of our low prices, however, sales fell far below my expectations. Now I have a warehouse full of furniture that must be moved. What's more, there are new shipments on the way from several manufacturers.

The time for action has come. On Saturday, May 6, you will see in all the Santa Fe papers an announcement of stock-disposal sales. Prices will be low. In many cases, our furniture will be offered at cost and even less. Of course, we expect a great response. Because of this, I feel that you and a few other preferred customers should have the opportunity to shop in comfort before a public announcement is made of the sale.

Therefore, please consider this a personal invitation for you to shop at your convenience on May 3, 4, or 5. When you come, please give the enclosed card to one of our sales representatives.

Very truly yours,

Martin J. Foster

Martin J. Foster
Manager

re
Enclosure

4

inter-office memorandum

To	F. J. Marvin	From	A. R. Smith
Dept. or Pub.	Personnel Department	Dept. or Pub.	Foreign Department
Floor or Branch	4	Floor and Ext. or Branch	18
Subject	Job Replacement	Date	May 20, 19--

My assistant, Ms. Helen A. Jones, has just informed me that she is to leave the company on June 15. She is moving to France.

If it is possible, I would like to get someone to fill the vacancy immediately so that Ms. Jones can help in training the new person.

As you know, most of my correspondence is with customers in South and Central America. Consequently, it would be a great help to me if you could find a person who has some degree of proficiency in Spanish.

I will be in Cleveland on May 21 and 22, but I will be back on the morning of May 23. I will be able to interview anyone you send me after my return.

A. R. S.

bh

5

982 Underwood Avenue • New Orleans • Louisiana 70101

February 22, 19--

Mrs. Leona R. Strong, President
Harrison Manufacturing Company
4125 North Fifth Avenue
Denver, CO 80208

EMPLOYEES' HANDBOOKS

I am sending you today by express all the material that we have available on how to prepare an employees' handbook.

You will be interested, I am sure, in our experience in helping the Martin Miller Company prepare its latest handbook. When we were called in, that company already had a handbook, but it was out of date. The organization had grown considerably since that handbook was prepared; consequently, the handbook had to be completely rewritten. The new handbook was ready at the end of last year. It benefited by many lessons that had been learned during the work on the first handbook.

While working with the Martin Miller Company, we learned that the following three points are important in preparing a handbook:

1. It should not be a rule book listing things that should and should not be done by employees.

2. It should take advantage of the pleasant feeling of satisfaction with which an employee starts a new job. The handbook should play a definite part in maintaining that feeling of satisfaction.

3. It should set down facts that will make employees feel that they are important parts of the company. It should give them information on every phase of the company's organization and activities.

In the first edition of the handbook we tried to put in a section that was devoted to the history of the company. We had often felt a need for this. We also felt that this objective was not covered fully enough in the first handbook. This handbook was prepared with the employee exclusively in mind.

6 *Superior service for generations*

Mrs. Leona R. Strong 2 February 22, 19--

These are just a few thoughts that come to me at this time. I am sure that the Martin Miller Company would be glad to send you a copy of their new handbook. I believe that you may find many suggestions in it that you would be able to use when you prepare your handbook.

Needless to say, we are at your service. If you think that a visit with one of our representatives would be helpful, please call us. We will be glad to arrange an appointment.

R. L. Kane

R. L. Kane - VICE PRESIDENT, MARKETING SERVICES

irt

6

Developing Shorthand Writing Power

25 FREQUENTLY USED PHRASES

Illustrations of useful phrasing principles are presented in the fourth lesson of each chapter. You are already familiar with these phrases, so only a quick review is necessary. You should be able to read the lines below in half a minute or less.

Want

1

To

2

1. *I want, you want, we want, if you want, he wants, do you want, who wanted.*
2. *To be, to have, to see, to say, to plan, to paint, to blame, to share.*

26 GEOGRAPHICAL EXPRESSIONS

The fourth lesson in each chapter also contains a list of geographical expressions. You will find a number of these geographical expressions in the practice material of this lesson and of the following lessons.

The list is divided into three parts—names of cities containing a common beginning or ending, names of states, and names of foreign countries or foreign cities.

Read through the list quickly.

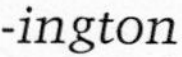

-ington

1

States

2

Foreign Countries

3

1. *Lexington, Washington, Wilmington, Arlington, Burlington.*
2. *California, Oregon, New Jersey, Connecticut, Kentucky, Tennessee, Alabama.*
3. *Italy, France, Rumania, Spain, Russia, Germany.*

Building Transcription Skills

27 Business Vocabulary Builder

scientifically Systematically determined through a study or experiment.

economical Thrifty; frugal.

remnant An unsold or unused end of piece goods.

conservation A careful preservation of something; planned management of a natural resource.

● Writing Practice

28 PREVIEW

☐ **29**

☐ **30**

☐ **31**

29 *Furnace, trouble, to be sure, scientifically, throughout, to make, performance, economical.*
30 *Quality, you want, to participate, hundreds, remnants, we hope you will, outstanding.*
31 *Emphasis, energy, conservation, American, obligation, few minutes, evaluating.*

LETTERS

29

Dear Mr. Bates: Has your furnace been giving you trouble lately? If it has, perhaps it needs a change of oil—[1] a change to California oil.

California oil is always a clean-burning oil. To be sure that it is, we[2] test it scientifically before we deliver it to your home. It has been tested in homes throughout California,[3] Oregon, and Washington to make sure it gives the best performance possible.

When you heat with our oil,[4] you use a fuel that is safe and economical. When you need oil, remember California oil. Sincerely,[5]

30

Dear Mr. Harrington: Are you getting just a little tired of increasing costs and decreasing quality in[6] many of the things you want to buy for your home? If you are, we would like to offer you a chance to participate[7] in one of the largest carpet sales ever conducted in Seattle, Washington.

We have purchased hundreds[8] of carpets and carpet remnants from a large manufacturer, and these items will be on sale in our main showroom[9] beginning next week. The prices will be much lower than you would ever expect.

We hope you will take advantage[10] of this outstanding sale by planning to be with us when our doors open next Monday. Very cordially yours,[11]

31

Dear Member: With so much emphasis being placed on energy conservation these days, the American Home[12] Association has been working hard to find ways to help our members save fuel.

Our research department has[13] recently published a guide on energy conservation. We are sending you a copy of this guide as a[14] consumer service at no cost or obligation. Our only request is that you read the material carefully[15] and apply those suggestions that might help you conserve energy in your home.

We want to emphasize that a[16] few minutes' time spent in evaluating your own use of energy now could save you hundreds of dollars over[17] the next few years. Please take a few minutes right now to read the guide. You will be glad you did. Very truly yours,[18] [360]

Reading and Writing Practice

32

con·do·min·i·um

Con·nec·ti·cut

geo

over·whelm·ing

intro

when

com·ple·tion

conj

va·ri·ety

pol·lu·tion

if

par

[169]

33

ap

15

8

re·pair·ing

nonr

145

ser

intro

board

if

and o

[154]

34

ap

guar·an·tee

ser

peel

intro

intro

intro

ex·cept

re·paint·ing

intro

[105]

Developing Shorthand Writing Power

35 WORD BEGINNINGS AND ENDINGS

A review of selected word beginnings and/or endings is presented in the fifth lesson of each chapter. You should be able to read all the words in 30 seconds or less.

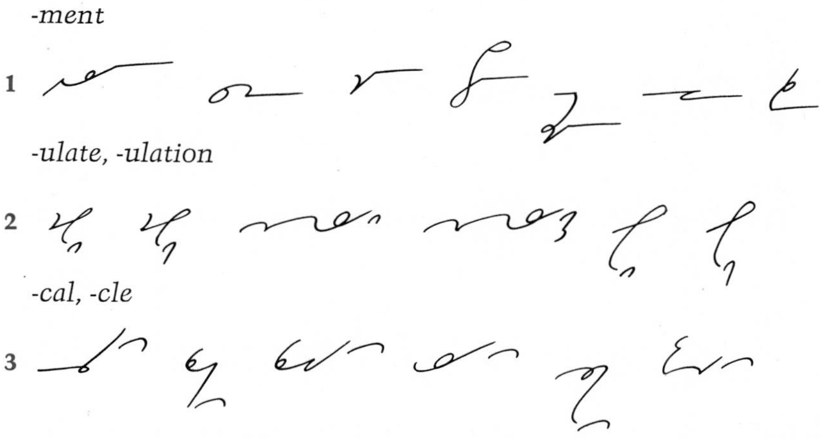

1. *Treatment, acknowledgment, statement, abatement, investment, moment, shipment.*
2. *Stipulate, stipulation, congratulate, congratulations, tabulate, tabulation.*
3. *Medical, surgical, periodical, radical, cubicle, spectacle.*

Building Transcription Skills

36 Business Vocabulary Builder

conspire To plot; to agree secretly.
distribution center Central warehouse.
sterling silver An alloy of almost pure silver.
tracer An investigation or inquiry.

Progressive Speed Builder (50-90)

The fifth lesson in each chapter contains a Progressive Speed Builder, the purpose of which is to force you to write faster.

Practice the preview for the Progressive Speed Builder by reading it, with the help of the key when necessary, and making a shorthand copy of it. The number preceding each preview line refers to the corresponding number of one of the five letters or memorandums that follow.

These letters, all of which are related to the same transaction, will probably be dictated to you by your teacher. The first letter is counted for dictation at 50 words a minute; the second, at 60; the third, at 70; the fourth, at 80; and the fifth, at 90. You should find the first two or three letters quite easy, but you will have to work a little harder on the fourth and fifth.

Your goal is to get something down for every word, even though the legibility of your outlines may suffer a little as the speed increases.

37 PREVIEW

38 *Purchased, August, delivered, today, has not yet, shipped, cancel.*
39 *Via, trucking, have been, by this time, immediate, tracer, touch, in a position.*
40 *Reports, however, distribution, center, it has been, September, if you will.*
41 *Unfortunately, uncrated, of course, condition, replace, as soon as possible, certainly.*
42 *You have been, difficulty, your order, occasionally, conspire, completion, replacement, we hope.*

LETTERS

Note: The first diagonal mark indicates the end of a quarter minute's dictation; two diagonal marks, the end of a half minute's dictation; three diagonal marks, the end of three-quarters of a minute's dictation; the number after each letter, the end of a minute's dictation.

38

[1 minute at 50]

Gentlemen: When I purchased one of your Model 18 lamps on August/18, the sales clerk told me that it would be delivered in about//ten days. Today is September 1, and the lamp has not yet arrived. Has///the lamp been shipped? If it has not, please cancel my order. Yours truly, [1]

39

[1 minute at 60]

Dear Mrs. Gates: Your Model 18 lamp was shipped via the National Trucking/Company on August 19. The lamp should, therefore, have been delivered by this time.

We//are starting an immediate tracer and will get in touch with you again when we///are in a position to give you a definite report. Very sincerely yours, [2]

40

[1 minute at 70]

Dear Mrs. Gates: The National Trucking Company reports that they tried to deliver your lamp/ on August 20. When their truck arrived, however, there was no one at home. The lamp was taken back//to the company's distribution center, where it has been lying since August 20.

The company///will deliver your lamp on September 8 if you will be at home on that day. Yours truly, [3]

41

[1 minute at 80]

Gentlemen: The National Trucking Company delivered my Model 18 lamp on September 8./ Unfortunately, when I uncrated the shipment on September 9, I found that the shade had been badly torn in//several places. I cannot, of course, accept the lamp in that condition. Please arrange to pick up the lamp and///replace it with a new one as soon as possible.

This order has certainly been a problem. Sincerely yours, [4]

42

[1 minute at 90]

Dear Mrs. Gates: We are very sorry that you have been having so much difficulty with your order for one of our Model/18 lamps. Occasionally, everything seems to conspire against the satisfactory completion of a customer's//order.

Today we sent you a replacement for the damaged lamp you received. We have crated the lamp with extreme care so that///it should arrive in good condition.

We hope, Mrs. Gates, that you derive a great deal of satisfaction from your lamp. Yours truly, [5] [350]

Reading and Writing Practice

43

intro

en·joy·ment

ser

prac·ti·cal

eco·nom·i·cal

intro

ex·te·ri·or

al·ready

li·censed

par

[118]

44

ser

when

kitch·en

ac·cept·ed

30

com·ple·tion

par

dead·lines

sup·pli·ers

ser

as

re·al·ize

and o

conj

com·mit·ment

ful·fill

conj

sum

le·gal

[164]

45

buy·ing

if

pieces

conj

ware·house

intro

30,

4

325

iden·ti·cal

480

210

8

20,

nonr

hand·some

[144]

46 BRIEF FORMS AND DERIVATIVES

Even though you already have considerable skill in writing shorthand, you can still profitably devote some time to a review of brief forms. Can you read this entire chart in 4 minutes or less?

	A	B	C	D	E	F
1						
2						
3						
4						
5						
6						
7						
8						
9						
10						
11						
12						
13						
14						
15						
16						
17						

CHAPTER 2

Office Systems and Equipment

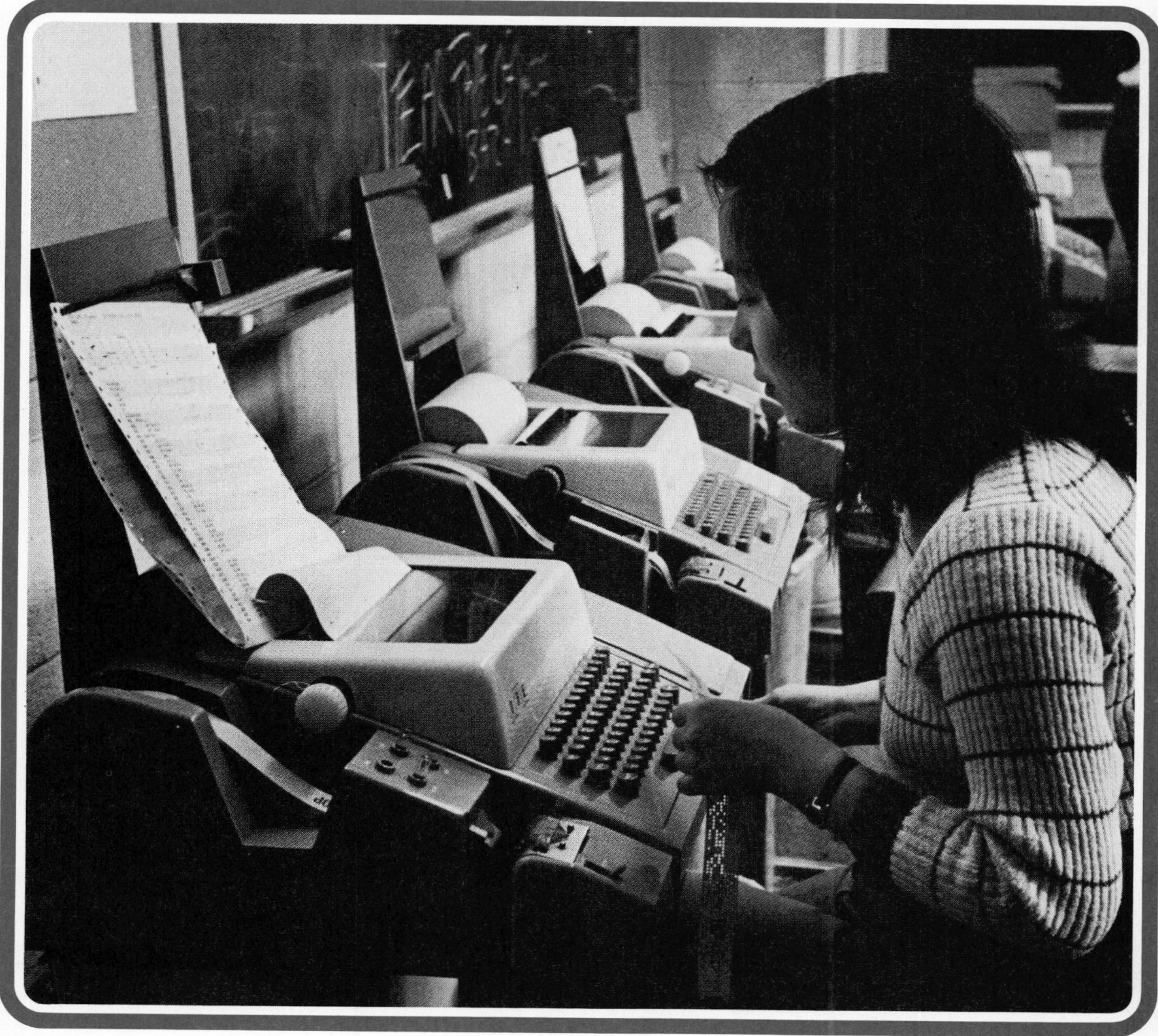

Punctuation Brushup

In the lessons of Chapter 2 you will review:

nc

; no conjunction

A semicolon is used to separate two independent but closely related clauses when a coordinating conjunction is omitted between them.

Jane passed the examination; Lou did not.

enu

: enumeration

A colon is used after an expression that introduces some illustrative material such as an explanation of a general statement, a list, or an enumeration.

Interest will be credited to your account on the following dates: January 1, April 1, July 1, and October 1.

We must now reach decisions on the following matters:
1. *When to announce the reorganization.*
2. *Who should make the announcement.*
3. *Where to hold the meeting.*

cr

. courteous request

When a request for definite action is put in the form of a question, a period is used at the end of the sentence.

Will you please send us your check immediately.

THE APOSTROPHE

1 A noun that ends in an *s* sound and is followed by another noun is usually a possessive, calling for an apostrophe before the *s* when the word is singular.

This company's advertising is very effective.

2 A plural noun ending in *s* calls for an apostrophe after the *s* to form the possessive.

All employees' data sheets will be reviewed.

3 An irregular plural calls for an apostrophe before the *s* to form the possessive.

We sell men's and women's clothing.

4 The possessive forms of personal pronouns and of the relative pronoun *who* do not require an apostrophe.

The books are theirs, not ours.
Whose paper is this?

THE DASH

Use a dash instead of other punctuation when *special emphasis* is required.

One part of the movie is particularly interesting—the opening scene.

When a parenthetical expression or an expression in apposition contains internal commas, set off the complete expression with dashes.

All of the students—Joan, Max, Lynn, and Lee—came to the meeting.

Use a dash to set off an afterthought.

The meeting was last Wednesday—or was it Thursday?

PARENTHESES

To de-emphasize explanatory expressions, place them in parentheses.

Our store is located in the National Bank Tower (formerly the Jones Tower) on the ground floor.

Place parentheses around reference information.

Our expenses are down substantially this year (see the attached page).

Use parentheses around numbers or letters accompanying enumerated items within a sentence.

I bought the following items: (1) a new sweater, (2) a new coat, and (3) a new hat.

EXCLAMATION POINT

An exclamation point may be used to express strong feeling, urgency, or enthusiasm.

I can't believe it!

An exclamation point may be used after a single word.

Congratulations! I knew you could win.

Developing Shorthand Writing Power

47 OUTLINE CONSTRUCTION

Vowel Written In -er, -ar, -or When the word endings *-er, -ar,* or *-or* follow *i*, left *s*, or *sh, ch, j*, more legible outlines result if the vowel is written in those word endings.

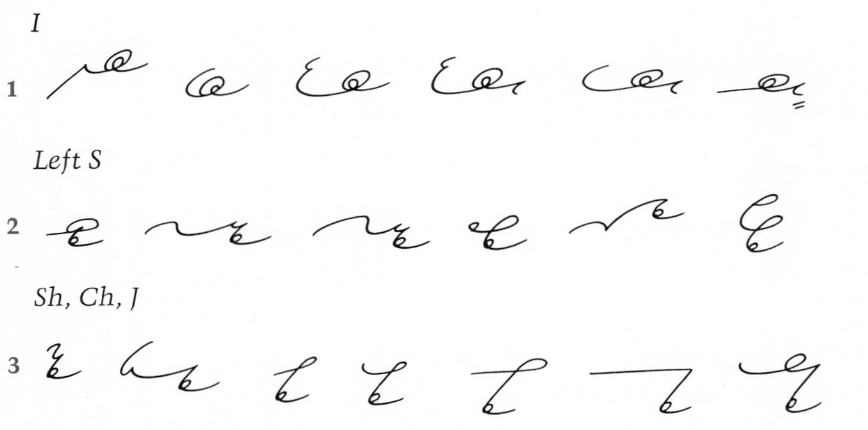

1. *Drier, prior, supplier, suppliers, pliers, Myers.*
2. *Nicer, closer, grocer, eraser, condenser, appraiser.*
3. *Washer, polisher, teacher, richer, major, manager, larger.*

Omission of Vowels in -el, -al, -ial, -eal When the endings *-el, -al, -ial,* and *-eal* are not accented, the vowels are omitted from those endings.

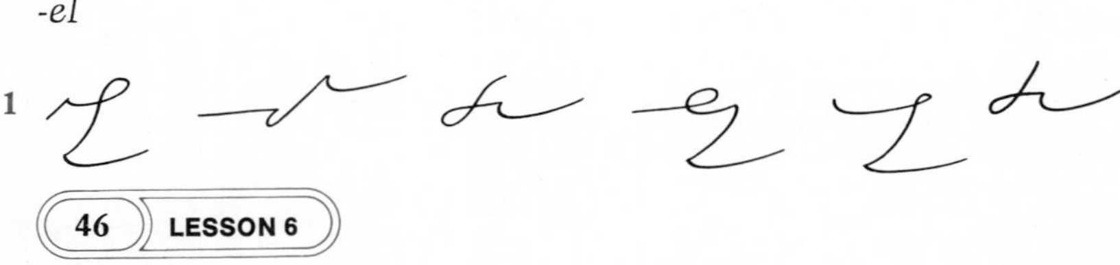

-al

2

-ial, eal

3

1. *Travel, model, panel, marvel, level, channel.*
2. *Formal, legal, original, central, total.*
3. *Material, managerial, secretarial, editorial, cereal.*

Building Transcription Skills

48 Business Vocabulary Builder

résumé A short account of one's career and qualifications.

collates Assembles in order.

overhead expense Operating cost.

Reading and Writing Practice

49 Modern Office Design

With modern office design,

[181]

50 LETTERS

its

year's

ser

sal·a·ries

gen·er·ous

as·sem·bly

geo

if

and o

yours

su·per·vi·sors

man·a·ge·ri·al

if

years'

nc

[141]

51

al·ways

as

bro·chures

mod·els

quite

intro

ap

ar·ea

if

vol·ume

conj

if

cr

[144]

52

if

ex·penses

Transcribe:
Model 450
copi·er

450

suc·ces·sor

450

410

enu

col·lates

stap·les

ser

[107]

Developing Shorthand Writing Power

53 RECALL DRILL k

This drill reviews all the different situations in which the shorthand stroke *k* is used in Gregg Shorthand.

K

1

Com-

2

Con-

3

-cal, -cle

4

-ic

5

---

1. *Keep, wreck, check, quick, because, actually, careful, cover.*
2. *Compare, compact, complain, complete, complex, combine, compensate.*
3. *Control, contract, contact, contain, content, continue, reconsider.*
4. *Medical, surgical, logical, identical, article, cubicle, ethical.*
5. *Tragic, basic, logic, specific, magic, scientific, graphic.*

Building Transcription Skills

54 Business Vocabulary Builder

profit margin Excess of income over expenditures.

reconditioning Restoring to a good condition.

programmers Those who prepare computer programs.

Writing Practice

55 PREVIEW

56 *Consultation, unusually, pinpoint, procedures, years ago, worthwhile, let us know, whether.*

57 *Pleasure, recommendation, recall, several months ago, Cleveland, Cincinnati.*

58 *American, thousands, recreation, facilities, daily, absenteeism, significantly.*

LETTERS

56

Dear Mrs. Katz: Would you be available to provide consultation services for our firm sometime in[1] January? Our basic expenses have been unusually high during the past several months, especially[2] during October, November, and December. We are unable to pinpoint the reason for this increase in[3] expenses. We have changed a number of our procedures to try to increase our profit margin. However, we[4] have had little success.

As you will recall, you worked with us a number of years ago (in 1975[5] and 1976) and suggested some very worthwhile changes at that time. Our executive staff[6] agreed that you were the logical person to contact regarding our present problem.

Will you please let us know[7] as soon as possible, Mrs. Katz, whether you are willing to accept this assignment for us. Sincerely yours,[8]

57

Dear Mr. Wilson: It is with a great deal of pleasure that I write a letter of recommendation for Mr.[9] Alvin Green. As you will recall, we spoke about Mr. Green several months ago when I visited your[10] office in Cleveland. I am delighted that you are considering hiring Mr. Green to manage your Cincinnati[11] office.

For two years Mr. Green worked for the General Office Supplies Company as a marketing[12] representative. He did his work efficiently and effectively. Both years he exceeded his sales budget,[13] and I was quite sorry when he left our organization to move to the Midwest to be near his family.[14]

Believe me, Mr. Wilson, if Mr. Green were to return to Miami, Florida, I would be very happy[15] to have him back on our staff. If you hire him, I am sure you will be making no mistake. Very truly yours,[16]

58

Mrs. Clay: In a recent issue of a news magazine, I read of an interesting trend in American[17] business. Over the last few years, thousands of companies have spent millions of dollars providing physical[18] recreation facilities for their employees to use while at work. Employees who use these facilities during[19] the day are actually producing more work, and they are better adjusted to their daily routines. In[20] addition, absenteeism has been reduced significantly in many of the businesses.

I am enclosing[21] a reprint of this article. In my opinion, providing for physical activity[22] might be an answer to some of our production problems.

Could we discuss this matter sometime soon? Fred Dayton[23] [460]

Reading and Writing Practice

59

month's

copi·er

nonr

intro

and o

nc

mi·nor

com·pet·ing

ad·just·ments

sug·ges·tion

par

lo·cal

ap

par

ob·li·ga·tion

[186]

60

ac·cept

cal·cu·la·tors

un·for·tu·nate·ly

intro

intro

re·con·di·tion·ing

of·ten

par

dis·cour·age

conj

4

ser

func·tions

ap

[201]

61

com·pa·nies

nc

com·pu·ters

intro

busi·nesses

cap·i·tal

rea·son

nc

pro·gram·mers

if

[160]

LESSON 8

Developing Shorthand Writing Power

62 WORD FAMILIES

-serve

1 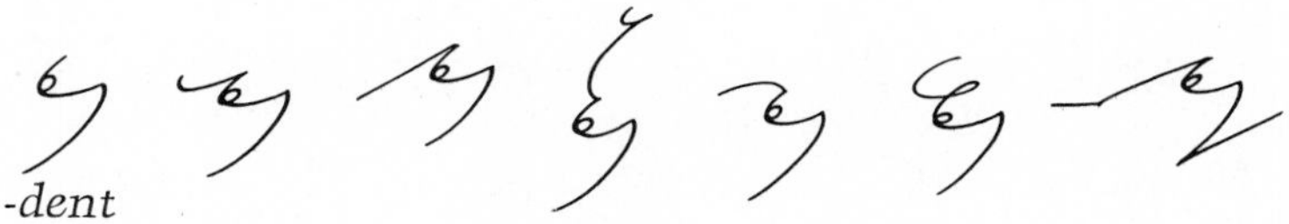

-dent

2 

---

1. *Serve, reserve, deserve, observe, conserve, preserve, undeserved.*
2. *Dent, indent, president, accident, resident, incident, confident.*

---

63 FREQUENTLY USED NAMES

Last Names

1 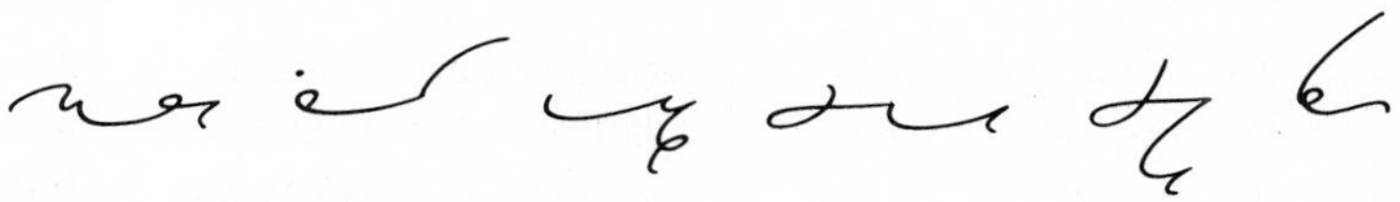

Men's First Names

2 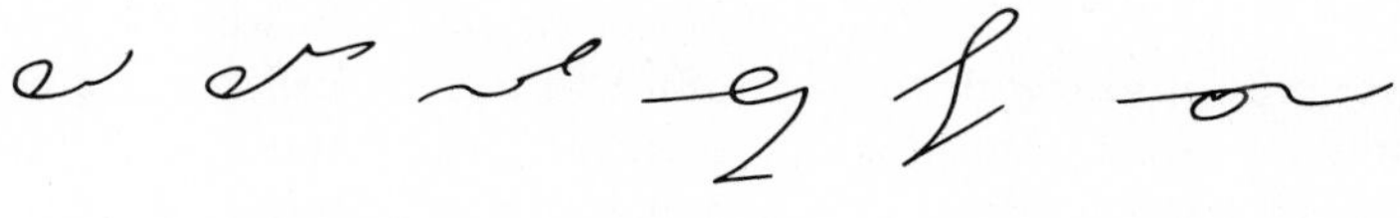

---

1. *Collins, Hilton, Lopez, Samuels, Chambers, Burke.*
2. *Arthur, Andrew, Curtis, Marvin, David, Michael.*

Building Transcription Skills

64 Business Vocabulary Builder

utilize To make use of.

microfilm A film bearing a photographic record on a reduced scale.

● Writing Practice

65 PREVIEW

☐ 66

☐ 67

☐ 68

66 *Furniture, showrooms, modular, assembled, however, I hope you will be able, week or two.*
67 *Probably, aware, efficiently, transfer, microfilm, storage, how much, we hope you will.*
68 *Capable, more than, receivable, payable, analyses, they will be able, valuable, management.*

LETTERS

66

Dear Ms. Collins: You may recall that last month I visited your furniture display showrooms. I was impressed with[1] your new modular office furniture that can be assembled to serve the needs of any particular[2] company.

I have discussed this type of furniture with our president, Mr. Arthur Hilton. He feels that now is[3] a good time for us to consider purchasing new furniture for our offices.

However, we need additional[4] details before we can make a decision on the purchase of office furniture. I hope you will be[5] able to come to our offices in the next week or two to discuss our office furniture needs. Please call Mr.[6] Hilton's secretary, Mr. Arthur Frank, at 555-1961 for an appointment. Sincerely,[7]

67

Dear Mr. Samuels: The last time you checked the cost of renting office space, you probably became aware of just[8] how important it is to utilize efficiently the space you now have. You probably began to look for[9] ways to conserve office space.

One way to conserve space is to transfer your valuable records to microfilm. If[10] you are not aware of how much space can be saved through the use of microfilm storage, we invite you or one of[11] your representatives to visit the General Office Equipment and Supply Company. Our current display[12] clearly illustrates how much space you can save by converting your old records to microfilm for storage.

We[13] hope you will plan to visit our offices soon; it will be a pleasure for us to serve you. Yours very truly,[14]

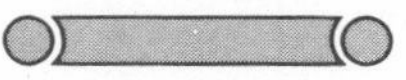

68

Dear Mr. Curtis: A good way to save on your accounting costs and speed up the work flow of your accounting[15] department is to buy or lease our Model 118 computer. This is a complete computer in every sense[16] and is capable of handling all your business information.

Your billing clerks will soon learn more than how to handle[17] accounts receivable, accounts payable, and payrolls with the computer. They will be able to make credit[18] checks for sales analyses and to handle inventory control. They will be able to compile all kinds[19] of information that will be valuable to the management of the business.

Send for our fact-filled brochure. It[20] will give you a complete picture of what the Model 118 computer can do for you. Very truly yours,[21]

[420]

Reading and Writing Practice

69

symp·tom

phys·i·cal

enu

ad·e·quate

lev·el

an·a·lyze

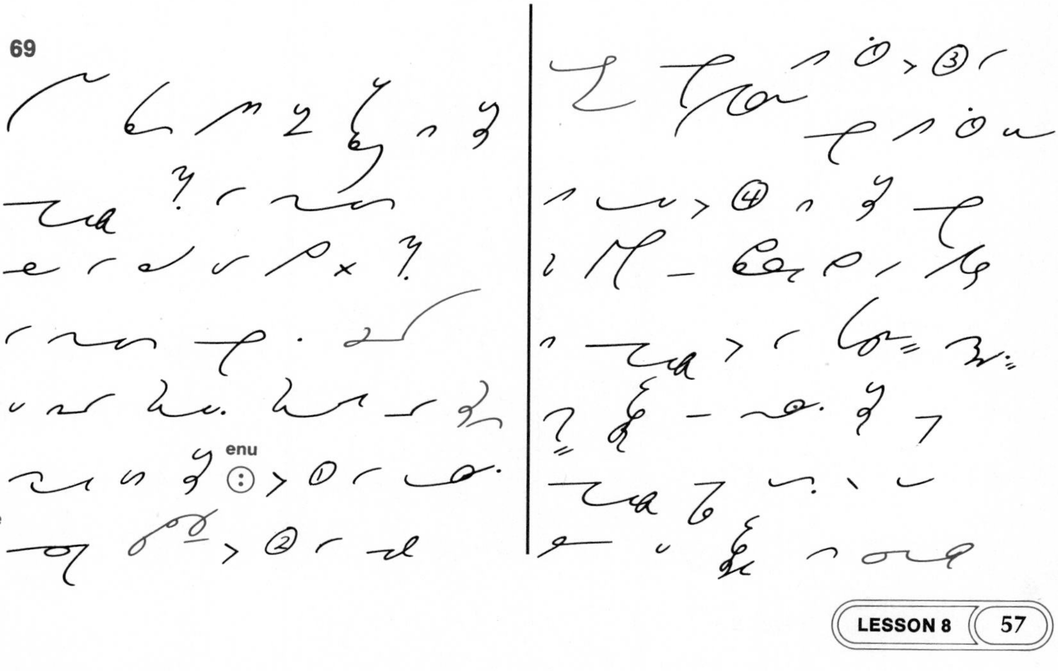

rec·om·mend·ed

if

ser

ef·fi·cient

intro

spe·cial·ists

intro

[187]

70

vice

ap

in·ven·to·ry

fre·quent

intro

intro

pre·vi·ous

conj

con·curs

par

soft·ware

cr

[90]

71

intro

be·com·ing

par

re·al·izes

clean·li·ness

its

ser

agen·cies

ac·com·mo·date

ex·am·ple

intro

ser

if

main·ten·ance

equip·ment

[157]

72

geo

nc

intro

eras·ing

track

ap

[107]

Developing Shorthand Writing Power

73 FREQUENTLY USED PHRASES

Glad

1

Few

2

1. *I would be glad, I will be glad, he will be glad, we would be glad, they will be glad.*
2. *Few days, few days ago, few months, few moments, few months ago.*

74 GEOGRAPHICAL EXPRESSIONS

-ford

1

States

2

Foreign Countries

3

1. *Hartford, Medford, Stamford, Bedford, Oxford, Bradford.*
2. *Massachusetts, Florida, Iowa, Indiana, Minnesota, Ohio, Pennsylvania, New Mexico.*
3. *Canada, Brazil, Argentina, Ecuador, Greece, India, Egypt.*

Building Transcription Skills

75 Business Vocabulary Builder

dry process A printing process that uses no liquid chemicals.

business administration A program of studies in college providing knowledge of business principles.

records management system A total system of organization for all records within a company.

Writing Practice

76 PREVIEW

□ 77

□ 78

□ 79

77 *Copier, inexpensively, almost, seconds, a hundred, bargain, showroom, we will be glad.*
78 *Few days ago, suppliers, senior, administration, graduates, period, circumstances.*
79 *Memorandum, be able, furthermore, square feet, retrieval, documents, records.*

LETTERS

77

Dear Mr. Bradford: With our latest model copier, you can get sharp, clear copies quickly and inexpensively.[1] Our new dry process produces perfect copies from almost any original. You can make one copy[2] in a few seconds; you can make a hundred or more in a few minutes.

Our new copier is a bargain. You[3] can buy one for much less than you might think. See it in operation at our showroom on Indiana Avenue.[4] If you prefer, we will be glad to bring a copier to your office for a demonstration. Yours truly,[5]

78

Mr. Brown: A few days ago I was in Medford, Pennsylvania, to speak with one of our suppliers. While I[6] was there, I met Mr. James Gardner, a senior in Tate College majoring in business administration. Before[7] beginning his studies there, he worked for several summers as a sales representative in Brazil and[8] Argentina. When he graduates from Tate College in May, Mr. Gardner would like to obtain a position[9] in sales with us.

I understand that our representative in Medford, Ms. Alice Jenkins, will be moving to[10] Canada in a few months, and it would not be a good idea to leave the Medford territory without a[11] representative for a long period of time. Under the circumstances, I feel that you should interview[12] Mr. Gardner as soon as possible. I will be glad to make the necessary arrangements. Mary Wilson[13]

79

Dear Mrs. Smith: Most large organizations have a problem handling all the mail they receive. They must store each letter[14] or memorandum and be able to find it in a matter of a few minutes if it is needed.[15] Furthermore, a regular filing system may take hundreds of square feet of office space.

The new General records[16] management system is designed to solve storage and retrieval problems. This system can store thousands of pieces[17] of correspondence in less space than a filing cabinet requires. Any paper can be found within a few[18] minutes because the system uses a quick, efficient coding system for storing all documents.

Take the first[19] step toward solving your records problems; invite our representative to give you all the facts. Very truly yours, [20] [400]

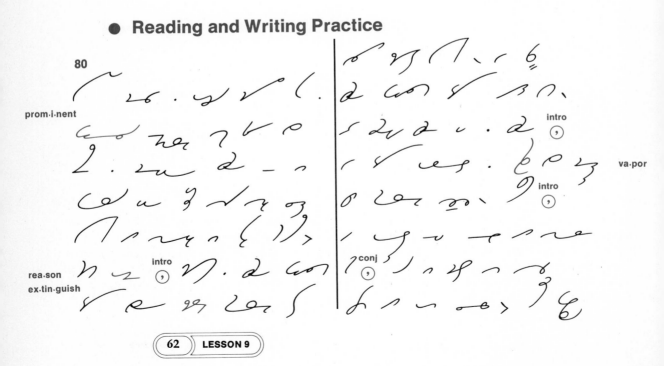

Reading and Writing Practice

80

prom·i·nent

intro

va·por

intro

rea·son

ex·tin·guish

intro

conj

[164]

81

intro

13

bought

com·pa·nies

if

intro

15

conj

conj

en·gi·neers

par

re·main

[131]

82

as

piece

han·dling

nc

[80]

Developing Shorthand Writing Power

83 WORD BEGINNINGS AND ENDINGS

For-, Fore-

1

-rity

2

-lity

3

1. *Fortunate, forward, forget, afforded, foreclose, forerunner, forever.*
2. *Integrity, authority, security, charity, sincerity, popularity, majority.*
3. *Quality, facilities, responsibility, locality, ability, flexibility.*

Building Transcription Skills

84 Business Vocabulary Builder

computerizing Equipping with computers.
consultations Acts of conferring or consulting.
simultaneously At the same time.

Progressive Speed Builder (50-90)

The letters in this Progressive Speed Builder range in speed from 50 to 90 words a minute. Practice the preview before taking the letters from dictation, and try to get something down during dictation for every word, even though your outlines may not be perfect. Do not stop writing!

85 PREVIEW

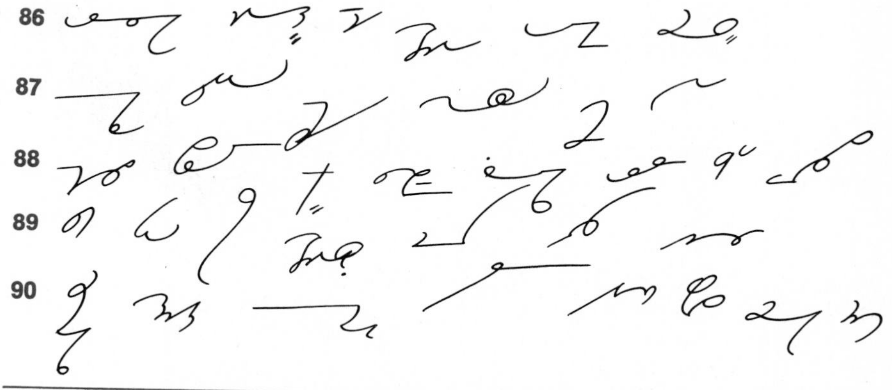

86 *Remember, St. Louis, interest, computer, luncheon, Philadelphia.*
87 *Manager, I told, invited, client, convenient, dinner.*
88 *Unfortunately, appointment, New Jersey, equipment, he will not be able, return, 9 o'clock, on that day.*
89 *I wish, board, I have been, computerizing, sometime, at that time, together.*
90 *Favorably, consultations, manufacturers, determine, discuss, I hope that, we will be, successful.*

LETTERS

86

[1 minute at 50]

Dear Helen: You will remember that when I saw you in St. Louis/last month you expressed an interest in meeting Bill Green, who is in charge//of our computer operations.

Can you have luncheon with him and///me when you are in Philadelphia on June 25? Sincerely yours, [1]

87

[1 minute at 60]

Dear James: Thank you for arranging for me to meet Bill Green, the manager of your/computer operations. As I told you, I will be in Philadelphia on//June 25, but I have invited a client to have luncheon on that day.

Would it///be convenient for you and Bill to have dinner with me in the evening? Sincerely, [2]

88

[1 minute at 70]

Dear Helen: Unfortunately, Bill Green made an appointment with the National Office Machines/ Company in Trenton, New Jersey, to inspect some of their new computer equipment, and he will// not be able to return to Philadelphia until 8 or 9 o'clock at night.

Can you///stay over until June 26? Both Bill and I are free for luncheon on that day. Very truly yours, [3]

89

[1 minute at 80]

Dear James: I wish I could stay over in Philadelphia until June 26, but that is the day on/which our board of directors meets in St. Louis, and I have been asked to outline for them my plans for//computerizing our accounting operations.

I will return to Philadelphia sometime early in///August, and I hope that at that time it will be possible for the three of us to get together. Sincerely yours, [4]

90

[1 minute at 90]

Dear James: The board of directors received my plans for computerizing our accounting operations favorably,/and for the last four weeks I have been having consultations with computer manufacturers to determine what type of//system we should install.

I have definite proposals from two manufacturers, and I would like to discuss them with you and///Bill on August 10 or 11 at 12 o'clock. I hope that this time we will be successful in getting together. Sincerely, [5] [350]

● Reading and Writing Practice

91

than

nc

;

si·mul·ta·neous·ly

conj

na·tion·wide

intro

par

[133]

92

copy·ing

conj

sim·i·lar·i·ty

intro

col·ored

par

au·to·mat·i·cal·ly

ad·justs

and o

if

and o

mod·ern

740

par

555-2097

[141]

93 Brief Forms and Derivatives

The following chart contains a number of brief forms and derivatives. First read the brief forms from left to right. Then read the chart down each column.

Reading goal: 3 minutes or less.

	A	B	C	D	E	F
1						
2						
3						
4						
5						
6						
7						
8						
9						
10						
11						
12						
13						
14						
15						
16						
17						

CHAPTER 3

Advertising and Sales Promotion

Typing Style and Punctuation Brushup

In the lessons of Chapter 3 you will review the correct method of typing addresses, amounts of money, expressions of time, and dates. You will also review the use of the hyphen and the correct way to type numbers, percentages, ages, anniversaries, fractions, and mixed numbers.

ADDRESSES

1 Always use figures in house numbers.

We live at 600 (not six hundred) *Elm Street.*

2 Spell out numbered street names from 1 through 10.

She worked at 310 Fourth Avenue.

3 Use figures in street names over 10.

His address is 37 East 68 (not 68th) *Street.*

AMOUNTS OF MONEY

1 When transcribing even amounts of dollars in business letters, do not use a decimal point or zeros.

The check for $360 (not $360.00) *was mailed yesterday.*

2 In business letters, use the word *cents* for amounts under $1.

The booklet cost only 68 cents (not $.68 or 68¢).

3 Even millions and billions of dollars may be transcribed in numbers and words for easier reading.

The budget is $32 million.

TIME

1 Use figures in expressing time with *o'clock.* (Remember the apostrophe!)

She should be here at 11 (not eleven) *o'clock.*

2 Use numbers in expressing time with *a.m.* and *p.m.*

He left at 9:30 a.m. and returned at 6 p.m.

DATES

1 If the name of the month precedes the day, do not use *th, st,* or *d* after the number.

On October 25, 1978, he retired.

2 If the day precedes the month, *th, st,* or *d* should be included.

On the 16th of November she will move to Maine.

HYPHENS

You can quickly decide whether to use a hyphen in compound expressions like *past due* or *well trained* by observing these rules:

1 If a noun follows the expression, use a hyphen.

We are concerned about your past-due bill (noun).

2 If no noun follows the compound expression, do not use a hyphen.

Your bill is now past due.

3 No hyphen is used in a compound modifier when the first part of the expression is an adverb that ends in *ly.*

She was editor of a widely read magazine.

NUMBERS

1 Spell out numbers 1 through 10.

We saw the show four times.

2 Use figures for numbers above 10.

There were 14 attendees.

3 If several numbers both below and above 10 are used in the same sentence, use figures for all numbers.

The vote was 5 for Bill, 15 for Helen, and 6 for Kay.

4 Spell out a number at the beginning of a sentence.

Thirty students were there.

5 Express percentages in figures and spell out the word *percent.*

We will receive a 7 percent commission.

6 To express even millions in business correspondence, use the following style:

30 million *110 million*

COMMAS IN NUMBERS

1 Numbers that contain four or more digits require a comma to separate thousands, millions, billions.

6,000 *915,691* *3,608,492* *10,500,000,100*

2 No comma is used, however, in large serial numbers, house or street numbers, ZIP Codes, telephone numbers, page numbers, and year dates.

No. 32426	*Model 55012*	*1800 First Street*
555-1482	*page 1901*	*1979*
		Houston, TX 77004

AGES AND ANNIVERSARIES

When ages are used as *significant statistics,* express them in figures.

You may vote at the age of 18.

When ages are not considered significant statistics, spell them in full.

My five-year-old daughter is learning to read.

Spell out ordinals (*first, second* and so on) in birthdays and anniversaries.

They are observing their second anniversary.

Figures may be used, however, when more than two words would be needed.

This is the company's 130th anniversary.

ADJACENT NUMBERS

When two numbers come together in a sentence and one is a part of a compound modifier, spell out the first and express the second in figures.

We rented three 6-room houses.

However, if the second number would make a significantly shorter word, spell it out and express the first in figures.

We received 700 three-page brochures.

FRACTIONS AND MIXED NUMBERS

1 Spell out most fractions that stand alone. Separate the elements with a hyphen.

We send brochures to three-fourths of the members.

2 In technical reports express fractions in figures, using a diagonal to separate the elements.

1/84 *3/92*

3 Mixed numbers should be expressed in figures.

We expect the sales to be 6½ times greater than last year.

4 Spell out a number that begins a sentence. Hyphenate a fractional element.

Three and one-half inches of rain fell.

Developing Shorthand Writing Power

94 OUTLINE CONSTRUCTION

Omission of Vowel From -er, -ar, -or When the endings *-er, -ar, -or* are not stressed or accented, the vowel is omitted from those endings.

-er

1

-ar

2

-or

3

1. *Wiser, greater, folder, printer, retailer, container.*
2. *Dollar, popular, grammar, similar, collar.*
3. *Supervisor, operator, contractor, error, honor, humor, vendor.*

Inclusion of Vowel In -er When the ending *-er* is stressed or accented, the vowel is written. It is also written in derivatives of words ending in accented *-er*, even though the *e* may no longer be accented in the derivatives.

1

2

1. *Transfer, transferred, transferring, confer, conferring, refer, prefer, defer, infer.*
2. *Transference, conference, reference, preference, deference, preferable, transferable.*

Building Transcription Skills

95 Business Vocabulary Builder

billboard *(one word)* A large panel designed to carry outdoor advertising.

notarized Certified that a document is authentic.

medium *(singular of media)* A method of communication.

Reading and Writing Practice

96 Advertising

50

160

70

While eating

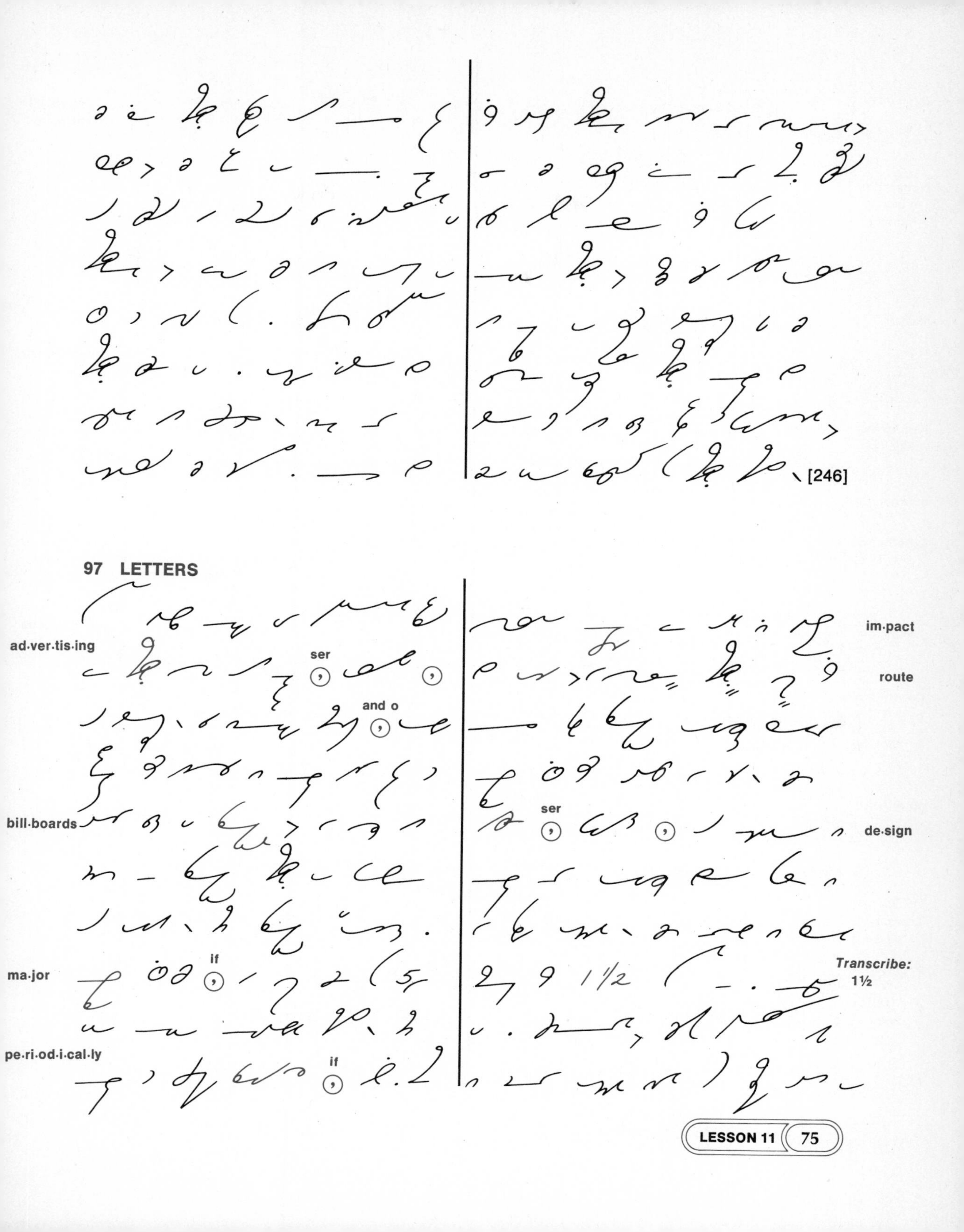

[246]

97 LETTERS

ad·ver·tis·ing

ser

and o

bill·boards

ma·jor

if

pe·ri·od·i·cal·ly

if

im·pact

route

ser

de·sign

Transcribe:
1½

Transcribe: 9 a.m. 5 p.m.

555-0458 nc ; [194]

98

Transcribe: five

equip·ment

func·tion·al

conj ,

intro ,

con·trac·tors

ac·cept·ing

and o ,

no·ta·rized

Transcribe: 700 South First

geo ,

Transcribe: nine

Transcribe: 4 p.m. August 8 trans·ferred

ac·quir·ing

if ,

su·per·vi·sor

[173]

99

pref·er·ences

intro ,

intro ,

nc ;

[81]

Developing Shorthand Writing Power

100 RECALL DRILL sh

This drill illustrates the different situations in which the *sh* stroke is used in Gregg Shorthand.

Sh

1

-ish

2

-tion

3

-tial, -cial

4

-ship

5

1. *Shift, shame, sharp, shield, shoes, appreciate, rush, shirt, machine.*
2. *Accomplish, flourish, finish, furnish, establish, vanish, polish.*
3. *Connection, selection, vacation, addition, condition, nation, mention, station.*
4. *Special, official, partial, essential, initial, substantial, preferential, credentials, circumstantial.*
5. *Membership, leadership, ownership, friendship, kinship, authorship.*

Building Transcription Skills

101 Business Vocabulary Builder

subscribers Receivers of a periodical or service by order on a regular basis.

auction A public sale of property to the highest bidder.

dividends Return on money invested.

Writing Practice

102 PREVIEW

103 *In our opinion, circulation, February, readership, subscribers, newsstands, supermarkets.*
104 *Annual, front, promotional, bicycles, various, articles, auctioneer.*
105 *Furniture, beautiful, top-quality, substantial, incentive, shoppers, suites, to make.*

LETTERS

103

Dear Mrs. Day: What is the most talked-about magazine in the country today? In our opinion, it is[1] *National Issues*. After only ten months of publication, *National Issues* has built up a circulation[2] of over 200,000. In February our readership was 201,000. Within three or four[3] years we expect the circulation to be at least 2 million.

We think this says a lot because we do not have[4] any subscribers. *National Issues* is sold only at newsstands and supermarkets. In our ten months of[5] publication, stories have been picked up by many newspapers, radio stations, and wire services. Never before[6] has a magazine had such an impact on other media.

If you want 200,000 people to[7] learn about your products, advertise in *National Issues*. You will be making no mistake. Yours very truly,[8]

104

Miss Harman: Our annual police auction will be held Saturday, June 12, at 10 a.m. on the front lawn of[9] the local police station at 121 South Main Street. Will you please prepare a promotional piece for the[10] local newspaper by this Thursday.

In addition to bicycles, this year we will also auction skis, tennis[11] rackets, and various other items. The new items will be furnished by Shell Sporting Goods; the used articles,[12] all of which are in excellent condition, will be provided by the members of the police force.

Roy Price, a[13] professional auctioneer, will conduct the sale and will establish the initial price for each item. George Sharp[14]

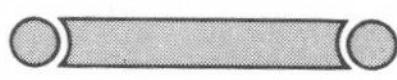

105

Dear Miss Shields: Our annual furniture sale will take place the week of February 3 at our main store at[15] 400 East 62 Street in Lansing. This year we are offering beautiful, top-quality furniture[16] worth more than $1 million. We will have a complete selection of furniture in the most popular styles.[17] Each piece will be offered at a substantial discount.

As an added incentive, we will give away the following[18] door prizes to lucky shoppers:

1. Three 5-piece living room suites.
2. Four 3-piece bedroom suites.
3. Two 4-piece[19] dining room suites.

Our doors will open at 9 a.m. sharp; come early to make the best selection. Sincerely yours,[20]

[400]

Reading and Writing Practice

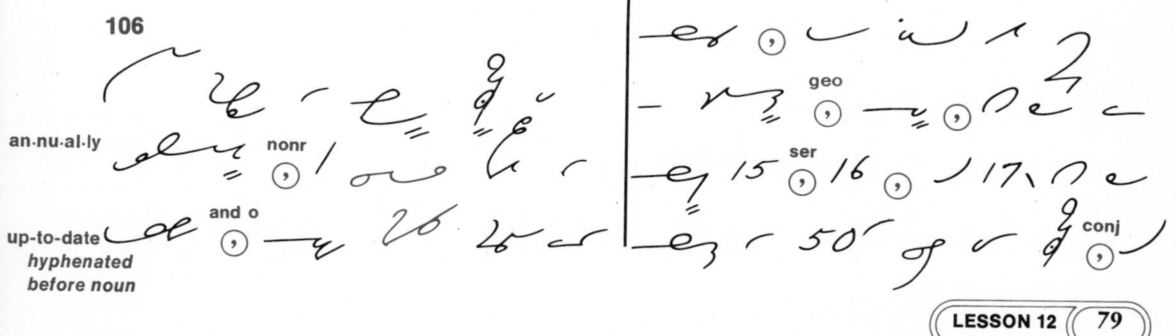

plan·ning

and o

al·ready

Transcribe: 1,000

[169]

107

ap

di·rec·tor

of·fi·cers

intro

ap

Transcribe: 8 p.m.

known

and o

cre·ative

Transcribe: ten

par

[121]

108

Transcribe: 6 percent

par

al·most

if

los·ing

com·pet·i·tors

3, 5

ser

well-trained *hyphenated before noun*

and o

[156]

109

dis·trib·u·tor

ser

if

intro

555-1164

par

ad

[84]

110

ap

intro

4

Transcribe: four $15 million

15

to·ward

com·pa·ny's

[124]

LESSON 13

Developing Shorthand Writing Power

111 WORD FAMILIES

-ified

1 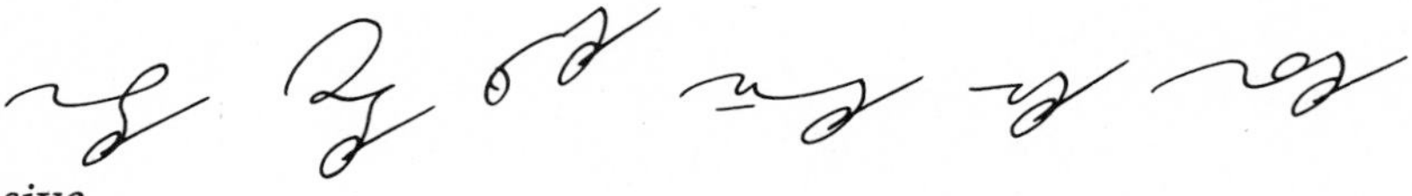

-sive

2 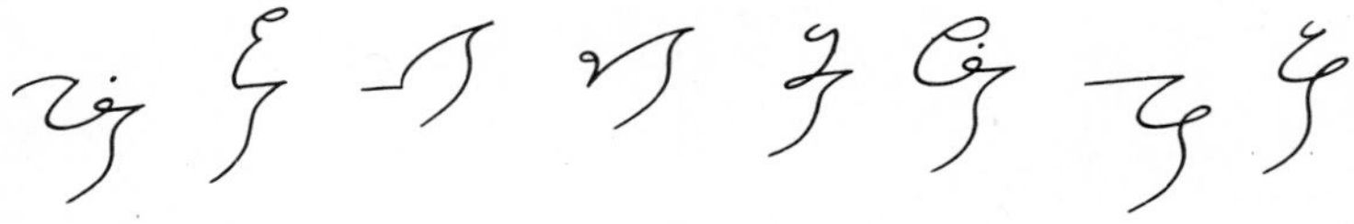

1. *Classified, diversified, identified, qualified, notified, gratified.*
2. *Comprehensive, expensive, intensive, extensive, offensive, apprehensive, impressive, oppressive.*

112 FREQUENTLY USED NAMES

Last Names

1 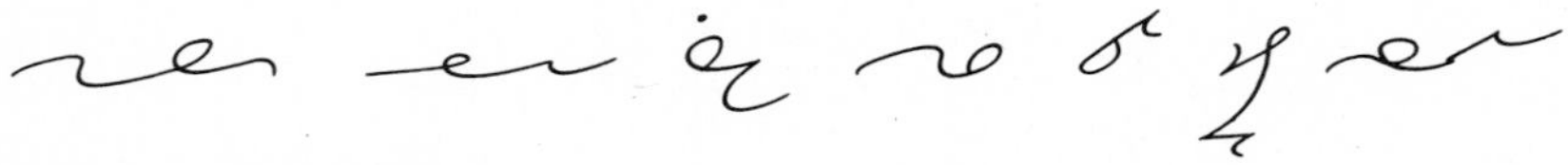

Women's First Names

2 

1. *Clark, Miller, Harper, Gray, Yates, Stevens, Carter.*
2. *Helen, Caroline, Louise, Terry, Susan, Diana.*

Building Transcription Skills

113 Business Vocabulary Builder

seldom Rarely; not often.

devote To concentrate on; to give to.

Writing Practice

114 PREVIEW

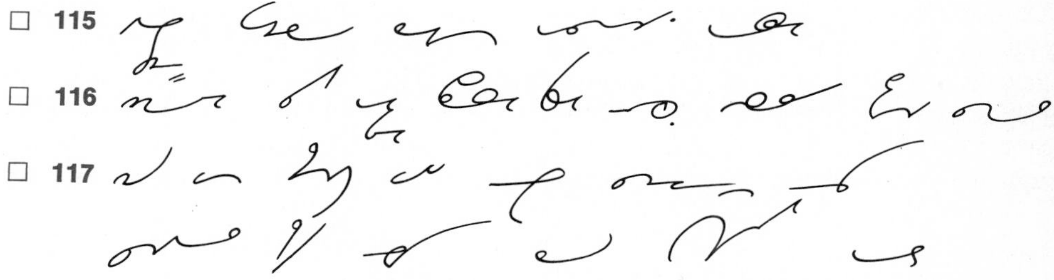

115 *Tribune, personnel, years ago, recruiting, lion's.*
116 *Woolens, edition, response, appearance, buyers, inquiring, carried, expect, equally.*
117 *You want, of course, effective, although, may be, economical, medium, actually, each dollar, next time, yield, dividends, let us.*

LETTERS

115

Dear Mr. Smith: I feel that I must write you about the impressive success we have had with our advertising[1] in the classified ads section of the *Tribune.*

We started our personnel agency ten years ago and have[2] enjoyed extensive growth since then. The success of our recruiting efforts for management and sales positions has[3] been the result of our advertising in the *Tribune*. The *Tribune* is our most vital link to the employment[4] market.

The *Tribune* will again receive the lion's share of our next year's advertising budget. Sincerely yours,[5]

116

Gentlemen: You will find enclosed the ad for Johnson woolens that we wish to run in the special fashion edition[6] of *Today* magazine for Sunday, June 16. The response we have received in past years from our advertising[7] in your special fashion edition has been most impressive.

Last year, in the week following the appearance[8] of our ad, we had buyers from all over the country visiting our showrooms with our ad in hand inquiring[9] about our woolens. Readers wrote us from all over the country asking for names of stores that carried our merchandise.[10]

We expect an equally satisfactory result from our ad in the June 16 issue. Sincerely,[11]

117

Dear Ms. Harper: When you want to increase your company's sales, the use of effective advertising should play a[12] major part in your planning.

Of course, you want to spend your money in the most effective way possible, and we[13] believe television advertising will do the best job for you. Although television advertising may[14] seem expensive, it may be the most economical medium for you to use because you actually reach[15] more people for each dollar spent.

The next time you want to get your message across to more people in a way that[16] will yield real dividends, let us show you how effective television advertising can be. Sincerely yours,[17] [340]

Reading and Writing Practice

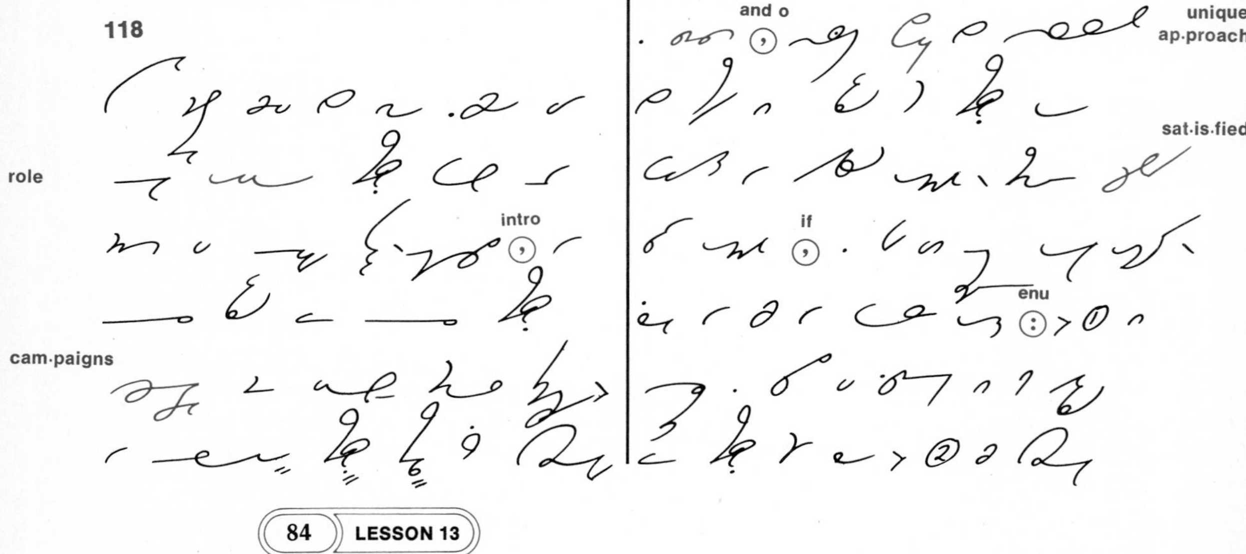

if

pro·gres·sive

par

[193]

119

re·al·ize

par

intro

sel·dom

when

ser

ach·ing

fa·tigue

and o

well-trained *hyphenated before noun*

[152]

120

fash·ion-con·scious *hyphenated before noun*

fam·i·lies

Transcribe: 77 percent

fur·ther·more

intro

ap·peal

sense

par

men's

wom·en's

if

555-6109 [152]

121

intro

as

conj

if

if

[99]

122

ap

guid·ed

ser

if

coun·tries

ser

Transcribe:
5
10
20

if

ap

31 [110]

Developing Shorthand Writing Power

123 FREQUENTLY USED PHRASES

1. You have been, I have been, I have not been, we have been, would have been, could have been, should have been, it has been, has not been.
2. Few months ago, some time ago, several days ago, years ago, weeks ago.

124 GEOGRAPHICAL EXPRESSIONS

-field

1

States

2

Foreign Countries

3 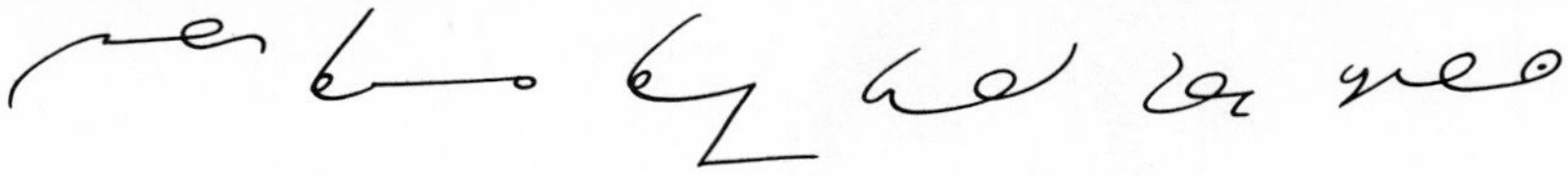

1. *Brownfield, Plainfield, Bakersfield, Fairfield, Springfield, Greenfield.*
2. *Arizona, Virginia, Delaware, Texas, Wisconsin, Rhode Island, Idaho, Nevada, New York.*
3. *Denmark, Germany, Belgium, Poland, France, Australia.*

Building Transcription Skills

125 Business Vocabulary Builder

authorities Individuals considered experts.

consultants Those who give professional advice or services.

consumer goods Commodities that directly satisfy human wants.

● Writing Practice

126 PREVIEW

☐ **127**
☐ **128**
☐ **129**

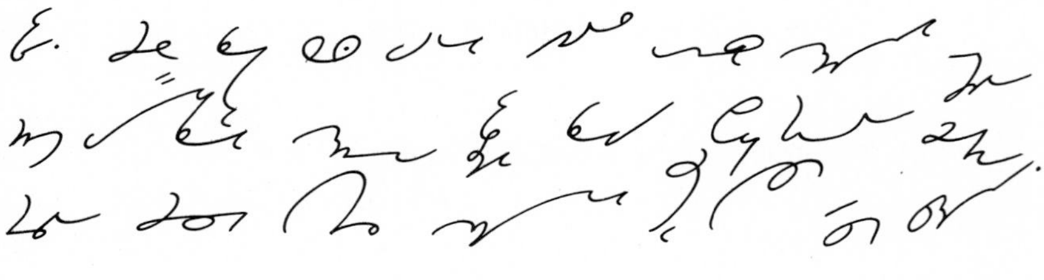

127 *Sporting, Phoenix, suburbs, area, authorities, two or three, recognize, consultants, in the future.*
128 *Successful, automobiles, consumer, specialists, period, approach, folder, we are sure.*
129 *Furniture, financial, difficulty, customers, savings, to make, transaction, outstanding.*

LETTERS

127

Dear Mr. Bates: Several weeks ago we opened a sporting goods store at 235 Fairfield Avenue[1] here in Phoenix, Arizona. The new store, which is the largest in our chain, replaces our old store that was[2] located in the suburbs. The new store will more effectively serve the needs of our customers in this area.[3]

During the first two months of operation, a number of well-known sports authorities will spend two or three days[4] each consulting with our customers. I am sure you will recognize the names of many of the authorities[5] listed in the enclosed brochure.

Make it a point the next time you are in our area to visit our new store,[6] look at our high-quality sporting goods, and meet our consultants.

It has been a pleasure serving you in the past,[7] Mr. Bates, and we hope we will have many opportunities to serve you in the future. Very truly yours,[8]

128

Dear Dr. Andrews: The successful marketing of real estate requires a different approach than is necessary[9] in selling food, automobiles, or other consumer goods. It requires specialists in the field of real estate.[10]

The General Real Estate Company has a team of experts who have had experience in every phase[11] of real estate sales. We began operating in Brownfield only ten years ago. However, in that short[12] period of time we have been able to expand our operations greatly. We now serve 43 cities and[13] towns in Delaware.

If you have been thinking about using a new approach in selling real estate, read about[14] our successful approach in the enclosed folder. We are sure you will like the way we do business. Sincerely yours,[15]

129

Dear Mr. Farmer: A few days ago we received a large shipment of furniture in our Plainfield showroom. This[16] furniture came to us from a manufacturer in Denmark who had financial difficulty and had to[17] sell all stock immediately.

We purchased the stock at a bargain price, and we are going to pass along to[18] you and our other customers the savings we were able to make on this transaction at a special sale on[19] August 15, 16, and 17. This sale will not be open to the general public; you will have to[20] present this letter to be admitted.

If you want a really outstanding furniture bargain, Mr. Farmer,[21] plan to be with us on one of the days of the sale. Our doors will open promptly at 9 a.m. Cordially yours,[22] [440]

Reading and Writing Practice

130

daugh·ter

ap

as

Wis·con·sin

pre·cise

conj

five-year *hyphenated before noun*

if

ques·tions

nc

to·mor·row

[138]

131

as

de·signed

nc

ex·pen·sive

intro

re·ceive

conj

Transcribe: 60 percent

ar·ea

pri·ma·ry

nc

me·di·um

and o

en·ve·lope

[125]

if

[174]

133

per·son's

ser

de·pend·able

ad·ver·tise

par

intro

self-ad·dressed

[97]

132

1615

10

Transcribe: ten 2-page

ap

par

Transcribe: $218

218

as

nec·es·sary

ser

par

re·quest

Developing Shorthand Writing Power

134 WORD BEGINNINGS AND ENDINGS

Ex-

1

Be-

2

-ingly

3

1. *Examine, exclude, explain, expenses, expressive, expert, expenditure.*
2. *Believe, because, become, before, beforehand, between, besides, unbecoming, beneath.*
3. *Increasingly, accordingly, seemingly, willingly, unwillingly, approvingly, knowingly, unknowingly.*

Building Transcription Skills

135 Business Vocabulary Builder

median income Income level reached by half the population.

site The location of an actual or planned structure.

visualize To form a mental image.

Progressive Speed Builder (60-100)

136 PREVIEW

137 *Retailer, daily, quickly, connection, telephone, if you need, provide.*
138 *Sporting, 4 million, more than, cities, products, special, issue.*
139 *To think, devote, entire, ideal, why not, advantage, power, section, submitting.*
140 *Customers, postage, insert, ordinary, newspaper, median, income, $20,000.*
141 *Advertisers, economical, route, results, brochure, eagerly, prospects, audience.*

LETTERS

137

[1 minute at 60]

Dear Mr. Green: If you are a retailer wishing to sell your business, advertise/the fact in the *Daily Times*. Your advertising will quickly help you make the right//connection.

To place your ad, telephone us at 555-8151. If you need///help in preparing your ad, a member of our staff will provide it. Yours truly, [1]

138

[1 minute at 70]

Dear Mr. Green: In the Sunday, April 21, issue of the *Daily Times* we will include/a special sporting goods shopping guide. With your advertising in this guide, you can reach the 4 million//readers of our paper. These people live in more than 10,000 cities and towns from coast to coast.///

Place an ad for your products in this special issue; it will pay off in more sales. Very truly yours, [2]

139

[1 minute at 80]

Dear Mr. Green: Fall is the time when people start to think about new cars. That is why in the September 16/*Daily Times* we will devote an entire section to new cars. This is the ideal place to tell more//than 4 million people about your new models.

Why not take advantage of the pulling power of this special///new-car section of the *Daily Times*. The closing date for submitting your advertising is August 1. Sincerely, [3]

140

[1 minute at 90]

Dear Mr. Green: Would you like to get your advertising message to your customers without spending money on postage? You/can do this if you will place an insert in the *Daily Times*. The *Daily Times* will carry your insert to more than 4 million//readers. These are not ordinary newspaper readers; they are people who have a median income of $20,000///a year.

Get your message to these people at a fraction of direct-mail costs; place an insert in the *Daily Times*. Cordially, [4]

141

[1 minute at 100]

Dear Mr. Green: More and more advertisers are including an insert in the *Daily Times* because they find that it is an economical/and quick route to sales results. Why not follow their lead.

Instead of inserting your advertising folder or brochure into an//ordinary envelope, put it into one of the most eagerly opened packages your prime prospects get every day—the *Daily Times*./// When you tell your story in the *Daily Times*, you reach an audience of more than 4 million readers.

Call us for all the details. Very truly yours, [5] [400]

● Reading and Writing Practice

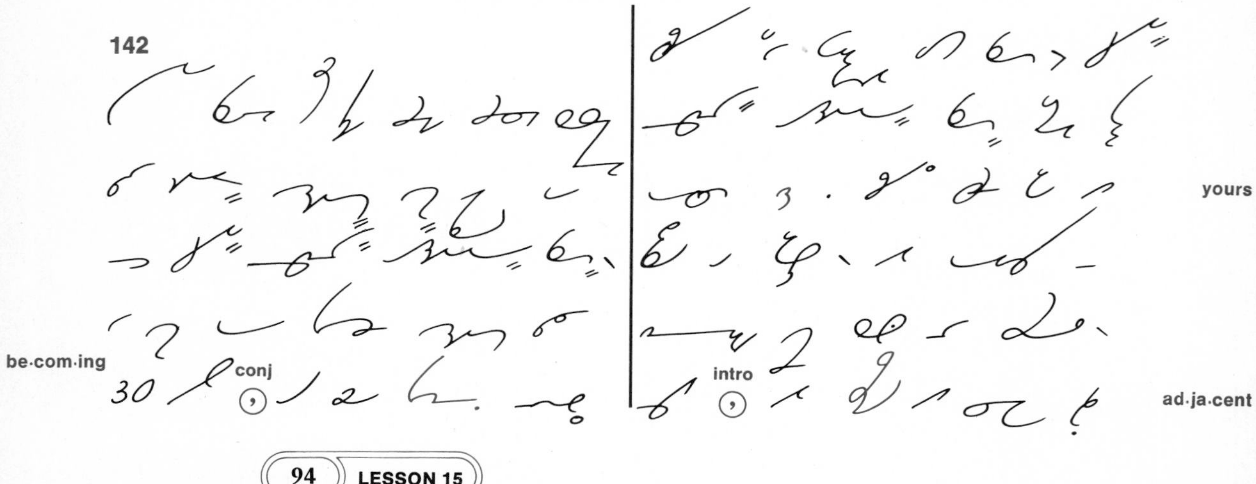

Transcribe:
one-half
ar·chi·tect

nonr

ap

site

[177]

143

ser
wheth·er
pho·tog·ra·phy

intro

en·joy·able

vi·su·al·ize

nc

de·scrib·ing

[129]

In meeting the public, your best approach is a polite, interested manner, and your best technique is to smile. A smile has an amazing effect, even over the telephone.

144 Brief Forms and Derivatives

How fast can you read the brief forms and derivatives in this chart? You should be able to read the entire chart in 2 minutes or less.

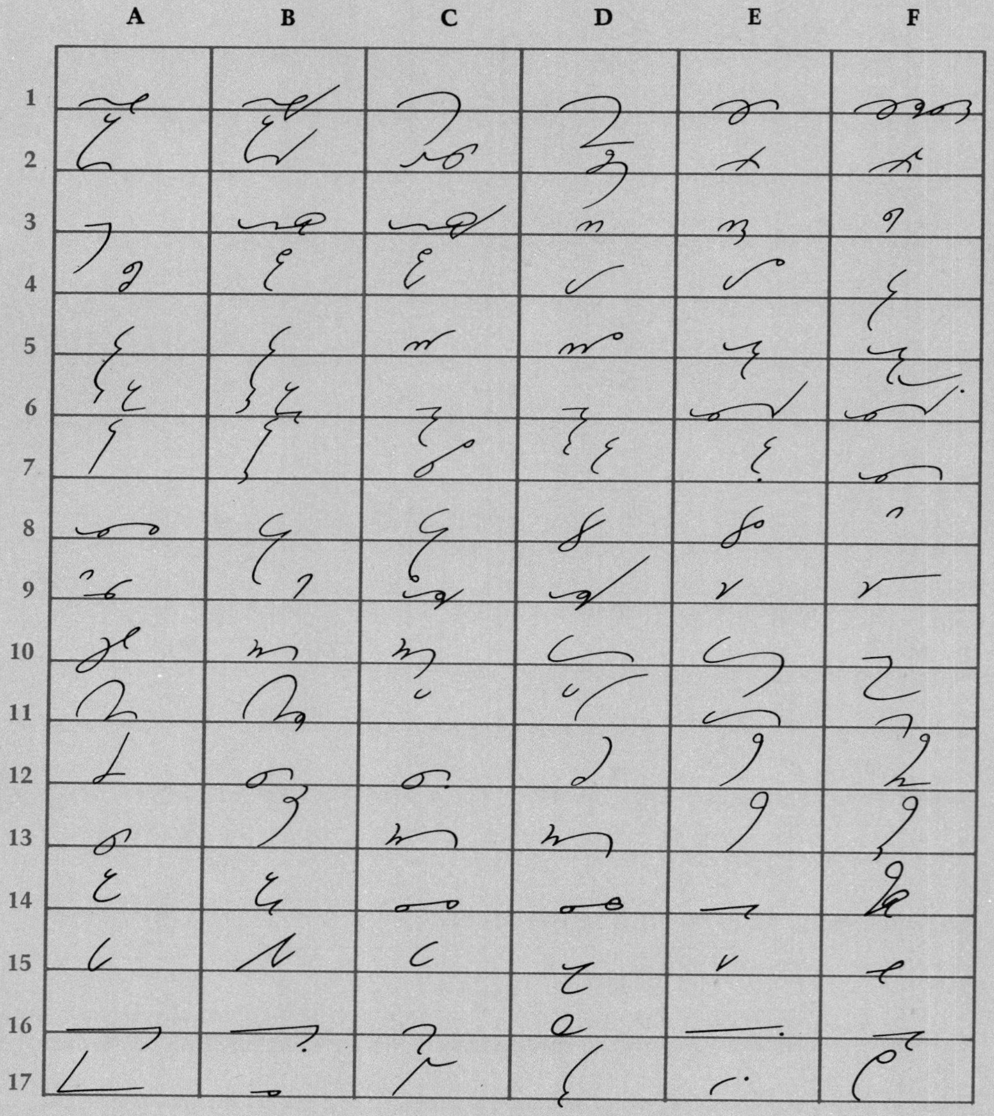

	A	B	C	D	E	F
1						
2						
3						
4						
5						
6						
7						
8						
9						
10						
11						
12						
13						
14						
15						
16						
17						

CHAPTER 4 Real Estate

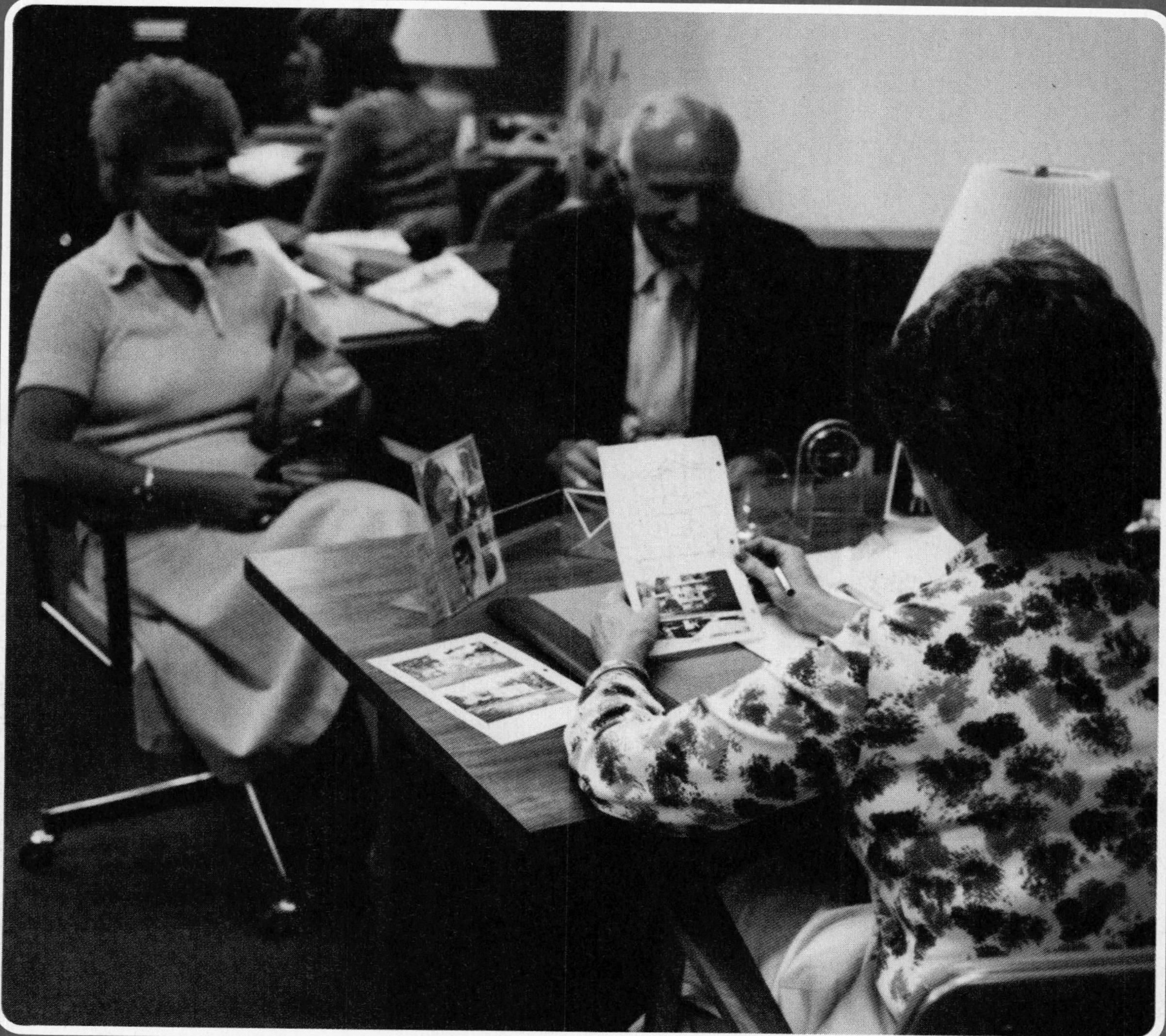

Typing Style and Punctuation Brushup

In the lessons of Chapter 4 you will review methods of typing literary and artistic titles, punctuation with quotation marks, and several rules for capitalization.

TITLES

1 In business letters, titles of books, pamphlets, magazines, and newspapers are underscored.

Our book, Jogging for Fun, just came off the press.

A copy of our booklet, Writing Effective Letters, is enclosed.

She subscribes to a magazine entitled World News.

I read the speech in yesterday's Chicago News.

2 Titles that represent a part of a complete published work are enclosed in quotation marks.

The article entitled "The Age of Automation" was published in the News Magazine.

The last chapter of his book is entitled "The Administrator Looks Ahead."

3 The titles of complete but unpublished works, such as manuscripts and reports, are enclosed in quotation marks.

We prepared a report entitled "Marketing in Europe."

The first word and all the main words in a title are capitalized. Words such as *in, the, of, and* are not capitalized.

Caution: These styles are recommended for general business letters; they are the styles followed in your textbook. However, some publishers prefer to have the titles of their publications typed in all capital letters; others prefer to have them quoted.

PUNCTUATION WITH QUOTATION MARKS

, introducing short quote isq (,)

1 Short quotations are introduced by a comma.

The owner said, "I am accepting applications for the job."

: introducing long quote ilq (:)

2 Long quotations are introduced by a colon.

Mr. Levy said: "I cannot attend the managers' conference in Chicago. I have several previously scheduled appointments that will necessitate my remaining here. I am asking Miss Jane Brown to represent me."

. inside quote iq (.)

, inside quote iq (,)

3 The period and comma are placed inside the final quotation mark.

The manager remarked, "There should be two more desks in the office."
The complaint, "I have been waiting for an hour," was ignored.

? inside quote iq (?)

4 The question mark is placed inside or outside the final quotation mark according to the sense of the sentence.

She asked, Have you tried the new computer?"
Why did he say, "I am not happy with the work"?

5 Semicolons and colons are placed outside the final quotation mark.

Be sure to mark the letter "Personal"; then place the carbon in a sealed envelope.
Shipments of the following goods should be marked "Fragile": glasses, plates, and cups.

CAPITALIZATION

1 Company Names and Divisions

Capitalize the first letter in the main words of a company name. Capitalize the word *the* only when it is part of the legal name of the organization. (Check the letterhead of the company to be sure.)

I work for The National Bank of Lexington.
He worked for the First State Bank.

Common organizational terms, such as *advertising department, manufacturing division, finance committee,* and *board of directors,* are not ordinarily capitalized.

He heads an advertising department.
She is a member of the finance committee.

2 Compass Points

Capitalize *north, south, east, west,* etc., only when they designate definite regions or when they are an integral part of a proper name.

I live in the South.
We went to the East Coast.
We are traveling west.

3 Days, etc.

Capitalize the names of the days of the week, months of the year, and holidays.

Our first class meets on Tuesday.
School begins in February.
The store will be closed Labor Day.

The names of the seasons are not usually capitalized.

We are enjoying spring weather.
Last winter was very cold.

4 General Classifications

Do not capitalize common nouns like *company* that represent general classifications.

Our company is opening a new branch office.

Use the following forms for the titles in the inside address, salutation, and body of business letters.

Mr. Keith	*Miss Washington*	*Dr. Pulaski*
Mrs. Kelley	*Ms. Lopez*	

Other titles, such as *professor* or *senator,* are spelled in full. They are capitalized only when they are used with names.

We will visit the professor.
The address was given by Professor Jenkins.

Developing Shorthand Writing Power

145 OUTLINE CONSTRUCTION

Omission of Vowel In cur, ker Omitting the minor vowel in the sounds *cur, ker* results in a very fluent joining.

1. *Current, incur, occur, recur, courage, curved, concur.*
2. *Courteously, excursion, curtail, courtesy, skirmish, curtain.*

Omission of Unaccented Circle Vowel The unaccented circle vowel is omitted between:

K and R

1

G and R

2

K and L, G and L

3

1. *Taker, maker, broker, thicker, career, locker.*
2. *Bigger, stagger, eager, tiger, sugar.*
3. *Local, focal, vocal, frugal, legal.*

Building Transcription Skills

146 Business Vocabulary Builder

panoramic Complete; unobstructed.

concurs Agrees.

moratorium A delay; a waiting period.

Reading and Writing Practice

147 A Home of Your Own

The selection of a home

Owning your own

[274]

148 LETTERS

company's fiscal

intro

reconsider

reapply

if

enu

assessment

when

process

[126]

decision

149

application

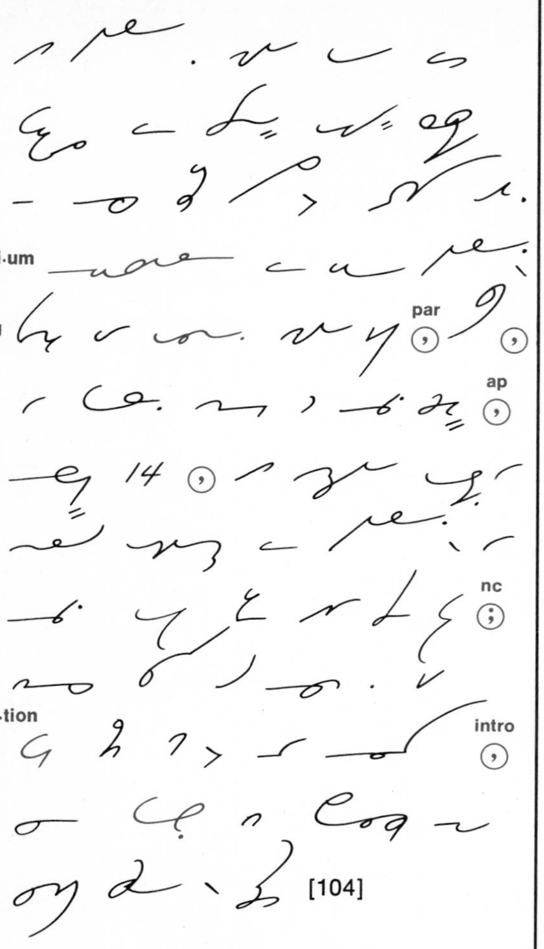

mor·a·to·ri·um

re·cur·ring

pre·sen·ta·tion

plac·ing

[104]

150

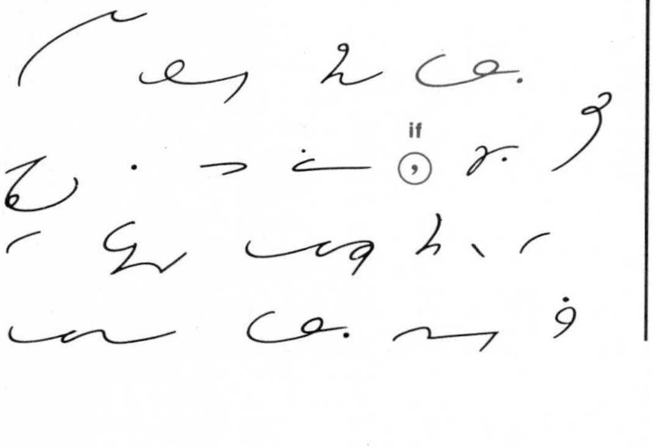

plan·ning

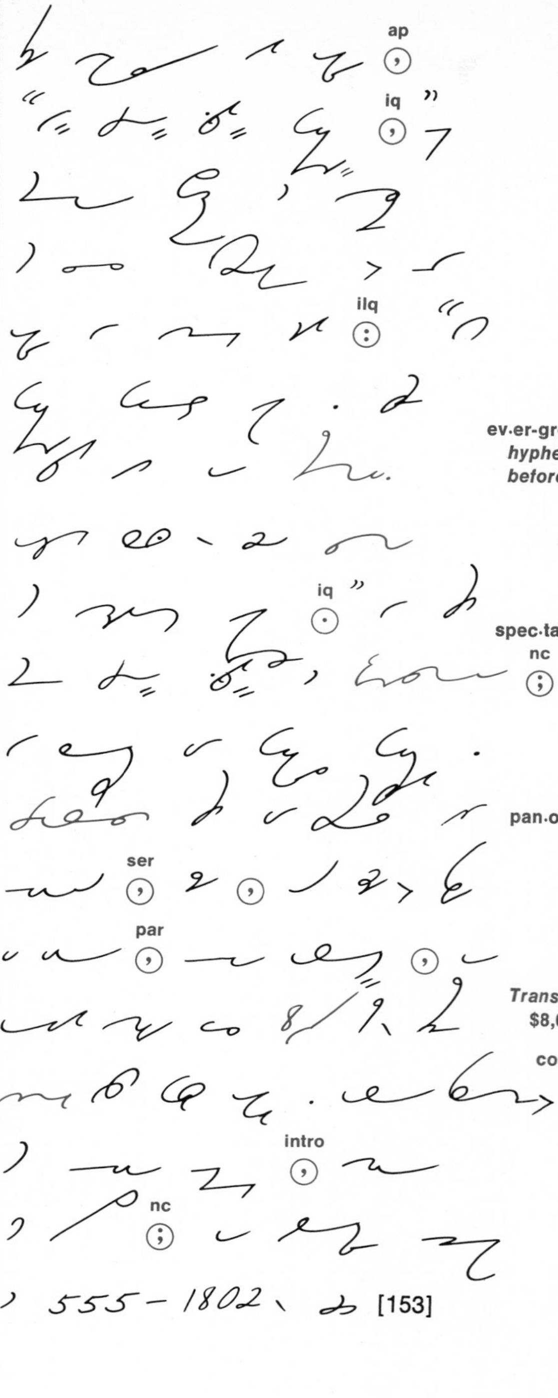

ev·er-grow·ing *hyphenated before noun*

ea·ger

spec·tac·u·lar

pan·oram·ic

Transcribe: $8,000

con·curs

[153]

Secretarial Tip
Turning Pages

Turning a notebook page efficiently may seem like a small thing. It is a minor matter, but knowing how to turn a page smoothly and quickly may sometimes make the difference between getting or losing several words of the dictation. Therefore, you should spend a few minutes to check your page-turning technique.

Perhaps the simplest method of turning the pages of a notebook is to treat the notebook as a solid block of wood. When you use this method, you push the notebook up with your left hand as you write down the first column with your right hand. When you are ready to begin writing in the second column, you pull the notebook down with your left hand until your right hand is at the top of the second column.

As your right hand goes down the second column, the left hand pushes the notebook up. When your writing hand is within a few lines of the end of the second column, the left hand prepares to turn the page by turning up the corner of the page. (See Figure 1.) As you are writing on the last line of the second column, the left hand grasps the turned-up corner. When you have written the last outline on the page, the left hand turns the page as the right hand moves up to begin the new column of the next page. (See Figure 2.)

▶ Note: If you are a left-handed writer, see page 410.

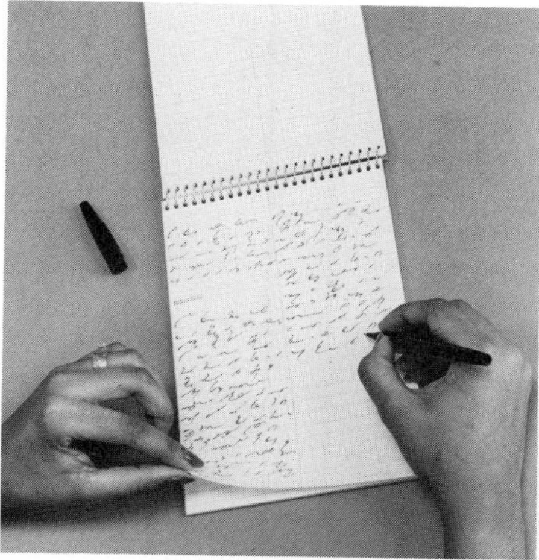

Figure 1: As the writer nears the bottom of the second column, the left hand turns up the corner of the page.

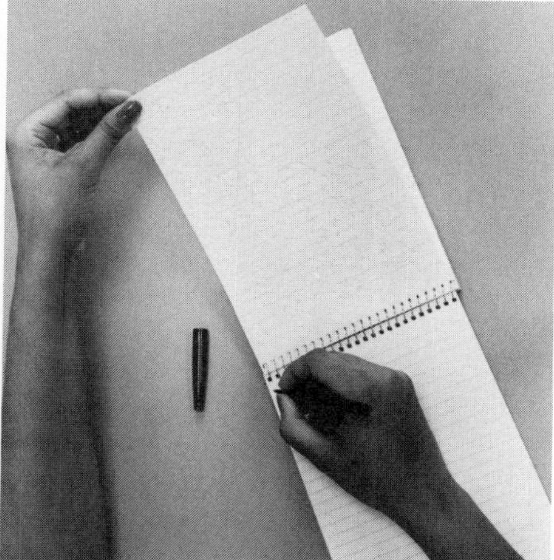

Figure 2: After the writer has written the last outline in the second column, the turned-up corner of the page is grasped with the left hand and the page can be turned quickly.

Developing Shorthand Writing Power

151 RECALL DRILL oo

In this lesson you will review the various uses of the *oo* hook.

Diphthong U

1

Diphthong Ow

2

Ul

3

-ulate

4

Under

5

---

1. *Unit, unite, unique, view, few, human, pure.*
2. *Now, how, vow, power, proud, loud, outside.*
3. *Consult, result, insult, multiply, ultimate, ultimately.*
4. *Calculate, regulate, stipulate, simulate, congratulate, tabulate.*
5. *Undertake, undergo, undertow, underdeveloped, underneath, understand, understood.*

Building Transcription Skills

152 Business Vocabulary Builder

obstacle Something that blocks or prevents action.

liens Rights to property as payment of debts.

collateral Something promised as security for a loan.

Writing Practice

153 PREVIEW

☐ 154

☐ 155

☐ 156

154 Enjoyed, discussion, requested, commercial, excellent, substantial, united.
155 Underwood, various, acquainted, incorporate, unique, financing, opportunity.
156 Council, annexed, unfortunately, granted, because, access, forthcoming.

LETTERS

154

Dear Mrs. Powers: I enjoyed our short discussion yesterday at Ms. Jane Mason's dinner party.

As you[1] requested, I have prepared some figures on the tax advantages of investing in commercial property that[2] I believe you will find interesting. Based on the information you gave me, I feel you are now in an excellent[3] position to make a substantial real estate investment.

Will you please call my secretary, Ms. Mary[4] Johnson, here at the United Real Estate Agency to arrange a time to come in to discuss the matter[5] in detail. I will be available to meet with you any time next week during the morning hours. Yours truly,[6]

155

Dear Mr. Underwood: Thank you for your request for information about the various homes we build. The best[7] way to become acquainted with the designs of our homes is to inspect our model homes in Shadow Brook Estates.[8]

We have four model homes on display that incorporate many unique features. There are sales representatives[9] at the homes to answer your questions concerning prices, location, and financing.

We hope you will take advantage[10] of this opportunity to see our homes and to get acquainted with our sales representatives. Yours truly,[11]

156

Ladies and Gentlemen: As you know, I appeared before the City Council in January to request that[12] my property east of the city be annexed. Unfortunately, my request was not granted. Please consider[13] this letter as my second formal request for this action.

The city refused to annex my property because[14] there was no access road. Since January, however, I have had an access road constructed.

Therefore, the[15] obstacle that prevented my property from being annexed is now removed. I trust your forthcoming[16] decision will be an affirmative one. I look forward to hearing from you at an early date. Cordially yours,[17] [340]

Reading and Writing Practice

157

buy·er

enu

ex·cel·lent

de·bris

nc

and o

[118]

158

re·cord·er's

intro

dis·cov·ered

dis·may·ing

col·lat·er·al

conj

sought

judg·ment

intro

ex·e·cut·ed

nc

intro

intro

un·der·mines

intro

conj

dis·ap·point

intro

else·where

[173]

159

intro

conj

ul·ti·mate·ly

mis·take

intro

to·tal·ing

liens

pro·ceed·ings

intro

when

par

if

nc

[169]

160

when

enu

ac·cess

80,

Transcribe: 80 percent

ul·ti·mate

iq

[138]

Developing Shorthand Writing Power

161 WORD FAMILIES

-cation

1

Out-

2

1. *Vacation, vocation, location, communication, duplication, education.*
2. *Outside, outstanding, outdone, outcome, outfit, outlay, outnumber.*

162 FREQUENTLY USED NAMES

Last Names

1

Men's First Names

2

1. *Garcia, Parks, Harris, Pulaski, Reynolds, Gilbert, Johnson.*
2. *Charles, Daniel, George, Barry, David, Don, Dennis.*

Building Transcription Skills

163 Business Vocabulary Builder

exclusive Limited to one; single.

formal Following strict or accepted form; proper.

rough-hewn Shaped without finishing.

Writing Practice

164 PREVIEW

☐ 165

☐ 166

☐ 167

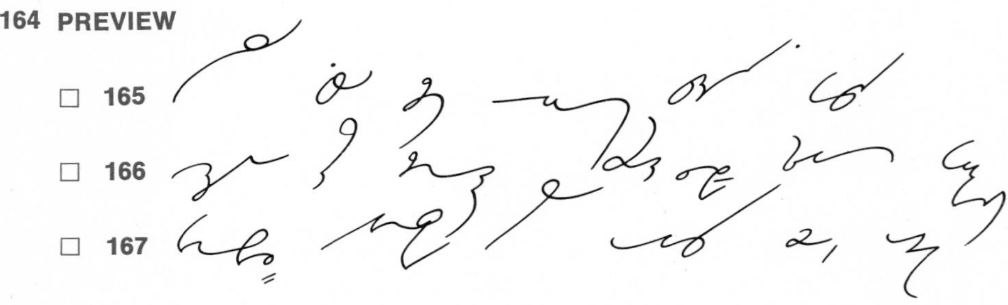

165 *Demand, hired, executive, mortgage, outstanding, proud.*

166 *Consider, advantages, exclusive, various, equipped, photograph, prospective.*

167 *Pulaski, described, detail, located, worship, reasonable.*

LETTERS

165

Dear Mrs. Harris: Because of the growing demand for real estate financing in our area, we have hired[1] Mr. Charles Parks as the manager of our new real estate department. Mr. Parks has been an executive[2] in the mortgage financing business for the past ten years. He has an outstanding record with two of the largest[3] companies in the area. He has a complete understanding of the financial problems of the real estate[4] field, and we are proud to make him a member of our staff.

Our company now has money available for[5] financing real property purchases. If you are in the market to buy or sell a piece of real property,[6] come to our office and let Mr. Parks outline the many services we offer customers. Cordially yours,[7]

166

Dear Mr. Harris: If you are planning to sell your home in the near future, may we suggest that you consider[8] the many advantages of an exclusive listing with National Realty.

We have 100 offices[9] in various locations throughout the nation. Our offices, which are located in the major poulation[10] centers of the United States, are all equipped with machines that print an actual photograph of your[11] home for prospective buyers. When you list your home with us, you will have the advantage of having more than 1,000[12] outstanding sales representatives working for you.

If you would like to have more detailed information about[13] how our organization works, write to us today; we look forward to hearing from you. Very truly yours,[14]

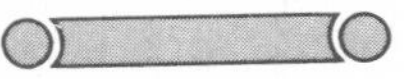

167

Dear Mr. Pulaski: Yesterday Mr. and Mrs. Daniel Davis came into our real estate office to[15] place their home for sale. When they showed me a picture of their home, described it in detail, and mentioned the location,[16] I thought of you. This home meets your requirements better than anything I have seen recently.

The house is located[17] in southeast Seattle and is near schools, stores, and houses of worship. The house has four bedrooms, a large family[18] room, a formal dining room, and 2½ baths.

The owners are asking $80,000, but they[19] will consider any reasonable offer. Call me immediately if you are interested. Yours truly,[20] [340]

Reading and Writing Practice

168

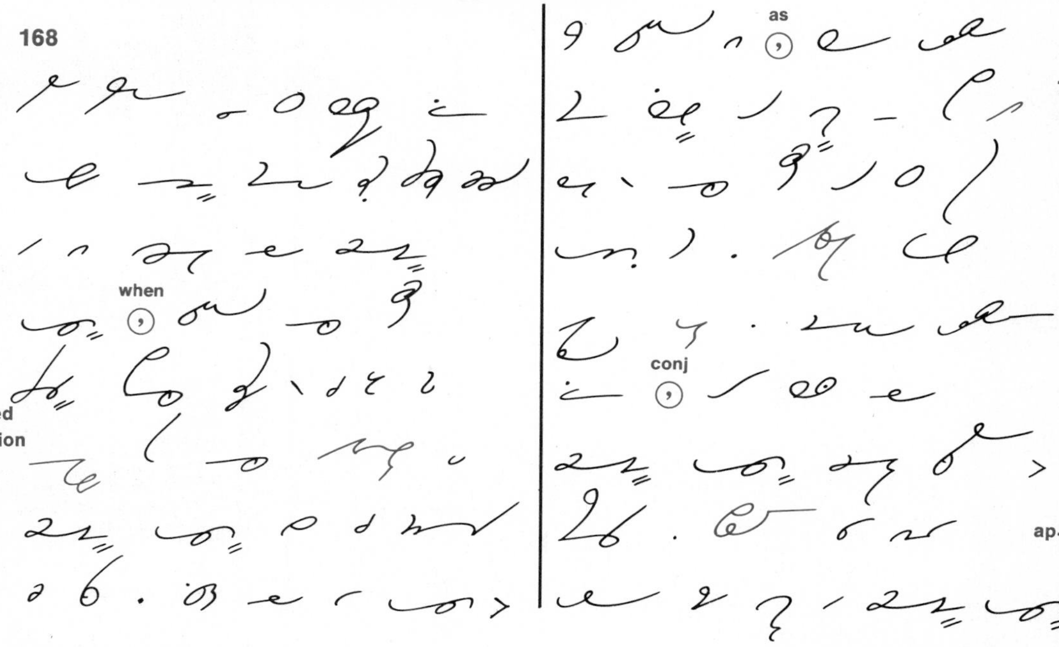

when

im·pressed

de·scrip·tion

as

Transcribe: two

de·sir·able

our·selves

conj

ap·point·ment

15

[131]

169

conj

award

wood·en

conj

rough-hewn

stained

par

built-in *hyphenated before noun*

ser

co·or·di·nat·ed

conj

cr

[155]

170

week's

intro

Transcribe: 410 North Pine Road

410

conj

buy·er

intro

ad

if

ex·clu·sive

intro

conj

ver·i·fy

qual·i·fy·ing

intro

po·ten·tial

when

[176]

171

ap

ap

poses

lay·out

intro

some·time

breaks

its

intro

cre·den·tials

pro·spec·tive

and o

[144]

Developing Shorthand Writing Power

172 FREQUENTLY USED PHRASES

To

1

Hope

2

1. To the, to that, to them, to these, to their, to this, to you, to get.
2. I hope, we hope, I hope that, I hope you will, we hope that, we hope you will be able, I hope you are, I hope you can.

173 GEOGRAPHICAL EXPRESSIONS

-ingham

1

States

2

Foreign Countries

3 

1. *Birmingham, Cunningham, Framingham, Nottingham, Buckingham.*
2. *Nevada, Maryland, West Virginia, South Carolina, North Carolina, Tennessee, New Jersey.*
3. *Australia, Burma, Colombia, Cuba, Israel.*

Building Transcription Skills

174 Business Vocabulary Builder

hedge Protection, especially financial.

parcels Plots of land.

● Writing Practice

175 PREVIEW

☐ 176
☐ 177
☐ 178

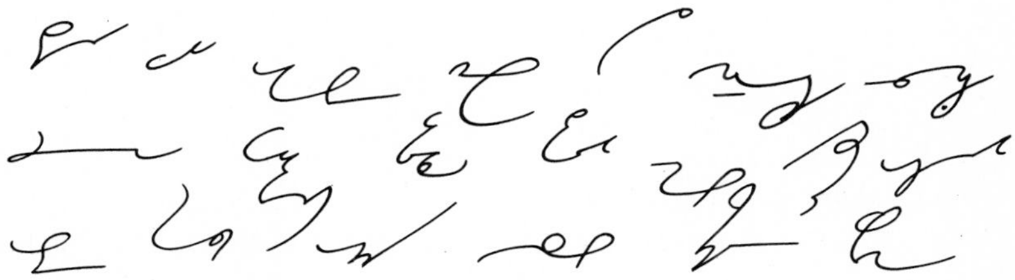

176 *Assistant, although, replacement, unable, to me, qualified, negotiate.*
177 *Seminar, prospective, sponsored, experts, inflation, disadvantages, residents.*
178 *Reassessment, valuation, resulted, garage, adjustment, I hope you will.*

LETTERS

176

Dear Mr. Tate: As you may know, Ms. Nancy Smith, who was my assistant for many years, recently retired and[1] moved to Columbia, South Carolina. Although we tried to find a replacement for her before she left, we[2] were unable to do so.

It occurred to me that you might know someone who is qualified for this position.[3] I need a person who would be able to make initial contacts with customers, negotiate real estate[4] contracts, and handle the general management of the office. I am willing to pay a qualified person[5] up to $1,500 a month.

If you know any people who could meet my needs, I would consider it[6] a personal favor if you would refer them to me. I will be in my office every day next week from 8[7] until 11 a.m. My telephone number is 555-8627. Very cordially yours,[8]

177

Dear Ms. Smith: A special seminar for prospective home buyers will be held on Thursday, March 25, at[9] 7:30 p.m. in the Nottingham Room of the Baker Hotel. The seminar is being sponsored by the[10] Nevada Real Estate Board.

A panel of experts will be on hand to answer the following questions regarding[11] real estate:

1. How can money invested in a home serve as a hedge against inflation?
2. Is land purchase[12] a good long-term investment?
3. What are the advantages and disadvantages of owning a home?

If[13] topics such as these interest you, we hope you will be with us next Thursday evening. There is no charge for this program;[14] it is being held as a special service to county residents. Yours truly,

P S. You may use the free parking[15] lot that is located east of the Baker Hotel near the Virginia Avenue entrance to the building.[16]

178

Dear Mrs. Cunningham: I recently received a notice of the reassessment of my property at[17] 326 East Main Street. The assessed valuation has been raised from $50,000 to $80,000,[18] which is an increase of 60 percent.

I called your office and talked to Mrs. Moore, the person who made[19] the reassessment. She said that the increase resulted from the construction of a new garage. This garage[20] represents less than 10 percent of the value of my home. I am, therefore, requesting an adjustment of my assessed[21] valuation to reflect the true increase.

I hope you will give me your decision soon. Very truly yours,[22] [440]

• Reading and Writing Practice

179

ap

auc·tion
par·cels

some time

pri·or·i·ty

rec·om·men·da·tions

[93]

180

re·as·sess·ment

intro

Transcribe: $950

par

cr

op·tion

self-ad·dressed

pro·vid·ed

[116]

Developing Shorthand Writing Power

181 WORD BEGINNINGS AND ENDINGS

Al-

1

-ther

2

-gram

3

1. *Almost, also, altogether, already, alter, alternate, alternative.*
2. *Brother, mother, father, neither, whether, bother, rather, leather.*
3. *Telegram, radiogram, diagram, monogram, program.*

Building Transcription Skills

182 Business Vocabulary Builder

tenants Those who temporarily occupy a building; renters.

coincidence Accidental sequence of events that appear to be related.

convalesces Returns to health.

Progressive Speed Builder (60-100)

183 PREVIEW

184 Mentioned, friend, interested, renting, cabin, decided.
185 Touch, expressed, trip, office, coincidence, summer, July.
186 Finally, able, whether, to change, to spend, Miami, directly.
187 Few days ago, learned, reasons, United States, cancel, disappointed.
188 Happening, sister, broke, therefore, convalesces, welcome, let me.

LETTERS

184

[1 minute at 60]

Dear Fred: Last January you mentioned that you had a friend who might be interested/in renting my cabin in August. Is he still interested?

Mary and I//decided that we will spend our vacation in Europe this year; consequently, our/// cabin is for rent. I am asking $500 for the month. Sincerely yours, [1]

185

[1 minute at 70]

Dear Jim: I have tried to get in touch with Harry Bates, the person who expressed an interest in renting/your cabin, but he is on a business trip and will not be back in his office until next Monday.//I will call him the first thing Monday morning.

As a strange coincidence, my wife and I are/// also going to Europe this summer, but we are leaving in early July. Very truly yours, [2]

186

[1 minute at 80]

Dear Jim: I finally was able to reach my friend, Harry Bates, this morning. I asked him whether he is still/interested in renting your cabin. He says that he has had to change his vacation from August to May and that//he and his wife have decided to spend the month in a hotel in Miami.

I will ask some of my other///friends, and if any of them are interested, I will have them get in touch directly with you. Sincerely yours, [3]

187

[1 minute at 90]

Dear Jim: A few days ago I learned that for business reasons I will have to stay in the United States during the month of/August. As a result, my wife and I have had to cancel our trip to Europe.

We are extremely disappointed because we// looked forward eagerly to the trip. If your cabin is still unrented, we would like to take it either for the first two weeks///or the last two weeks of August.

If you would be willing to rent it for two weeks, what would be the rental charge? Very truly yours, [4]

188

[1 minute at 100]

Dear Fred: Strange things seem to be happening to both of us. We, too, have had to cancel our trip to Europe. My wife's sister, who is 76/years old, fell down and broke her hip, and my wife has to take care of her. We are, therefore, going to take her to the cabin for two months//while she convalesces.

Perhaps you and Mary can spend a weekend with us in August. The cabin has a large guest room that you are welcome///to use. During your stay we can do some fishing; there are lots of fish in our lake.

Let me know how this idea appeals to you. Sincerely yours, [5] [400]

Reading and Writing Practice

189

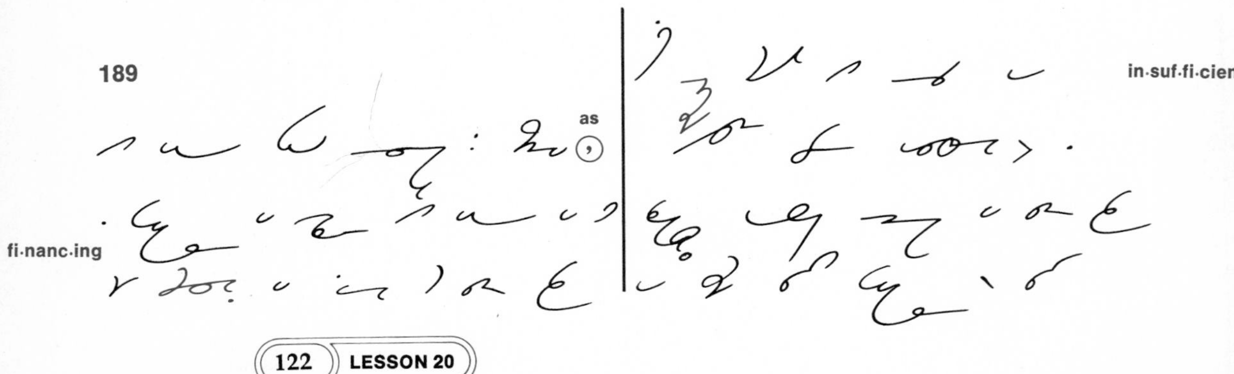

av·er·age
al·most
Transcribe:
$50,000
30 percent
re·quire·ment
qual·i·fy
conj
intro
rec·om·mend
pro·cess
[162]

190

intro
geo
intro
ten·ants
li·cense
intro
intro
ac·knowl·edge
cr
Smith's
[124]

191 Brief Forms and Derivatives

The following chart contains many brief forms and derivatives. Can you read the brief forms as rapidly going up and down each column as you can read them going from left to right?

Reading goal: 2 minutes or less.

	A	B	C	D	E	F
1						
2						
3						
4						
5						
6						
7						
8						
9						
10						
11						
12						
13						
14						
15						
16						
17						

PART

Secretarial Tip
Page from a Secretary's Notebook

On page 127 there is a page from an efficient secretary's notebook. Let us examine some of the techniques that were used.

▶ Note: The numbers of the following paragraphs correspond to the encircled numbers on page 127.

1 The end of a letter is indicated with a double line.

2 There are several blank lines between letters. Instructions from the dictator are written on these lines either during or after the dictation.

3 The dictator inserted a word in a sentence that was previously dictated. The point of the insertion is indicated with a caret and the word is written directly above it.

4 The employer dictated the punctuation in this particular sentence. The punctuation is inserted and circled.

5 The heavy colored pencil mark down the side of this letter indicates that the letter is to be transcribed first.

6 This shorthand outline represents the expression *Basic College Typing.* The secretary devised a shortcut for the term because it was used frequently.

7 The date is always placed at the bottom of the page.

8 The dictator spelled out this name. Whenever the dictator spells a name or a word, the secretary writes it in longhand.

9 The dictator decided to make a long insertion in a paragraph that had already been dictated. The secretary placed a large *a* at the point of the insertion.

10 A double line is drawn after the last sentence that had been dictated.

11 A large *a* is written underneath the double line followed by the material to be inserted.

12 Another double line is drawn to indicate the end of the insertion.

13 The dictator decided to make a transposition.

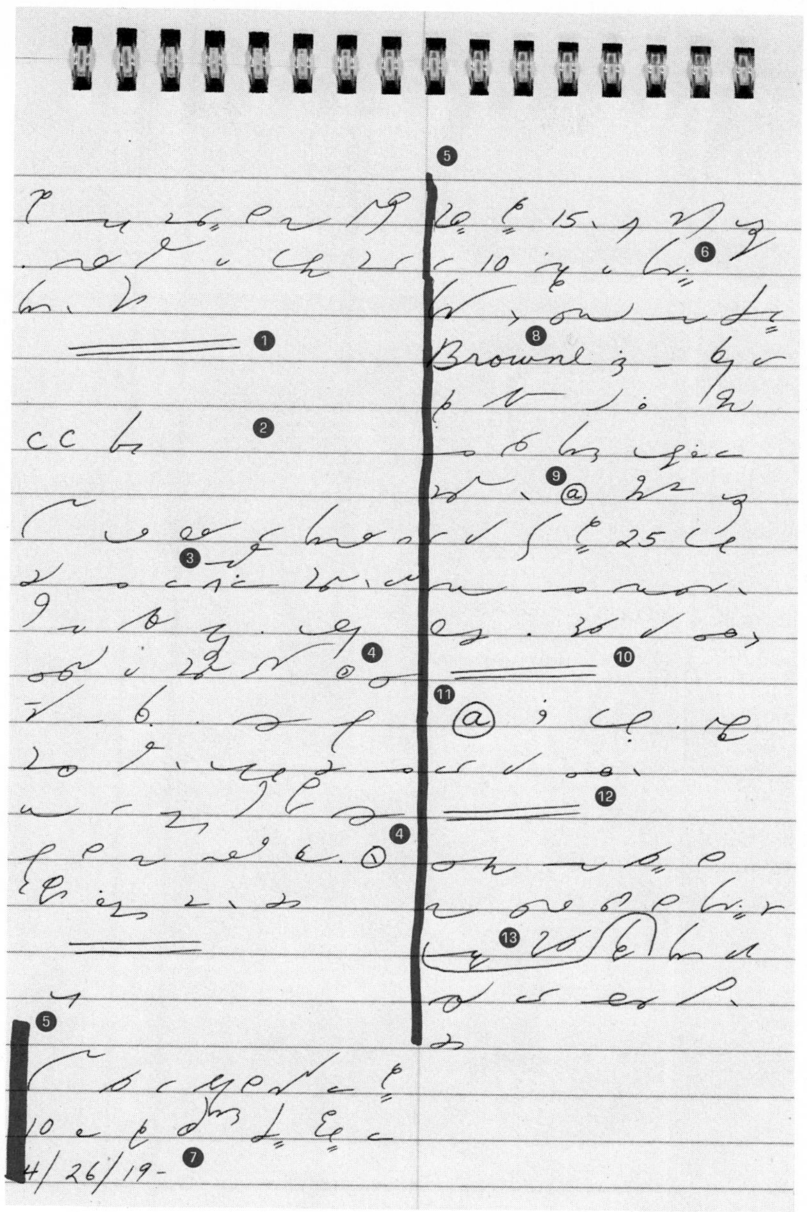

CHAPTER

5

Schools and Education

Developing Shorthand Writing Power

192 OUTLINE CONSTRUCTION

Vowel Written In -ant, -ent The vowel is written in the endings *-ant, -ent* when those endings follow *i, n, r,* or *l.*

I

1

N

2

R

3

L

4

---

1. *Compliant, defiant, client, giant, reliant, self-reliant.*
2. *Prominent, permanent, component, dominant, indignant.*
3. *Ignorant, inherent, grant, restaurant, fragrant, tyrant.*
4. *Implant, transplant, silent, talent, excellent, propellant.*

Building Transcription Skills

193 PUNCTUATION PRACTICE , contrast Contrasting expressions are set off by commas.

I need your reply today, not next week.

The higher we climb, the more we will be able to see.

▶ Note: When such phrases fit smoothly into the flow of the sentence, no commas are required.

It was a luxurious but very practical house.

Whenever this use of the comma occurs in the Reading and Writing Practice exercises, it will be indicated in the shorthand thus: cont (,)

● Reading and Writing Practice

194 Educated People

There are two

We must

[201]

195 LETTERS

ilq

sal·a·ries

Transcribe: five 25 percent

iq

conj

ex·cel·lent

ad·mis·sion

if

ap·pli·cants

intro

cont

[161]

ac·cept·ed

196

tech·nol·o·gy

ap

Transcribe: 9 a.m.

com·pre·hen·sive

intro

and o

up-to-date
hyphenated before noun

cont

intro

intro

equal·ly

if

high·ly re·ward·ing
no hyphen after ly

[192]

197

ap

15

enu

1

straight-copy
prob·lem-solv·ing
• *hyphenated before noun*

2

3

intro

pro·ce·dures

well in·formed
no noun, no hyphen

intro

rec·om·mend

be·gin·ning

[113]

Developing Shorthand Writing Power

198 RECALL DRILL f

In this drill you will review the various situations in which the shorthand *f* is used.

F

1

-ful

2

Fur-

3

For-, Fore-

4

-ification

5

Feet

6 10, 405, 6, 1/2, .

1. *Fame, free, fact, effect, affect, leaf, roof.*
2. *Grateful, wonderful, successful, handful, painful, careful.*
3. *Furnish, furnished, furniture, furnishings, further, furthermore, furtive, furnace.*
4. *Forget, forgot, fortunate, foreclose, foreclosure.*
5. *Ratification, justification, notification, verification, qualification, classification.*
6. *10 feet, 405 feet, 600 feet, 1,000 feet, a few feet.*

Building Transcription Skills

199 PUNCTUATION PRACTICE , words omitted A comma is used to indicate the omission of a word or several words that are clearly understood from the meaning of the sentence.

One of our automobiles is bright red; the other, drab blue.

In March our branch sales increased 18 percent; in April, 15 percent.

You may pay one-half of the purchase price now; the balance, in three months.

Whenever this use of the comma occurs in the Reading and Writing Practice exercises, it will be indicated in the shorthand thus: wo (,)

Writing Practice

200 PREVIEW

☐ 201

☐ 202

☐ 203

201 *College, character, education, borrow, necessary, unforeseen.*
202 *Picture, yearbook, Fletcher, appointment, immediately, until, requires.*
203 *Maintenance, modifications, classroom, bookshelf, display, adjustable.*

LETTERS

201

Dear Mr. Fleming: Working your way through college is a fine way to build character. Unfortunately, it has[1] a tendency to interfere with the primary purpose of going to school—learning.

You can make things easier[2] for yourself, Mr. Fleming, by arranging for an education loan from the Mutual Trust Company.[3] Our loans are available to all college students, and you may apply for a loan at any time. You may borrow[4] as much as $16,000 and use it for tuition, books, or any other necessary college[5] expenses.

After you graduate, you will have as long as four years to repay the loan. For a small fee we[6] furnish repayment insurance so that the loan will be paid in full should you die, become disabled, or if any[7] other unforeseen circumstance should arise.

For more detailed information, write or call us soon. Yours truly,[8]

202

Dear Students: In order for your picture to appear in the school yearbook, it will be necessary for you to[9] have your photograph taken before school begins.

Please call the Fletcher Photography Studio at 555-3121[10] and make an appointment to have your picture taken. Because only three weeks' time remains before[11] the school term begins, we suggest you make your appointment immediately. Monday through Friday the studio[12] is open from 9 a.m. until 5 p.m.; on Saturday, from 9 a.m. until noon.

The sitting requires[13] only a few minutes; please call the studio as soon as possible for an appointment. Very truly yours,[14]

203

Dear Mr. Allen: I am enclosing the maintenance-request form that outlines in detail the modifications[15] I would like to have made in my classroom for the next two school years. I would like to have some of the work done this[16] summer; the rest, next summer.

This year I would like a special bookshelf 6 feet by 5 feet placed next to the display[17] board in the back of the room. I prefer open shelving on adjustable brackets rather than permanent shelves.[18] Next year I would like to have two 6-drawer file cabinets to hold my curriculum materials.

Last week[19] when you changed the electrical wiring in my room, your construction foreman, James Smith, left several hundred feet[20] of heavy-gauge wire in my storage closet. Would you ask him to pick it up as soon as possible. Yours truly,[21]

[420]

Reading and Writing Practice

204

co·op·er·a·tion

intro

in·sti·tut·ed

city's

Transcribe:
five

stu·dio

Transcribe:
9 a.m.

nc

wo

en·rich·ment

for·tu·nate

[150]

205

as

intro

nc

wo

Feb·ru·ary

conj

intro

conj

intro

[123]

Admin
Dept Ch

LESSON 23

Developing Shorthand Writing Power

206 WORD FAMILIES

-ness

1 

-stic

2 

---

1. *Fairness, willingness, helpfulness, carelessness, happiness, freshness, illness.*
2. *Artistic, realistic, drastic, elastic, plastic, mystic.*

---

207 FREQUENTLY USED NAMES

Last Names

1 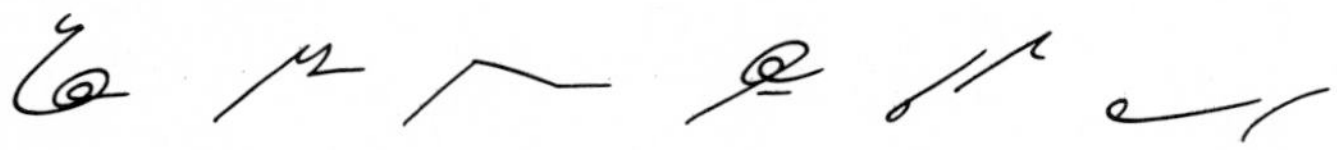

Women's First Names

2 

---

1. *O'Brien, Dawson, Duncan, Dwyer, Edwards, Ellington.*
2. *Charlotte, Cynthia, Diane, Evelyn, Ellen, Eve.*

Building Transcription Skills

208 PUNCTUATION PRACTICE , interruption of thought

When a word, phrase, or clause is inserted in a sentence and interrupts the thought of that sentence, use commas to set off the insert.

Programming a computer, I am told, *requires much skill.*

Our school building, you must admit, *is in the best of condition.*

Our new building will be as big as, if not bigger than, *any other building in town.*

Caution: Be sure to enclose the complete interrupting expression, not just part of it.

no

Our business volume is as great as, if not greater, than it was a year ago.

yes

Our business volume is as great as, if not greater than, it was a year ago.

Each time this use of the comma occurs in the Reading and Writing Practice exercises, it will be indicated in the shorthand thus: it (,)

Writing Practice

209 PREVIEW

☐ 210

☐ 211

☐ 212

---

210 Concerned, discussed, superintendent, deduct, prior, willingness.
211 Adult, Los Angeles, painting, qualified, artistic, talent.
212 Academy, launched, strong, institution, continue, contribute.

LETTERS

210

To the Staff: I am very much concerned about the matter of absence at our regular monthly staff meetings.[1] I have discussed the problem with Ms. Ellen James, our school superintendent. She recommends that we deduct an[2] hour's wages from the paychecks of those who miss these required meetings without prior approval.

Some of you will[3] probably think that this is a

drastic step, but I am sure you realize the importance of our communicating[4] with each of you at least once a month to discuss current problems. Therefore, we feel the proposed action is entirely[5] justified.

Your willingness to cooperate with us will be appreciated. Diane Fox, Principal[6]

211

Dear Miss Dawson: The adult education department of the Los Angeles City Schools will sponsor an advanced[7] painting class at the East Hills High School beginning at 7 p.m. on Thursday, September 21. The[8] course will run for six weeks and is intended for those who have had some experience in painting.

Our instructor,[9] Miss Charlotte O'Brien, is particularly well qualified to teach advanced techniques of painting. If you have[10] artistic talent, and I suspect that you do, here is an opportunity to develop it under the[11] expert guidance of Miss O'Brien.

You may register at the principal's office, which is located near the[12] Baker Avenue entrance to the building, at any time prior to the first class meeting. Very truly yours,[13]

212

Dear Mr. Duncan: The Evans Academy annual fund-raising drive was launched a few weeks ago, and we[14] are encouraged by the strong support we have received.

Our drive comes at a time when Evans Academy, like every[15] other institution of learning, is in greater need of financial support than ever before. If the[16] excellent programs for which Evans Academy has long been known are to continue, and we hope they will, all[17] alumni will have to contribute generously to our drive.

Will you please help by sending your check soon? Just make[18] it out to the Evans Academy Fund. Your willingness to help will be appreciated. Sincerely yours,[19] [380]

Reading and Writing Practice

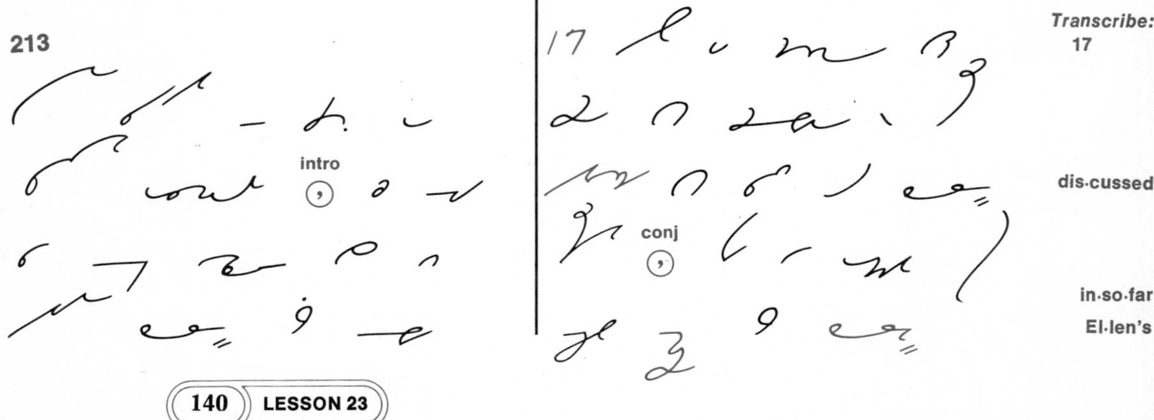

at·ten·dance

as

re·al·is·tic

con·tin·u·a·tion

intro

al·ter·nate

its

ac·cept

rec·om·men·da·tion

intro

conj

if

[214]

214

as

great

ser

ad·min·is·tra·tors

com·prise

par

it

par·tic·i·pa·tion

[181]

215

it

ev·i·denced

wel·come

par

Transcribe:
40

ap

[80]

Developing Shorthand Writing Power

216 FREQUENTLY USED PHRASES

Time

1

As

2

1. *On time, in time, the time, at the time, at that time, this time, from time.*
2. *As you, as you know, as you can, as you can see, as you say, as you will, as well, as good.*

217 GEOGRAPHICAL EXPRESSIONS

-wood

1

States

2

Foreign Countries

3

1. *Elmwood, Greenwood, Maplewood, Oakwood, Ridgewood.*
2. *Arkansas, Wisconsin, Rhode Island, Louisiana, Mississippi, Georgia, New Jersey, Connecticut.*
3. *Spain, Mexico, Peru, Bolivia, Poland, Russia.*

Building Transcription Skills

218 Business Vocabulary Builder

critical Inclined to judge severely.
strategy A plan of action.
flawless Without defect.

Writing Practice

219 PREVIEW

☐ 220

☐ 221

☐ 222

220 *Spanish, enough, Colombia, studying, language, flawless, vocabulary.*
221 *Greenwood, critical, influence, discipline, rigid, associated.*
222 *Homecoming, alumni, canceled, reception, auditorium, forward.*

LETTERS

220

Dear Mr. James: Do you know that in just a few short months you can learn Spanish well enough to feel at home in Spain,[1] Mexico, or Colombia? You can do this by studying Spanish with the aid of our new language recordings,[2] which employ a new and easy method that is used by some of the country's leading colleges.

With this method[3] you listen to and imitate the flawless Spanish of native speakers. As you listen, you quickly pick up[4] the correct accent and develop your vocabulary.

More than 100,000 students have learned Spanish[5] with our recordings. Why not join them the next time you want an interesting challenge. Mail the enclosed circular to[6] receive a free brochure. It will show you how you can learn Spanish quickly and easily. Very sincerely yours,[7]

221

Dear Miss Allen: I have written you several times over the past ten years concerning the experiences[8] our children had while attending Greenwood High School here in Rhode Island. As you know, the letters were sometimes quite[9] critical.

As I look back over the years, however, I am inclined to acknowledge that Greenwood High School exerted[10] a very positive influence on my children. Your school's discipline was quite rigid, which I now believe[11] contributed to a good academic atmosphere. The fact that my children have adjusted so well to college[12] indicates that your staff did a fine job in preparing them.

I am very happy to have been associated[13] with you over the years. Even though I have no children in your school at the present time, you may count on[14] my unqualified support for the many excellent programs you operate at Greenwood High. Cordially yours,[15]

222

Dear Ms. Smith: Homecoming this year will be held on Friday, November 15, at Elmwood College.

The fee for members[16] of the Elmwood College Alumni Association is $5, and it is due now. Please send us your[17] check for this amount in the enclosed envelope as soon as possible. Your canceled check will serve as your receipt.[18]

We have planned many special events this year. We will have a reception, a concert by the college orchestra,[19] and a dinner honoring those professors who will be retiring at the end of the year. All events will be[20] held in our new auditorium at 121 Louisiana Street.

We are confident that you will[21] enjoy your return to Elmwood College once again this year. Please come; we look forward to seeing you. Yours truly,[22] [440]

Reading and Writing Practice

223

ap

its

an·nu·al

Transcribe: 5 p.m.

chil·dren's

turn·out

intro

some·time
ap·point·ments

ad·here

nonr

en·joy·able

wel·come
prin·ci·pal

ap

11:20

[157]

224

Transcribe:
seven
Room 712

712

strat·e·gy

ap

per·son·nel

as

sim·i·lar

[124]

Developing Shorthand Writing Power

225 WORD BEGINNINGS AND ENDINGS

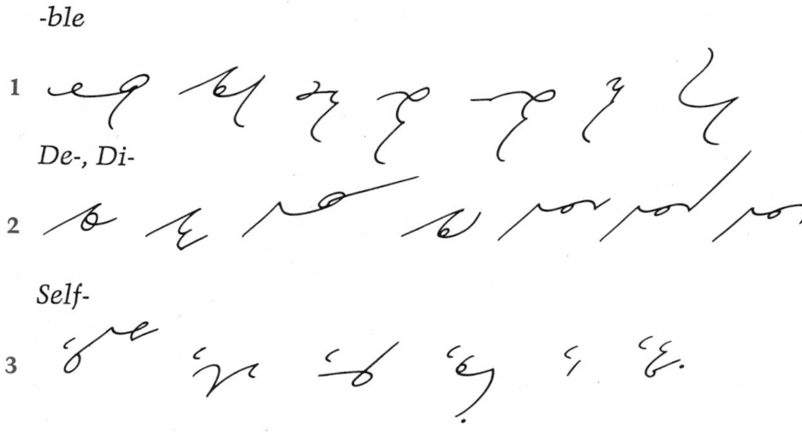

1. Reliable, dependable, sensible, capable, incapable, washable, valuable.
2. Desire, deposit, delighted, depend, direct, directed, direction.
3. Self-addressed, self-confidence, self-made, self-serving, selfish, self-supporting.

Building Transcription Skills

226 PUNCTUATION PRACTICE connecting words repeated

When a connecting word such as *and*, *or*, or *nor* is repeated before items in a series, the items are not separated by commas. Example:

The shipment of strawberries was not spoiled or discolored or damaged in any way.

but

We need a desk, a file, and a chair for our new office.

Progressive Speed Builder (70-110)

Once again, the speed range of the letters in this Progressive Speed Builder will be increased. The letters in this Progressive Speed Builder begin at 70 words a minute and run to 110 words a minute.

If you practice the preview before you take the letters from dictation and pay close attention to the vocabulary of the early letters in this Progressive Speed Builder, the 110-word-a-minute letter will be easy for you.

227 PREVIEW

228 Description, convinced, similar, program, discuss, perhaps.
229 Complete, details, pleased, rather, thanks, invitation.
230 Luncheon, suggestions, install, ourselves, turnover, personnel.
231 Discussion, also, running, ahead, submit, members, concerned.
232 Management, committee, dissenting, outlining, difficulty, visual.

LETTERS

228

[1 minute at 70]

Dear Mr. Davis: After listening to the description of your sales training program at the/meeting of the Management Club yesterday, I was convinced that my company would profit greatly//from a similar program.

Would it be possible for you sometime in the near future to discuss///this program with me and perhaps tell me how we should go about starting such a program? Sincerely, [1]

229

[1 minute at 80]

Dear Mr. James: I will, of course, be glad to give you complete details about our sales training program. While we/are pleased with the program in general, it does present some rather difficult problems, not the least of which//is expense. I will give you the whole story when I see you.

Thanks for your invitation to have luncheon with you///at your executive dining room. Will Thursday, June 20, at 12 o'clock be convenient? Sincerely, [2]

230

[1 minute at 90]

Mr. Jones: I had luncheon yesterday with Mr. William H. Davis, and he told me about the sales training program they/use at Best and Company. He made many suggestions on how we can install such a program ourselves and what the cost would//be.

I am sold on the idea of starting such a program here because it will help us reduce our turnover of personnel,///which has been very high in recent years.

When will it be convenient for me to discuss this program with you? Abe James [3]

231

[1 minute at 100]

Mr. James: After our discussion last week, I am also convinced that we will be taking a smart step by running our own sales training/program.

Please go ahead and outline a plan for the program and submit it to me by January 15, if possible. On that date I//will meet with the management committee and take that opportunity to present the plan to them.

I think the members of the committee///will buy the idea because they, too, have been very much concerned about the high turnover of personnel in recent years. William Jones [4]

232

[1 minute at 110]

Mr. James: You will be happy to know that the management committee approved your idea for the installation of a sales training program in/our organization without a dissenting vote. You did such a fine job outlining your plan that after I presented it, there were only two or three//questions that were asked. I was able to answer each of them without any difficulty at all.

I am attaching a color circular that describes/// some printed and visual materials that might be helpful to you in the sales training course. Perhaps you might want to investigate them. William Jones [5] [450]

Reading and Writing Practice

233

quan·ti·ty

if

intro

em·ploy·ees

com·pe·tent

Transcribe: ten

guar·an·tee

per·son·nel

ap

nc

fur·ther

com·pli·men·ta·ry

[171]

234

de·vel·op

per·suad·ed

train·ees

pos·sess

de·sir·able

intro

cat·a·log

nonr

six-month *hyphenated before noun*

if

poise

Transcribe: 302 East 21 Street

302 21

nc

par

[210]

235

as

an·nu·al

intro

intro

en·coun·tered

par

[82]

CHAPTER 6

Travel and Transportation

Developing Shorthand Writing Power

236 OUTLINE CONSTRUCTION

Vowel Omitted In -ant, -ent The vowel is omitted in the word endings *-ant, -ent* in the following families:

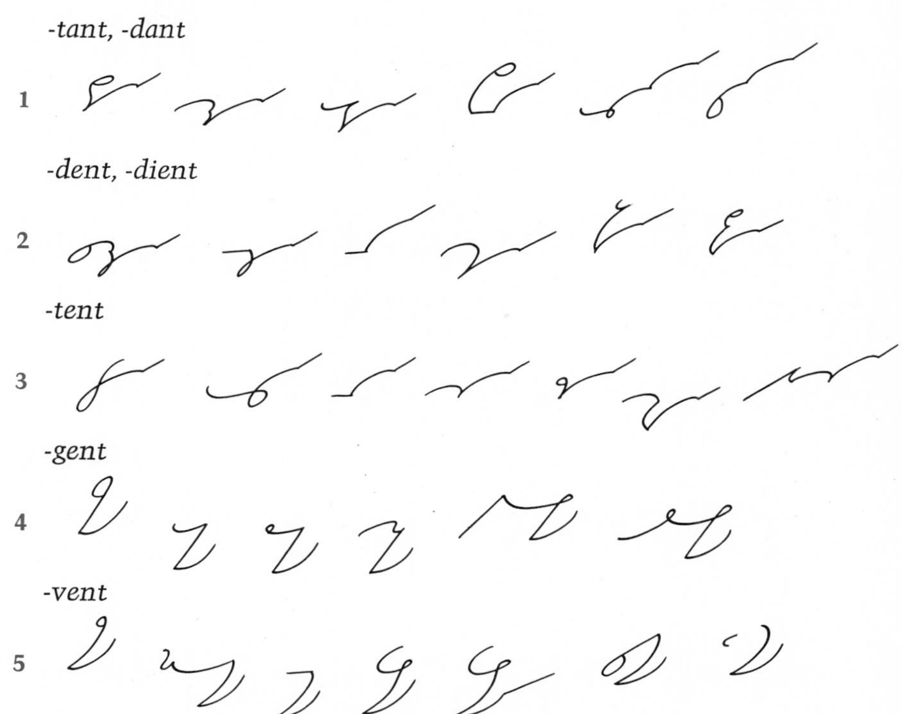

1. *Assistant, constant, resistant, abundant, redundant, attendant.*
2. *Accident, incident, indent, confident, obedient, expedient.*
3. *Patent, latent, intent, content, extent, competent, discontent.*
4. *Agent, regent, urgent, cogent, diligent, intelligent.*
5. *Event, solvent, invent, prevent, prevented, advent, circumvent.*

Building Transcription Skills

237 SIMILAR-WORDS DRILL You are already familiar with the Similar-Words Drill through your work with previous volumes of Gregg Shorthand, Series 90. You will recall that these drills call your attention to groups of words that sound or look alike or almost alike so that you will be on the alert to choose the correct word when you transcribe.

Study the definition of each word and read the examples.

SIMILAR-WORDS DRILL adapt, adopt

adapt To modify; to change.

We will adapt *the plans to fit our needs.*

adopt To accept formally and put into effect.

We must adopt *the resolution as it is written.*

Reading and Writing Practice

238 Traveling by Air

During takeoff

[233]

Government regulations

239 LETTERS

con·sis·tent·ly

ap

ev·i·dent

high-qual·i·ty
hyphenated before noun

de·layed

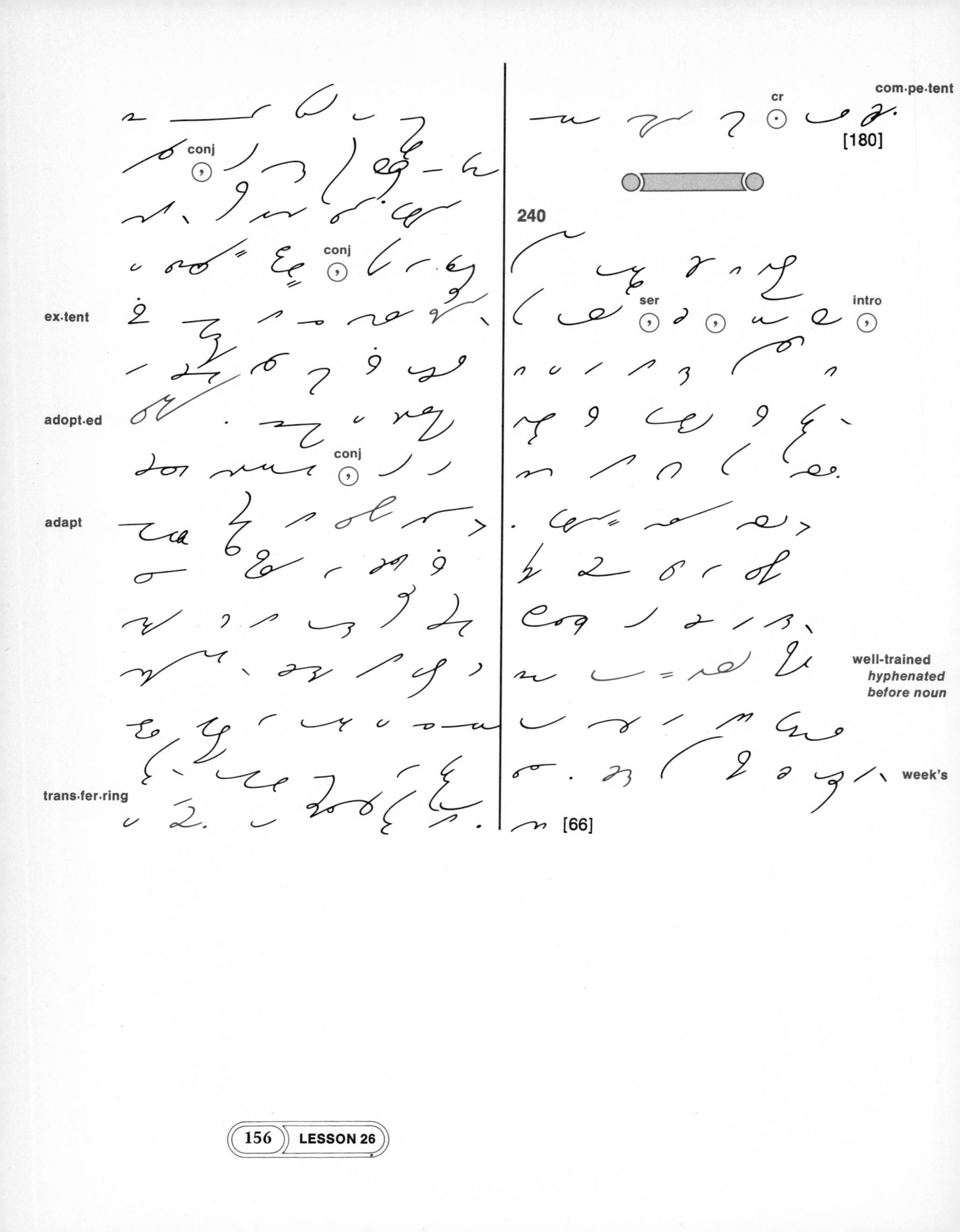

conj

conj

ex·tent

adopt·ed

conj

adapt

trans·fer·ring

cr

com·pe·tent

[180]

240

ser

intro

well-trained
hyphenated before noun

week's

[66]

Developing Shorthand Writing Power

241 RECALL DRILL n

In this drill you will review the several uses of the alphabet stroke *n*.

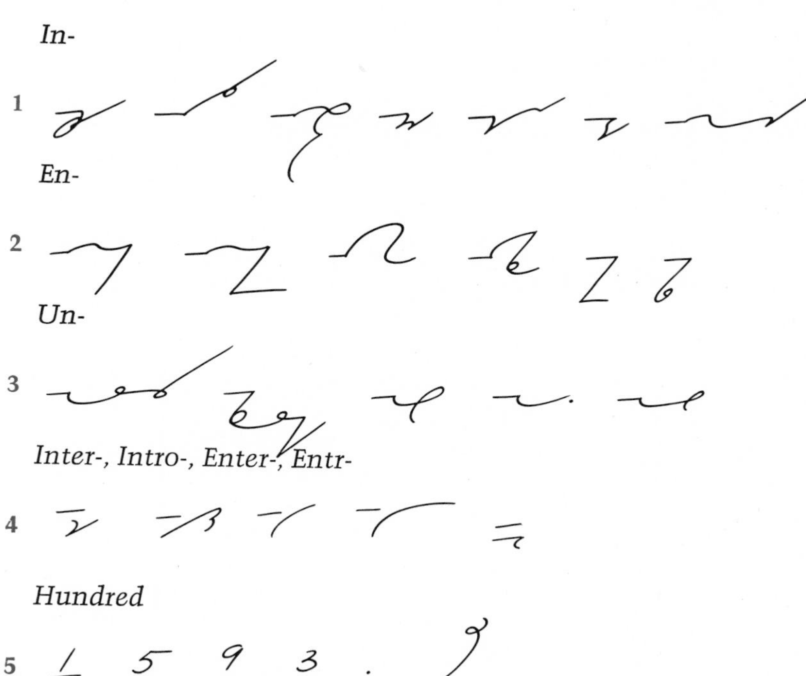

1. *Inside, indeed, incapable, insult, instant, insist, include.*
2. *Encourage, encouragement, endeavor, endanger, engine, enjoy.*
3. *Unlimited, unchallenged, unwrap, unwilling, unless.*

4. *Interstate, introduce, entertain, entertainment, entrance.*
5. *100, 500, 900, 300, a hundred, several hundred.*

Building Transcription Skills

242 ACCURACY PRACTICE

The speed and the accuracy with which you can read your shorthand notes depend to a large extent on how well you write your notes. The notes do not have to be as beautiful as those in this book, but they should be readable. They will be legible if you are careful about one important thing—proportion.

The accuracy drills in this book are designed to help you develop proportions as well as to point out the correct joinings of the various strokes in Gregg Shorthand.

The drills in this lesson deal with groups of outlines that might look alike when they are written under the pressure of rapid dictation.

SUGGESTIONS FOR PRACTICE

In practicing this drill and the other accuracy drills in this book, you should follow this procedure:

■ 1 Read through the entire drill to be sure that you know the meaning of each outline.

■ 2 The outlines in each drill are written in groups. Write each group of outlines once, striving to see how accurately—rather than how rapidly—you can write each outline.

■ 3 Make another copy of the entire list.

The secret of writing the following outlines legibly is to keep the straight lines straight and the curves deep.

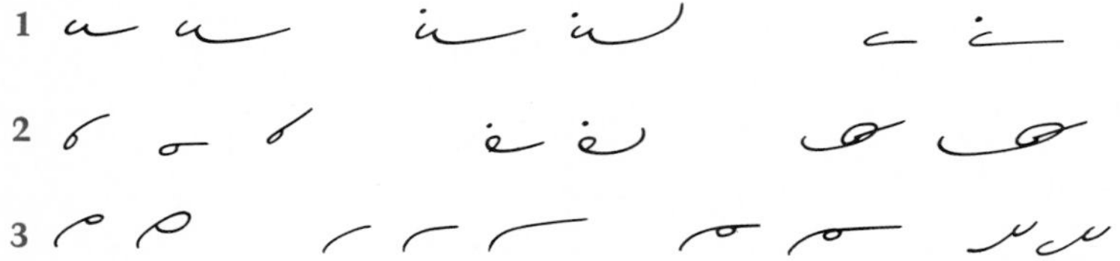

---

1. *Or, all; whole, hold; on, home.*
2. *With, when, yet; hear, heard; write, light.*
3. *They, that; the, than, them; then, theme; though, although.*

Writing Practice

243 PREVIEW

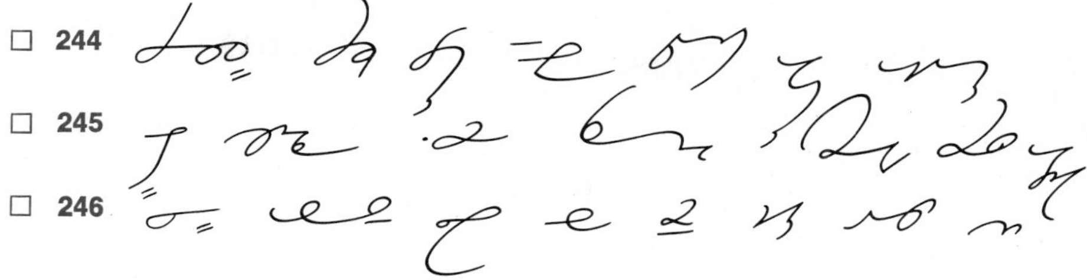

244 *Jamaica, vacation, packages, international, attractive, representatives, restrictions.*
245 *Nevada, council, aware, bargains, developed, variety, reputable.*
246 *America, railway, enable, anywhere, 200, stations, throughout, cordially yours.*

LETTERS

244

Dear Mr. Smith: No one has to tell you that Jamaica is a wonderful place for a vacation; it is truly[1] a beautiful island. Prices of the new tour packages just introduced by International Airlines[2] make it even more attractive. You can plan a vacation to Jamaica for three, four, or five days. Our prices,[3] which include air fare, hotels, and meals, begin at only $400.

When you arrive in Jamaica, one[4] of our representatives will meet you at the airport and drive you to your hotel, where you will have one of the[5] most delightful, entertaining, and carefree vacations you have ever experienced. You can spend the days swimming,[6] fishing, or boating. If you prefer, you can just relax in the warm sun.

You can leave from New York, Philadelphia,[7] or Houston. You may take any flight; there are no time restrictions. If you are interested, and at our[8] low prices it is hard not to be, just call the nearest office of International Airlines or your local[9] travel agent.

For a vacation of unlimited enjoyment, go to Jamaica. Very truly yours,[10]

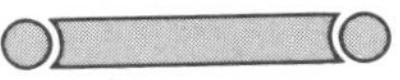

245

Ladies and Gentlemen: The Nevada Travel Council would like you to be aware of the many outstanding[11] travel bargains available to visitors to our state.

More than 100 travel agencies throughout the[12] nation have developed package plans for all our tourist areas. These plans include hotel accommodations,[13] meals, and a variety of entertainment features. The Nevada Travel Council has thoroughly[14] investigated each of the plans listed in the enclosed brochure and has found them to be backed by reputable,[15] established agencies.

For more information about a particular plan, write to the company listed in[16] the brochure. If we can be of help, call our toll-free number, (800) 555-1601. Yours truly,[17]

246

Dear Mr. Barnes: Thank you for your interest in traveling throughout America via the International[18] Railway System. As you may know from recent newspaper advertising, our company is selling "See[19] America" passes that enable the bearer to travel anywhere in the United States on one of our[20] trains for a flat rate of $150. The pass is good for any two-month period from March through[21] November.

We believe the "See America" pass is one of the best travel bargains ever offered. It can[22] be used as often as you wish during the two-month period.

You may purchase your "See America" pass at[23] any of the 200 International railway stations located throughout the country. Cordially yours,[24] [480]

Reading and Writing Practice

247

break·able

nc

stur·dy

shock

if

nc

[87]

in·vest·ment

248

intro

due

sur·plus

Transcribe:
300
one-half

in·cred·i·bly low
no hyphen after ly

if

extreme·ly
tem·per·a·tures

intro

add

[125]

249

when

Transcribe: 200

intro

ac·com·mo·da·tion
choose

ser

ex·er·cise
sau·na

Transcribe: three

[149]

LESSON 28

Developing Shorthand Writing Power

250 WORD FAMILIES

-claimed

1 

-tional

2 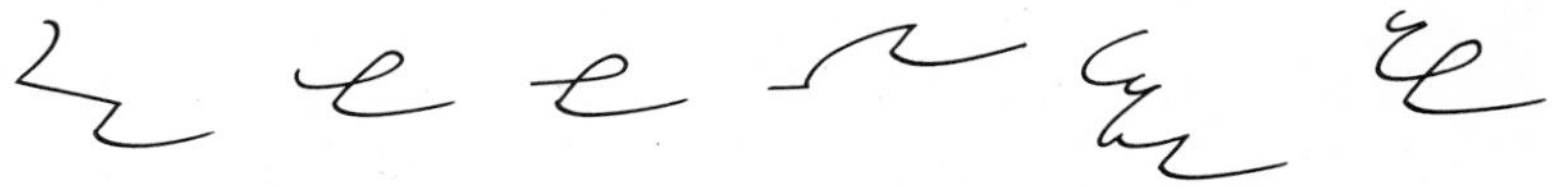

1. *Claimed, unclaimed, reclaimed, exclaimed, proclaimed.*
2. *Functional, rational, national, intentional, proportional, operational.*

251 FREQUENTLY USED NAMES

Last Names

1 

Men's First Names

2 

1. *Black, Gates, Ross, Kennedy, Gilbert, Andrews.*
2. *Cal, Darrell, Dennis, David, Douglas, Earl.*

Building Transcription Skills

252 Business Vocabulary Builder

destination The place arrived at after a journey.

excursion plan A plan by which trips are offered at reduced rates.

attaché case Briefcase.

segment Part; portion.

Writing Practice

253 PREVIEW

□ 254
□ 255
□ 256

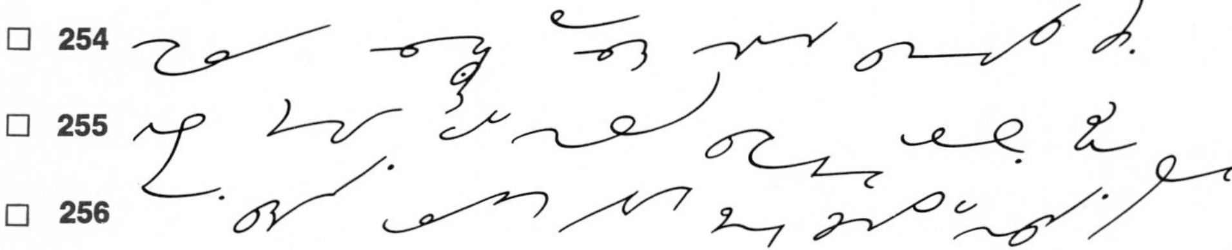

254 Completed, negotiations, electronics, contract, accommodate, interviewing.
255 Traveling, forgotten, although, claimed, accomplishments, relaxing, seashore.
256 Outstanding, reduction, destination, excursion, weekday, overcrowding, details.

LETTERS

254

Mr. Foster: I recently completed negotiations with National Electronics, one of the largest[1] electronics equipment manufacturers in the country, to handle the shipment of all their products.[2] We have signed a one-year contract and will begin delivering their products immediately.

We will need to[3] hire at least 50 additional staff members to accommodate this increased business. Please have our personnel[4] office begin interviewing applicants as soon as possible. I am sure we have many qualified people[5] on our list of prospective employees.

Please keep in touch with me about your progress in this matter. Cal Black[6]

255

Dear Mr. Gates: Many of us have grown so used to traveling around the world that we have forgotten the beauty[7] of our own country. Although we have claimed great pride in our country's industrial accomplishments, we have sometimes[8] forgotten that the United States includes some of the world's most beautiful scenery.

The National Bus[9] Company would like to help you and your family see some of the lovely country within the borders of the[10] United States. This summer plan to see and enjoy the United States by taking a comfortable, relaxing[11] bus tour. One of our well-trained, courteous representatives will be glad to help you plan a trip to the mountains,[12] to the seashore, or to any other place that you would enjoy visiting.

Our office is located at[13] 201 Main Avenue, and we are open from nine to five each day. Plan to stop in soon. Very truly yours,[14]

256

Dear Mr. Ross: When you travel on International Airlines this year, we will give you something more than the[15] outstanding service you have come to expect from us. We will also give you a 30 percent reduction in the[16] price of your ticket. All you need do is travel Monday through Thursday and stay a minimum of seven days at[17] your destination.

Our new excursion plan is good on any of our routes throughout the United States, Canada,[18] and Europe. The excursion plan will enable us to fill more seats on our scheduled weekday flights and avoid[19] the overcrowding we sometimes experience on Fridays, Saturdays, and Sundays. Since this will reduce our[20] operating expenses, we can pass our savings along to you through the fare reduction.

Contact us or your local[21] travel agency for additional details on our widely acclaimed new excursion plan. Very truly yours,[22] [440]

Reading and Writing Practice

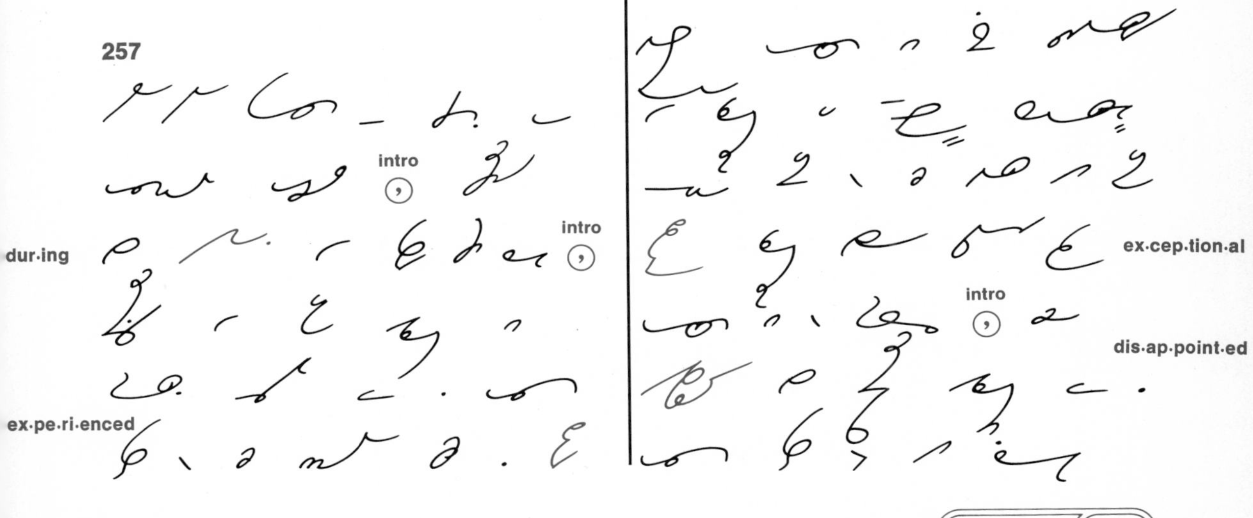

intro

brief
ques·tion·naire

Transcribe:
two

[163]

258

li·cense

Transcribe:
five

New Or·leans

nonr

much-needed
hyphenated before noun

intro

po·ten·tial

aware

edi·tions

route

[136]

259

nonr

hed·uled

·riv·al

intro

·ta·ché

when

s·cov·ered

is·tak·en·ly

it

ap

conj

intro

com·mend

and o

prompt

intro

its

[209]

LESSON 29

Developing Shorthand Writing Power

260 FREQUENTLY USED PHRASES

Done

1 

One

2 

1. *You have done, I have done, we have done, has done, could have done, I should have done, may be done.*
2. *One of the, one of our, one of the best, one of them, one of these, one or two, one of the most.*

261 GEOGRAPHICAL EXPRESSIONS

States

1 

Foreign Countries

2 

1. *Washington, Florida, Wyoming, Utah, California, Oregon, Kentucky.*
2. *Canada, Brazil, Mexico, Israel, Portugal.*

Building Transcription Skills

262 Business Vocabulary Builder

cuisine A style of cooking.

frequenting Visiting often.

moderate *(adj.)* Not expensive; reasonably priced.

Writing Practice

263 PREVIEW

☐ 264

☐ 265

☐ 266

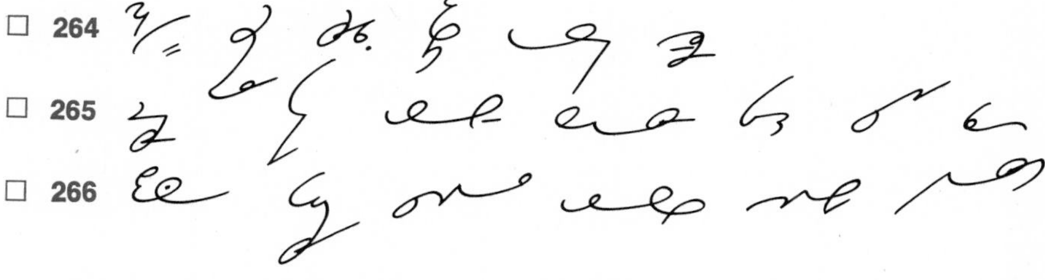

264 *Washington, favorite, sightseeing, spacious, language, cuisine.*
265 *Sunshine, budget, railways, airline, bonus, adult, circular.*
266 *Israel, provide, actually, relaxation, contrast, delightful.*

LETTERS

264

Dear Mr. Day: A Washington Inn is a favorite place to stay for thousands of vacationers in the[1] United States, Canada, and Mexico. After a long day of sightseeing, a spacious, comfortable room in[2] a Washington Inn is a wonderful place to rest.

Perhaps one of the nicest things about our inns is the fact[3] that our people speak your language. In Mexico our people speak both Spanish and English; in Canada, both English[4] and French.

Our dining rooms feature the local cuisine in a charming atmosphere. In addition, we serve[5] typical American foods at every location.

If you are planning a vacation, call (800) 555-9104[6] soon and make reservations at Washington

Inns in all the cities you plant to visit. When[7] you have done this, you can relax and look forward to a relaxing, pleasurable trip. Very sincerely yours,[8]

265

Dear Ms. Day: Now you can enjoy Florida sunshine without placing too great a strain on your budget. This can be[9] done with the new low-cost round-trip fare on Coastal Railways. Our rates are lower than the lowest airline fare and[10] possibly even cheaper than driving.

To make your stay in Florida brighter, Coastal Railways has a bonus for[11] you. You can lease a Nelson car for only $70 a week with free mileage. You pay only for the[12] gas and oil you actually use.

This plan is good for trips to Miami, Orlando, and several other cities.[13] You can leave and return any day of the week, and children ride at one-half the regular adult fare.

For[14] information and reservations, call one of the numbers listed in the enclosed circular. Sincerely yours,[15]

266

Dear Mr. Lewis: If you are looking for a place to spend a week's vacation, why not go to Israel. For[16] less than $1,000 we will fly you there, provide fine hotel accommodations and meals, and drive you to[17] and from the airport. In addition, we will plan a sightseeing tour for you; there is much to see in Israel.[18]

Actually, you can probably cram more history, more relaxation, and more contrast into a week in[19] Israel than anywhere else in the world. Israel is one of the most interesting, delightful countries that[20] you will ever visit.

We have a variety of one-week plans to choose from. Each is designed to show you the[21] real character of Israel. Our tourist office is open daily from nine to six; call soon. Cordially yours,[22]

[440]

● Reading and Writing Practice

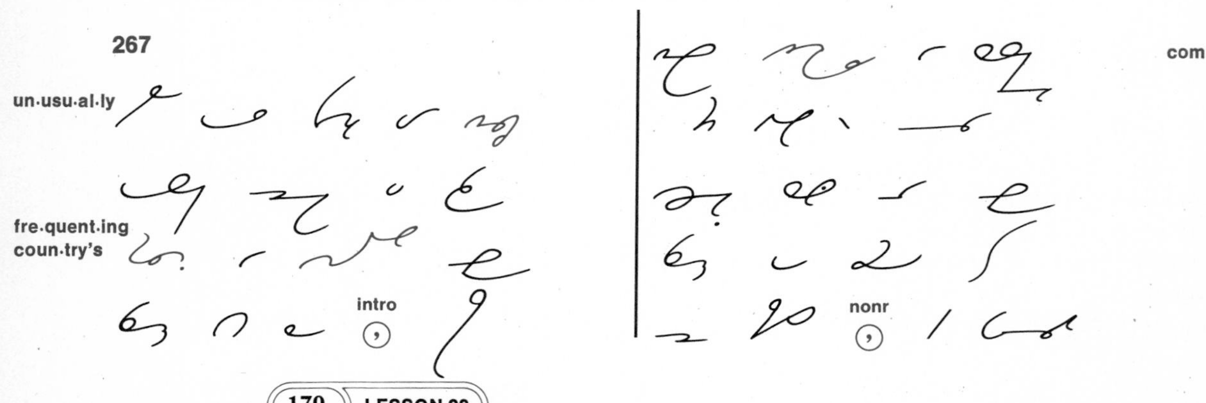

hours'

intro

ar·riv·al

enu

geo

geo

geo

Transcribe:
three

res·er·va·tions

[201]

268

intro

nc

wo

intro

mod·er·ate

ser

hos·pi·ta·ble

intro

[76]

Developing Shorthand Writing Power

269 WORD BEGINNINGS AND ENDINGS

Re-

1

Con-

2

-ings

3

1. *Receive, review, rebel, repel, rebuke, receipt, reception, resign, reject.*
2. *Confer, conference, condemn, confess, continue, contemplate, contain.*
3. *Hearings, holdings, meetings, workings, headings, openings, feelings.*

Building Transcription Skills

270 Business Vocabulary Builder

hardship Difficulty.

fragile Easily broken; delicate.

negative impact An unfavorable effect.

Progressive Speed Builder (70-110)

271 PREVIEW

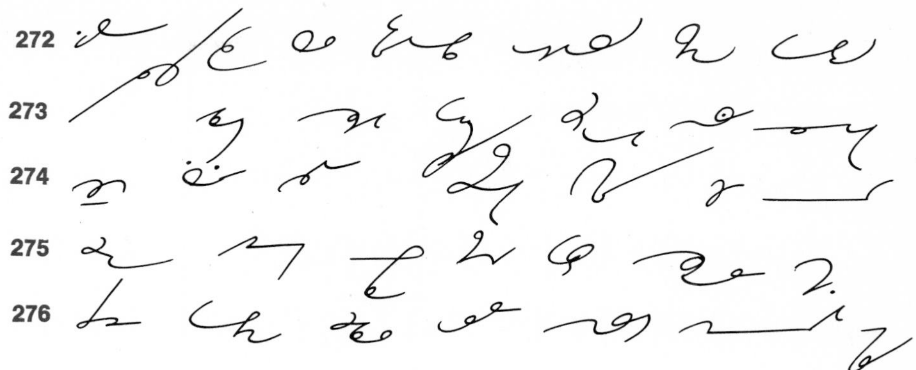

272 *Hotel, people, airy, spotlessly, restaurant, assured, pleasant.*
273 *Dedicated, to serving, guests, provided, facilities, create, memorable.*
274 *Quick, heart, theater, available, devoted, whether, month.*
275 *Single, too much, major, effect, prices, gasoline, comforting.*
276 *Genuine, pleasure, sincerely, return, grateful, comments, enjoyed.*

LETTERS

272

[1 minute at 70]

Dear Mr. Jackson: The Gates Hotel is a real hotel for real people. The rooms are bright, airy,/and spotlessly clean. At the Gates Hotel you don't have to go out to find a great restaurant because// there are three right in the hotel.

The Gates Hotel is everything a great hotel should be. So the///next time you are in Springfield, stay at the Gates and be assured of a pleasant visit. Sincerely yours, [1]

273

[1 minute at 80]

Dear Mr. Jackson: Gates hotels are dedicated to serving our guests the finest meals.

Our chefs are provided/with the best in food, in staff, and in facilities. They have everything they need to create great meals. What this means//to you is that when you stay at a Gates hotel, you have a memorable dining experience.

Stay at a///Gates hotel on your next trip. Once you have stayed with us, you will not want to stay anywhere else. Sincerely yours, [2]

274

[1 minute at 90]

Dear Mr. Jackson: Even if you come to New York for a quick meeting, you will get more out of New York if you stay at the/National Hotel. The National is in the heart of the shopping and theater area.

We will give you a fine room with a//fine view. We will give you excellent service. If you wish, we will make available to you a whole floor devoted to meetings.///

Why not make the National Hotel your headquarters—whether you are in New York for a day or a month. Very sincerely yours, [3]

275

[1 minute at 100]

Dear Mr. Jackson: If you must pay more than $12 a night for a single room at a motel, you are paying too much. At a Nelson/motel, our rate for one person is $12. That is the lowest rate of any major chain in the country. The rate of $12 is//in effect all year long. Our prices do not vary in any of our motels.

Today it is very expensive to travel. Gasoline///costs more, operating your car costs more, and eating costs more. It should be comforting to know that your motel room costs less. Yours truly, [4]

276

[1 minute at 110]

Dear Mr. Jackson: It was a genuine pleasure to have had you with us here at the Wilson Lodge. We sincerely hope that your visit was a pleasant one/and that you enjoyed every minute of your stay.

In order to make our lodge one to which our guests will want to return again and again, we invite your//comments on how we can improve our service and our facilities. We will be grateful if you will send us your comments on the enclosed card.

If you enjoyed///your stay, and we sincerely hope you did, perhaps you will tell some of your friends about us.

We look forward to having you with us again. Yours very truly, [5] [450]

Reading and Writing Practice

277

do-it-your-self *hyphenated before noun*

if

frus-tra-tion

frag-ile

ar-range-ments

intro

[125]

278

as

ei-ther

break

site

ad·e·quate
fa·cil·i·ties

geo

conj

hard·ship

par

re·tain

in·curred

[184]

279

as

leg·is·la·tive
freezes

year's

Transcribe:
3 percent

off·set

par

neg·a·tive

com·pre·hen·sive

[118]

Clothing

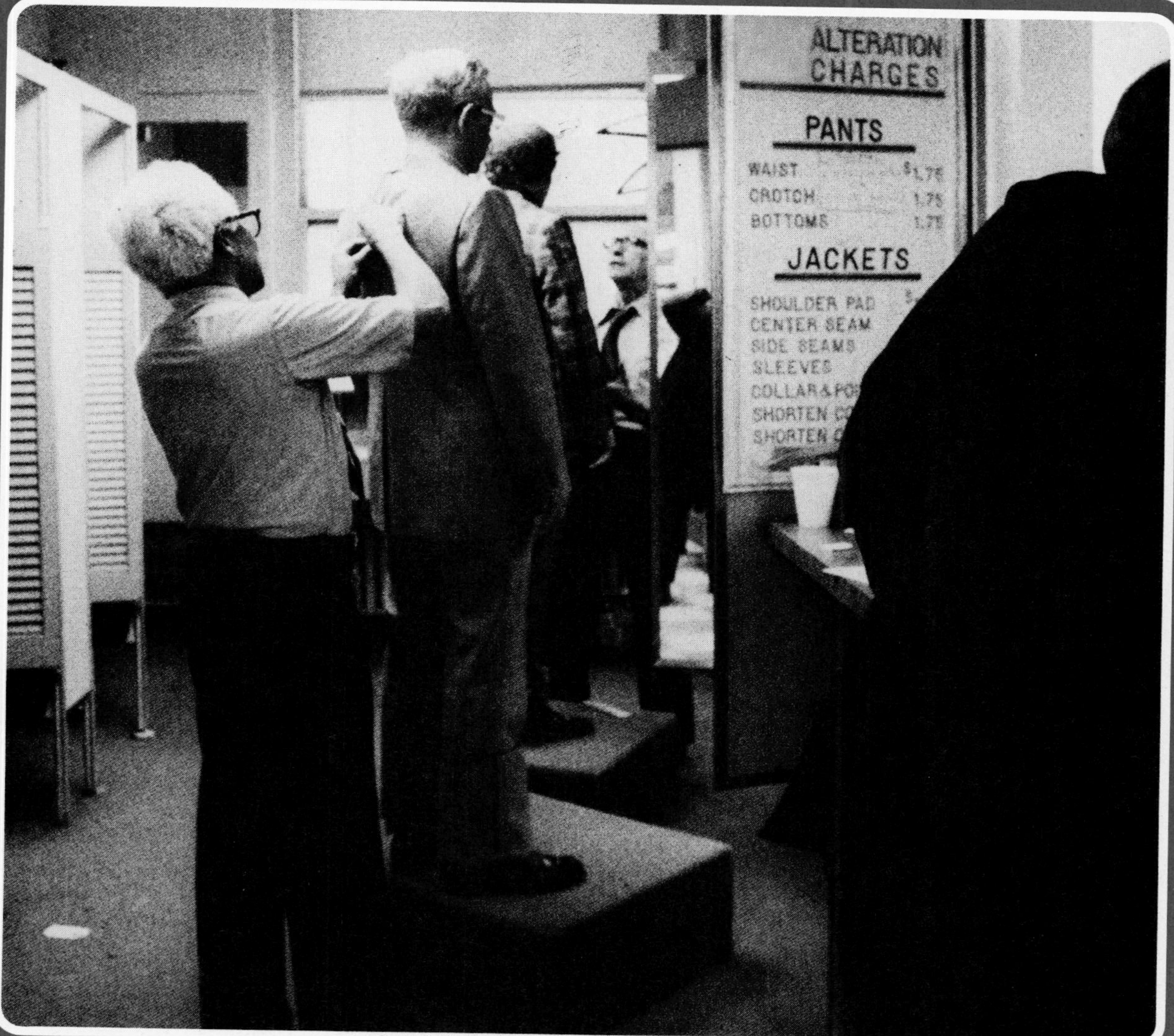

Developing Shorthand Writing Power

280 OUTLINE CONSTRUCTION

Word Endings -vity, -city In the interest of facility, the vowel is omitted in the endings *-vity, -city.*

Activity, brevity, creativity, capacity, publicity, simplicity.

Omission of Short E and I In order to obtain outlines that are easy to read, short *e* and *i* are omitted between:

P and N, T, D

1

B and N, T, D

2

1. *Open, happen, ripen, appetite, repetition, competition, rapid.*
2. *Combination, robin, rabbit, prohibit, habit, rabid.*

Building Transcription Skills

281 SIMILAR-WORDS DRILL confidently, confidentially

confidently With assurance or certainty; with conviction.

She spoke confidently.

confidentially Secretly; privately.

I was given the information confidentially.

Reading and Writing Practice

282 Clothing

The people

[178]

283 LETTERS

com·pa·ny's

pro·hib·its

yours
cus·tom·er's

intro

Transcribe:
two

over·due

conj

intro

self-ad·dressed

[154]

284

ap

man·u·fac·tur·er's

con·fi·den·tial·ly

com·pli·ments

im·pres·sion

com·pet·i·tors

col·leagues
de·vel·op

if

wear·ing

when

well-trained
hyphenated before noun
rep·re·sen·ta·tives

con·fi·dent·ly
Transcribe: ten

10

Transcribe: 9 a.m.

nc

wo

[206]

285

intro

rec·om·men·da·tion

zon·ing

out·weigh

[79]

Developing Shorthand Writing Power

286 RECALL DRILL e

In this drill you will review the different uses of the alphabetic stroke *e*.

E

1

-ly

2

-ingly

3

Ye-

4

---

1. *Knee, me, see, real, meal, feel, near, fear.*
2. *Friendly, falsely, reasonably, gladly, certainly, nicely, only.*
3. *Willingly, seemingly, correspondingly, knowingly, unknowingly, unfailingly, unwillingly.*
4. *Years, yet, yell, yellow, yearn, yield, yes.*

Building Transcription Skills

287 ACCURACY PRACTICE

The Accuracy Drills in this lesson also deal with groups of outlines that tend to look alike when they are written under the stress of rapid dictation. Practice the drills, following the suggestions given on page 158.

Writing these outlines legibly will give you no problem if you:

- 1 Keep the straight lines straight, the curves deep.
- 2 Make the *a* circle very large, the *e* circle tiny.
- 3 Watch your proportions closely.

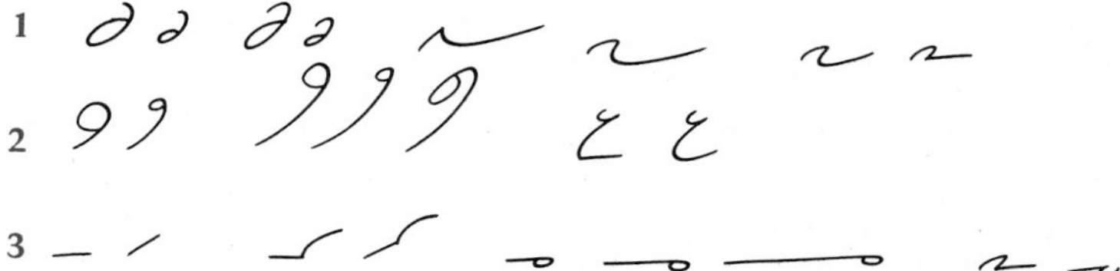

1. *Say, see; way, we; it will, you will; you are, one (won).*
2. *As, if; I have, ever-every, however; opinion, opportunity.*
3. *In-not, it-at; in the, at the; any, me, many; one (won), no.*

Writing Practice

288 PREVIEW

☐ 289

☐ 290

☐ 291

289 *Response, request, reviewed, outlining, distributed, ratification, vary, incentive.*
290 *Administrative, showroom, designers, preliminary, radical.*
291 *Husband, exceedingly, ideal, carrying, destination, wrinkle-free.*

LETTERS

289

To the Staff: In response to a formal request made through your employees' organization, the management of[1] the Baker Company has decided to increase the commissions paid on all clothing sales.

We have carefully[2] reviewed our present policy and prepared a circular outlining the new commission plan. The circular[3] will be distributed to all departments next week. The new plan is, of course, subject to ratification by[4] the employees' association.

The increases will be based on present department budgets and will vary[5] among departments. The increases range from 15 percent to 25 percent of the present commissions[6] paid. If you have any questions about this action, please speak to your department head.

We hope that these changes will[7] be satisfactory and provide a greater incentive for all our sales personnel. William H. Washington[8]

290

Mr. Perkins: Could you arrange to see the administrative officers of the company on Friday[9] afternoon at 2 p.m. in our fashion showroom? Our designers wish to display their sketches and other[10] preliminary work on next year's line of women's clothing.

The designers are working on styles that represent quite a[11] radical departure from those of the past three years. We feel that the designs are exceedingly good, but we want[12] your opinion of them.

The session should take approximately two hours; we have over 100 designs for[13] you to see. We will follow up with an executive meeting on Monday, February 26, at 8:30[14] a.m. At that time we will evaluate the display and make important decisions on the production[15] of next year's line.

I hope you will let me know immediately if you can meet with us. Alice Garcia[16]

291

Dear Mrs. Green: One of the nicest gifts you can give your husband—on his birthday, at Christmas, or for any special[17] occasion—is a Kelley garment bag.

A Kelley garment bag is an exceedingly nice gift. It is[18] ideal for business or pleasure trips because it can be hung on the coat rack of any plane or train and then folded[19] neatly for easy carrying. Your husband will arrive at his destination knowing that his clothes are fresh and[20] wrinkle-free.

Give your husband a gift that he will appreciate; give him a Kelley garment bag. Cordially yours,[21] [420]

Reading and Writing Practice

292

de·ci·sion

re·sign

as·sis·tance

conj

sub·mit·ted

as

sep·a·rate

au·thor·i·ty

es·sen·tial

intro

intro

an·tic·i·pate

par

[177]

293

for·ward·ed

intro

un.for.tu.nate.ly

com·plete

back-or·der *hyphenated before noun*

enu

men's

wom·en's

chil·dren's

com·ing

conj

cat·a·log

par

nc

[161]

294

en·e·my

fade

par

sci·en·tif·i·cal·ly de·signed
no hyphen after ly

nonr

intro

ser

moths

555-8926 conj

intro

[105]

Developing Shorthand Writing Power

295 WORD FAMILIES

-ser

1

-duct

2

1. *Answer, announcer, tracer, sponsor, freezer, blazer, nicer.*
2. *Conduct, product, deduct, misconduct, by-product.*

296 FREQUENTLY USED NAMES

Last Names

1

Women's First Names

2

1. *Golden, Grady, Grant, Green, Haines, Hale.*
2. *Edith, Eileen, Elaine, Eleanor, Ellen.*

Building Transcription Skills

297 Business Vocabulary Builder

coordinated Matching or complementing.

inventory Stock; the supply on hand.

goodwill A friendly attitude shown by one toward another.

● Writing Practice

298 PREVIEW

☐ 299
☐ 300
☐ 301

299 Stylish, comfortable, custom, tailoring, consequently, lifetime, wardrobe.
300 Purchased, representative, alterations, shipped, conducted, long, refund, money.
301 Problem, answers, stretch, dollars, coordinated, daytime, converted.

LETTERS

299

Dear Mr. Golden: No matter how much you pay for your clothes or how stylish they are, you will not feel comfortable[1] wearing them unless they fit properly. While most clothing stores no longer do custom tailoring, the Western[2] Clothing Store believes that your clothes must be fitted expertly.

Consequently, we provide lifetime tailoring on[3] any garment we make for you. Whether it is a blazer, a suit, or an overcoat, we will alter it for[4] you free of charge for the life of the garment. If you gain or lose a few pounds, just bring the garment in for free[5] alteration.

You might feel that a company that conducts its business in this manner would have to charge much more than[6] its competition. In spite of this outstanding service, however, our clothes cost about the same as you would pay[7] at any other fine clothing store.

The next time you plan to add to your wardrobe, stop by our store in San Francisco.[8] You may find that our products and services provide the perfect answer to your clothing needs. Cordially yours,[9]

300

Dear Mrs. Grady: On June 15 I purchased a dress from your San Diego store. Ms. Edith Green, the sales[10] representative, promised me that the simple alterations that had to be made would be completed in two or[11] three days and that the dress would be shipped to me within one week.

Here it is July 5, and I still have not received[12] the dress. If I conducted my own business in such a manner, I am afraid that I would not be in business[13] very long.

I am leaving on my vacation July 25, and I would like to take the dress with me. Can[14] you deliver it by that date? If not, please cancel the order and refund my money. Very sincerely yours,[15]

301

Dear Mrs. Haines: Inflation is a problem, but there are things that can be done about it. We do not have all the[16] answers, but we do have some of them. We at Elaine's Clothing Shop are showing customers how to stretch their clothing[17] dollars. We do not suggest that our customers buy lower-quality clothing; we suggest that they purchase[18] carefully coordinated fashions.

We have sports coats and blazers that can be worn with contrasting slacks. We have dresses[19] than can be worn in the daytime for work and then converted for evening wear simply by adding a smart jacket.[20]

Visit Elaine's Clothing Shop at 212 South State Street the next time you are in Chicago. Very truly yours,[21] [420]

● Reading and Writing Practice

302

col·lege

de·vot·ed

styles

pref·er·ences

add

wom·en's

oc·cu·py

Transcribe: third

ser

,

ap·peal

es·pe·cial·ly

intro

ap·par·el

West·port's

ap

for·mal·ly

ap

browse

[194]

303

conj

prompt·ly

enu

no·tice·able

intro

quite

intro

intro

mis·rep·re·sent·ed

intro

par

cr

[154]

LESSON 34

Developing Shorthand Writing Power

304 FREQUENTLY USED PHRASES

To do

1 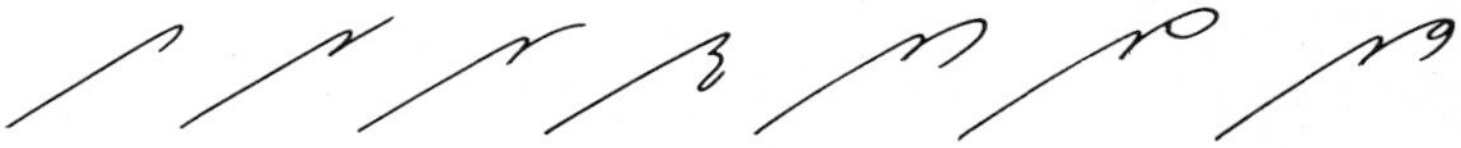

Say

2 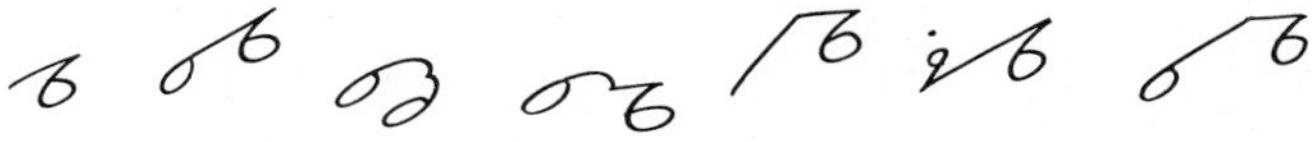

1. *To do, to do it, to do the, to do so, to do this, to do that, to do these.*
2. *To say, I would say, I can say, I cannot say, would not say, he should say, I would not say.*

305 GEOGRAPHICAL EXPRESSIONS

-son

1 

States

2 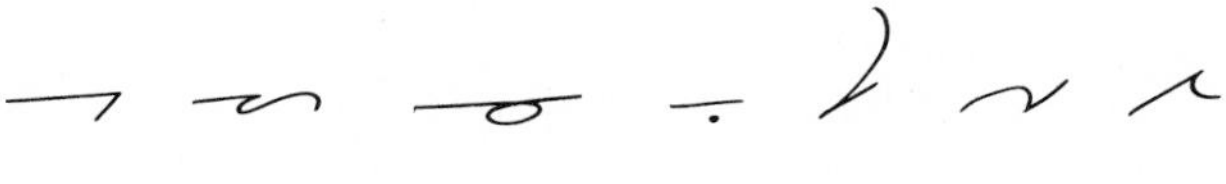

Foreign Countries

3 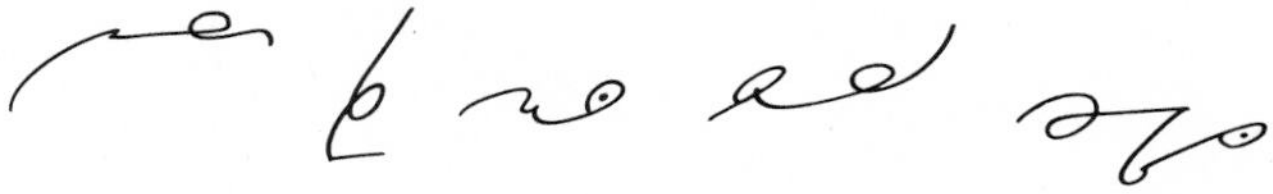

1. *Madison, Atchison, Dawson, Garrison, Harrison, Jefferson, Henderson.*
2. *Michigan, New York, Maine, New Hampshire, Vermont, Connecticut, Texas.*
3. *Denmark, Japan, Korea, Thailand, Cambodia.*

Building Transcription Skills

306 Business Vocabulary Builder

replenishing Restocking; filling up again.
fire retardant A substance having the ability to stop the spread of fire.
mandate Order.
bolts Rolls of cloth.

Writing Practice

307 PREVIEW

□ 308
□ 309
□ 310

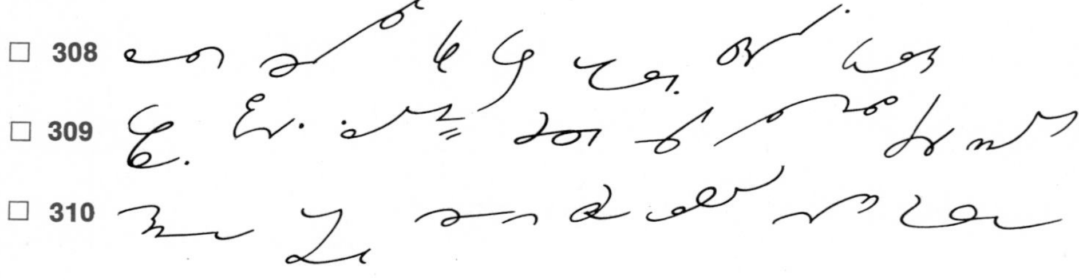

308 *Election, candidates, choice, privilege, replenishing, outstanding, politicians.*
309 *Preparing, expecting, Henderson, financial, in addition, dignity, jacket, wonderful.*
310 *Consumer, reveals, chemical, fire retardant, continuous, flannel.*

LETTERS

308

Dear Mr. James: Election Day this year comes on Tuesday, November 5. After you have voted for the candidates[1] of your choice, vote for the store that is to have the privilege of replenishing your wardrobe this fall. We hope[2] you will choose the Madison Men's Shop.

Our platform is simple. We are in favor of fashion, good taste, and outstanding[3] quality. We believe in personal service and old-fashioned courtesy. That is the only way we want[4] to do business. You see, unlike politicians, we are up for reelection every day.

If you don't have an[5] account at the Madison Men's Shop, don't let that sway your vote. It is easy to open one at any of our[6] 12 stores located throughout Michigan. All you need to say is, "Open an account for me today." Yours truly,[7]

309

Dear Band Member: As you know, we are preparing for our summer band concerts in the park. We are happy to say[8] that we are expecting our best year ever.

We have been working with the Henderson City Council on the[9] financial arrangements, and I am happy to say that we will receive the same amount of money from the council[10] as we did last year. In addition, the council has consented to purchase a sports coat for each musician. This[11] will add considerable dignity to the appearance of the band.

Our opening concert is scheduled for[12] Sunday afternoon, June 26. We are asking you to do the following things before that date:

1. Stop by[13] the New York Clothing Shop at 161 Madison Street to get your jacket.
2. Purchase a pair of black pants[14] to wear with the jacket.
3. Be sure that you have a pair of black shoes to complete your outfit.

We are looking forward[15] to a wonderful concert series, and we know that the residents of Henderson are too. Sincerely yours,[16]

310

Mr. Frank: The Consumer Safety Commission just published a report that may well affect our business operation.[17] The report reveals that some materials used to manufacture children's clothing have been treated with[18] a cancer-causing chemical. The chemical, which is imported from Japan and Korea, is a fire[19] retardant, and continuous contact with the skin has proved harmful.

Will you please write to our supplier to see if[20] this chemical has been used in the treatment of our flannel. Prompt attention to this matter is imperative.[21] I cannot say what the results of this report may be, but it is conceivable that all clothing treated with[22] the chemical may be recalled by government mandate.

Please call me when you have heard from our supplier. J. Boyles[23] [460]

● Reading and Writing Practice

311

Transcribe: 12 dozen

poly·es·ter

nc ;

for·eign

com·pet·i·tors

ser

Transcribe:
25 percent

25,

conj

par

[124]

312

rep·u·ta·tion

ser

girls'

par

boys'

po·ten·tial

large-vol·ume
hyphenated before noun

def·i·nite

cap·i·tal·ize

ex·pan·sion

intro

com·plete

pre·lim·i·nary

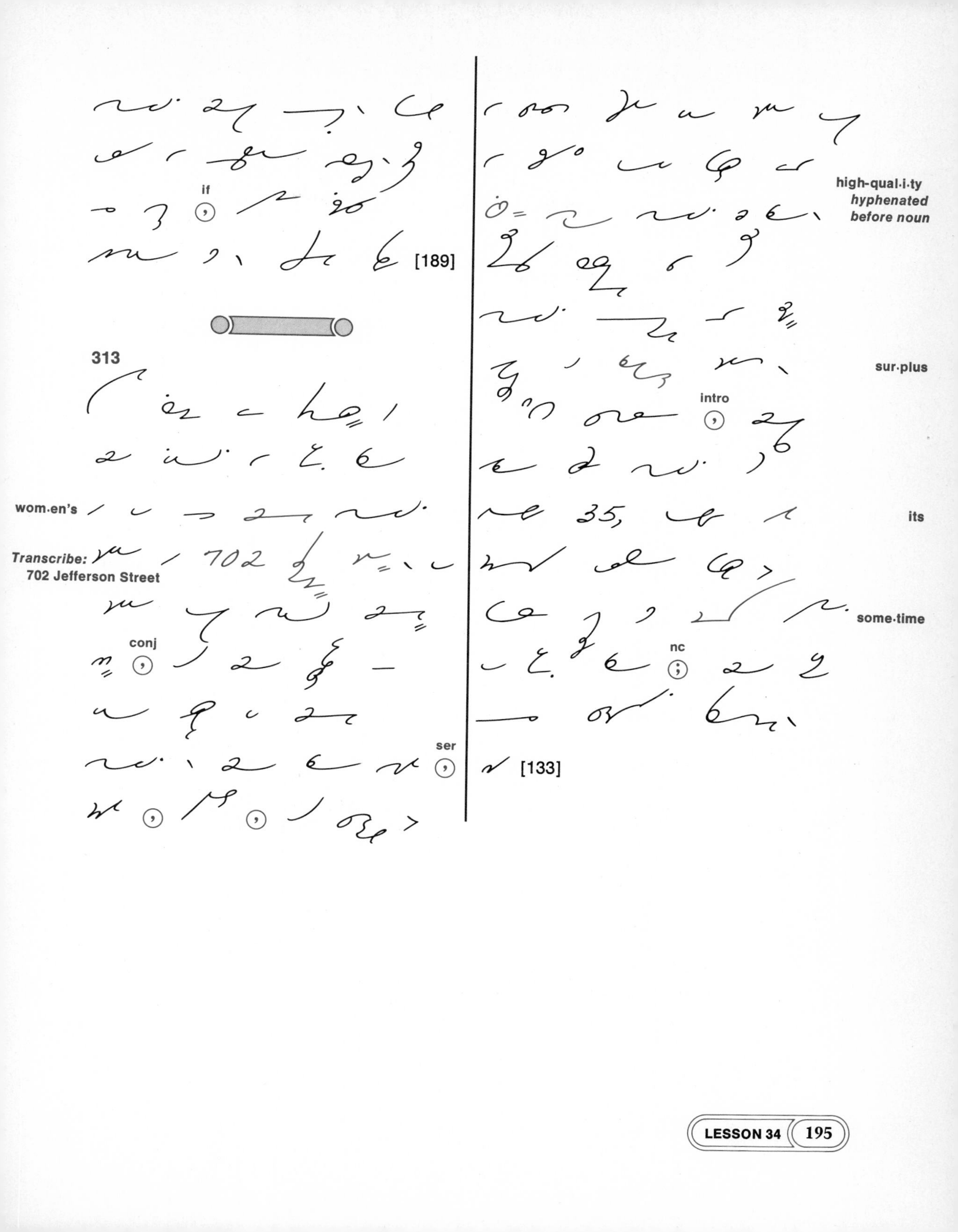

[189]

313

wom·en's

Transcribe: 702 Jefferson Street

[133]

high-qual·i·ty *hyphenated before noun*

sur·plus

its

some·time

Three Dictation Problems

All shorthand writers, while in the process of developing their shorthand speed, at one time or another encounter three problems that they must learn to handle. You will have to learn to handle these problems also.

1 What to do if you fall behind.
2 What to do when the dictator uses an unfamiliar word.
3 What to do when you do not hear a part of the dictation.

No doubt you have already encountered these problems in your speed-development practice.

Here are some suggestions that will help you cope with them.

1 **You fall behind.** It should not be a source of distress to you when you occasionally fall behind the dictator in your practice. It is only natural for you to fall behind sometimes when you are striving to reach a higher speed than the one at which you are proficient. If you were always able to get all the dictation easily, it would be a sign that the dictation rate was not rapid enough and that consequently your speed was not increasing. Of course, falling behind consistently is a different and more serious matter! When you occasionally find yourself falling behind:

a Keep up as long as you can. The dictator may pause to think through the rest of the sentence or paragraph, and the few seconds that this takes may be sufficient for you to catch up.

b When you can keep up no longer, skip the words that you have not written and leave a line or two blank in your shorthand notebook. When you transcribe, this blank space will indicate the point at which you have a break.

c Pick up the dictation at the new point. Never stop writing. If you do, you may never become a really rapid writer.

d When you transcribe incomplete notes, try, with the help of context, to supply the words that you had to leave out.

2 **You meet an unfamiliar word.** The most expert writer will occasionally have to write a shorthand outline for a completely unfamiliar word. When this happens to you, follow these suggestions:

a Try to write the word in full.

b If you cannot write it in full, try to get at least the beginning of the word. This beginning may help you find the correct word in the dictionary later.

c If the word completely escapes you, leave a space so that you can readily locate the spot at which the word occurs. The important consideration is that you do not become confused and lose precious time worrying about the word as the dictator continues speaking.

When you transcribe, you may be able to substitute a synonym for the word you missed that will not alter the meaning of the dictation.

The larger your English vocabulary, the less frequently this problem will confront you. Consequently, do all you can to increase your vocabulary through extensive reading and study.

3 **You do not hear a word.** All writers will occasionally fail to hear a word, either because the dictator did not enunciate clearly or because some noise interfered with hearing. These suggestions will help you to handle this problem:

a Leave a space when you do not hear a word. Once again, context may help you to supply the word—or at least a satisfactory substitute—when you transcribe. Do not stop writing with the hope that the context of the next few words may suggest the word you missed. If you stop writing, you may fall hopelessly behind.

b If you think you hear a word but the context tells you that it could not possibly be the correct one, write what you think you heard anyway. If you have time, circle the outline quickly. If you are pressed for time, leave a space. If you have written what you thought you heard, your outline will often suggest the actual word that was dictated. For example, if you think you hear, "There was a large increase in the building industry's *reduction* rate," write just that. When you transcribe, your outline for *reduction* will suggest to you that the correct transcription of the sentence is, "There was a large increase in the building industry's *production* rate."

c There will be occasions when a word that you misheard will occur to you sometime later. When this happens, resist the temptation to go back and insert it. The dictator will not wait while you do so, and you may lose more than you gain. It is better to try to remember the word when you transcribe—and the chances are that you will.

These suggestions are intended basically to apply to your speed-development work in class. When you fall behind, encounter an unfamilar word, or do not hear a word while you are taking dictation from your employer in the business office, you will generally interrupt the dictation. You must not risk the possibility of transcribing correspondence with an error in it.

Developing Shorthand Writing Power

314 WORD BEGINNINGS AND ENDINGS

Sub-

1

Per-, Pur-

2

-ification

3

1. *Submit, substandard, subcontract, substantial, suburbs, suburban.*
2. *Permit, perfect, perform, persuade, purple, purse, pursue.*
3. *Classification, verification, purification, notification, specifications, modifications.*

Building Transcription Skills

315 Business Vocabulary Builder

tedious Tiresome; boring.

modifications Changes.

expanding Making larger; adding to.

Progressive Speed Builder (80-120)

The Progressive Speed Builder in this lesson runs from 80 words a minute to 120 words a minute. Does 120 words a minute sound fast to you? You won't find it fast if you practice the words and phrases in the preview.

Remember, try to get something down for every word, and under no circumstances should you stop writing!

316 PREVIEW

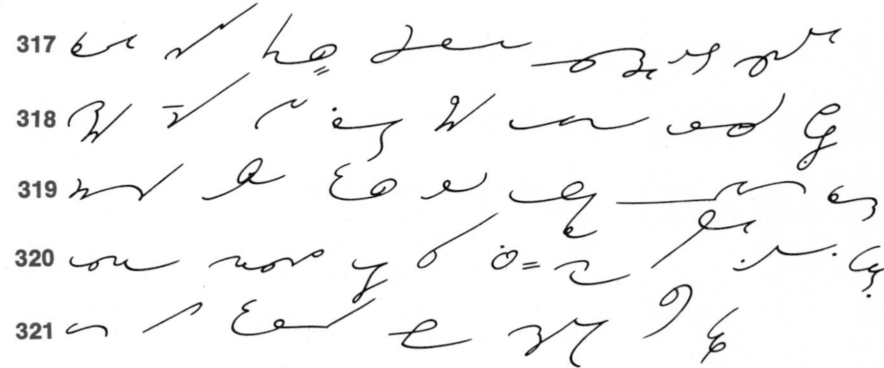

317 Shirts, you ordered, July, familiar, magazines, three or four, counters.
318 Thank you for your order, interested, to know, helpful, if you would, local, remind, appreciate.
319 Suggested, entire, supply, third, larger, months ago, circulars.
320 Recall, correctly, repeat, added, high-quality, details, handling, processing.
321 Of course, due, supplemented, national, considerable, however, position.

LETTERS

317

[1 minute at 80]

Dear Mr. Green: The shirts that you ordered on June 8 have been shipped. We will bill you for them in July.

You will like/the way our shirts sell. People ask for them by name. They are familiar with our shirts as a result of our advertising//in national magazines during the past three or four years.

In a few days we will send you a supply///of circulars featuring these shirts. We suggest that you place them on one of the counters in your store. Yours truly, [1]

318

[1 minute at 90]

Dear Mr. Green: Thank you for your order for 12 dozen shirts. They were shipped several days ago.

You will be interested to/know that in August we will advertise these shirts in four national magazines. This advertising should result in many fine//sales for you. It would be helpful if you would insert an ad in your local paper about July 3 to remind people///that our shirts are for sale in your store.

Once again, Mr. Green, thank you for your order. We appreciate it. Sincerely yours, [2]

319

[1 minute at 100]

Gentlemen: As you suggested in your letter of June 15, I placed an advertisement in our local paper on July 4. I sold/out my entire supply of shirts by July 10. You have probably received my third order by this time. You will notice that it is much//larger than my first two orders. When I decided to place your shirts in stock several months ago, I made a very wise move.

Please send me///another supply of your circulars as well as any other material you may have advertising your shirts. Yours very truly, [3]

320

[1 minute at 110]

Dear Mr. Green: As you know, since last June you have been selling our men's shirts successfully. If I recall correctly, we have received four repeat orders from/you.

You will be interested to know that we have just added men's shoes to our line. These will be high-quality shoes and will sell for $30. Details// about these shoes are included in the enclosed folder.

Would you be interested in handling our shoes? If you would, please fill out and return the enclosed///form. When we receive it, we will send you our usual dealer's contract that you simply sign and return to us for processing. Very truly yours, [4]

321

[1 minute at 120]

Gentlemen: You are, of course, correct when you say in your letter of February 18 that I have been very successful in selling your shirts. Much of my success/has been due to the fact that I have supplemented your national advertising with considerable advertising of my own in our local paper.

At this//time, however, I do not feel I can take on your line of men's shoes. That would mean expanding the floor space of our store, which I am not in a position to do.

I///appreciate your offer to handle your men's shoes, and perhaps sometime in the future it will be possible for me to take advantage of your offer. Sincerely yours, [5] [500]

Reading and Writing Practice

322

sub·mit·ting

cat·a·log

intro

Transcribe: $35

dis·trib·ut·ing

intro

ex·cess

bur·den

par

as

add

[141]

323

Men's

old-fash·ioned

prin·ci·ple

here

top·coat

wear·ing

if

ob·li·gat·ed

par

up to date
no noun,
no hyphen

intro

ward·robe

out·fit

high-qual·i·ty
hyphenated
before noun

par

[154]

324

due

avoid
te·dious

50

Transcribe:
$50
per·mit·ted

30

if

Sub·ur·ban

9

Transcribe:
9 a.m.

10

nc

wo

9

[157]

CHAPTER

Radio and Television

Developing Shorthand Writing Power

325 OUTLINE CONSTRUCTION

Word Ending -ion The word ending *-ion* is expressed by *oo-n* after *n*; by *n* in other cases.

Expressed by OO-N

1

Expressed by N

2

1. *Union, communion, reunion, onion, companion, dominion.*
2. *Million, champion, medallion, criterion, rebellion, pavilion.*

Word Endings -ious, -eous The word endings *-ious, -eous* are expressed by *us*.

1

2

1. *Industry, industrious; envy, envious; injury, injurious; study, studious.*
2. *Serious, various, curious, obvious, previous, erroneous, courteous.*

Building Transcription Skills

326 SIMILAR-WORDS DRILL lead, led

lead *(verb)* To guide or conduct; to pursue; to live; *(noun)* a metal.

She will lead *us on the tour.*
Most people lead *full, active lives.*
We cannot use gasoline that contains lead.

led The past tense of lead.

She led *us on the tour yesterday.*
Most people who have led *full, active lives are very happy.*

Note: A very common error that stenographers make is to spell both the present and the past tense of *lead* alike, perhaps because both the present and the past tense of *read* are spelled alike. Don't you make this mistake! The past tense of *lead* is spelled *l-e-d*.

Reading and Writing Practice

327 Modern Miracles

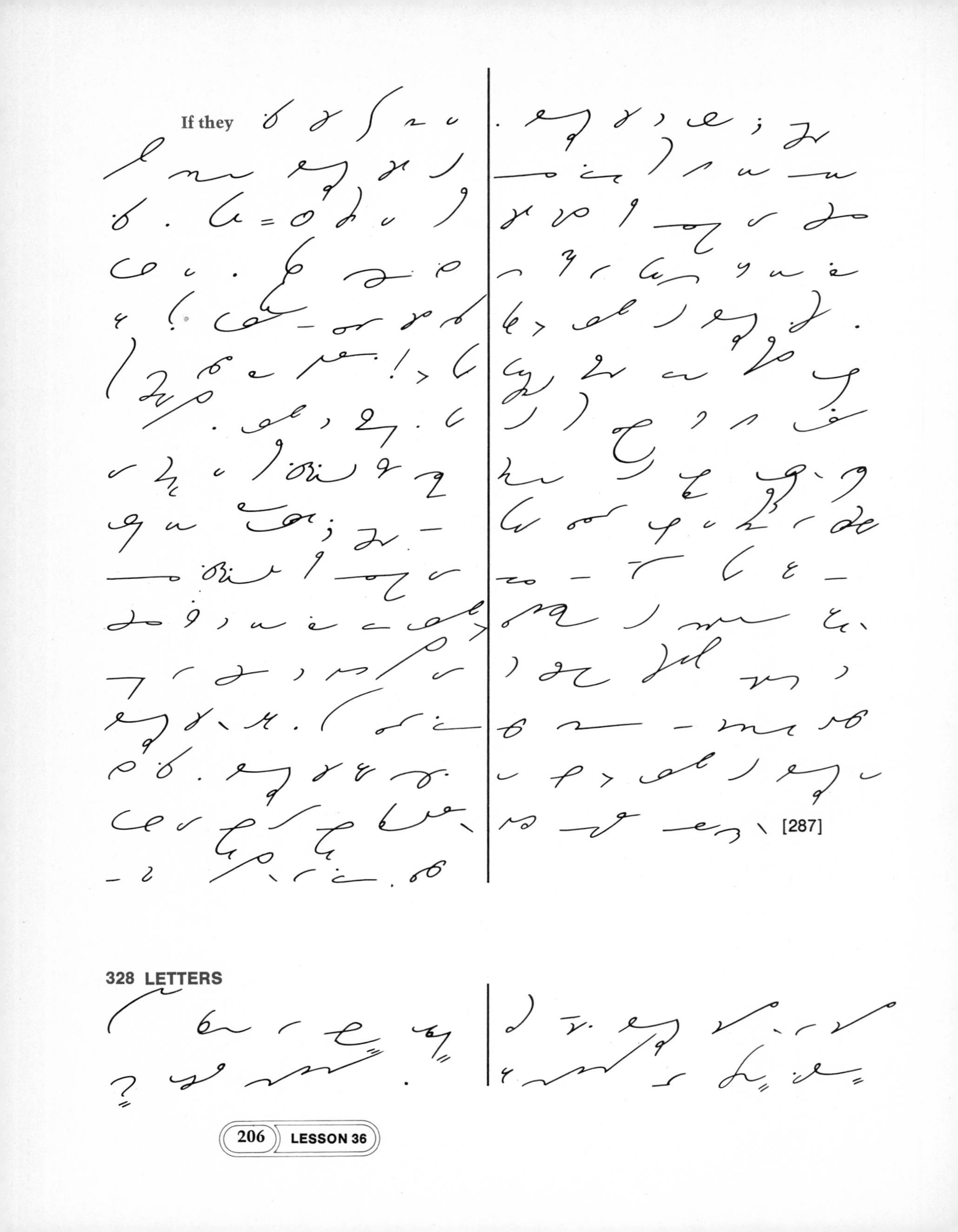

If they

[287]

328 LETTERS

Transcribe: six

lead·ing

iden·ti·fied

nc ;

vis·i·ble

conj ,

view·ers

day's

intro ,

ro·tat·ed

Transcribe: 2,000

intro ,

bal·lots

led

[177]

329

if ,

al·most

intro ,

conj ,

se·ri·ous·ly

high·lights

ath·letes

[125]

Developing Shorthand Writing Power

330 RECALL DRILL o

In this drill you will review the different combinations in which *o* is used.

O

1

Oi

2

Al-

3

Over

4

-ort

5

1. *Old, so, know, row, foe, flow, low, soap.*
2. *Oil, soil, boy, noise, voice, toy, boil, boiler.*
3. *Also, although, altogether, almost, alter, Albany, already.*

4. *Over, overcome, overcharge, overdo, overlook, overrule, overturn.*
5. *Sport, import, export, report, deport, mortal, quarter.*

Building Transcription Skills

331 ACCURACY PRACTICE

The drills in this lesson are designed to help you join circles to straight lines correctly. Follow the practice suggestions given on page 158.

In practicing these groups:

- 1 Keep the straight lines straight.
- 2 Close each circle.
- 3 Make the *a* circles large, the *e* circles tiny.

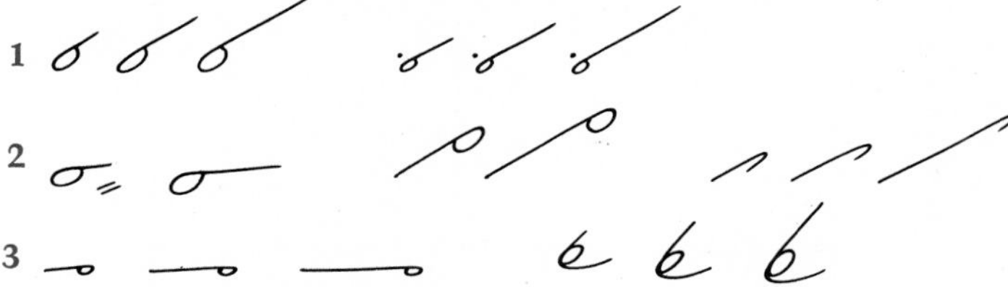

---

1. *Ate, aid, aided; heat, heed, heated.*
2. *Ann, I am; day, today; to, do, to do.*
3. *Any, me, many; share, chair, jar.*

Writing Practice

332 PREVIEW

☐ 333

☐ 334

☐ 335

333 First, anniversary, expected, annual, broadcasting, Albany, cable, justified.
334 Discussed, format, program, listening, appreciably, gained, license, support.
335 Recommend, consideration, electric current, trial, expectations, statement.

LETTERS

333

To the Staff: June 1 marked our first anniversary in the television business. How are we doing? We are[1] doing far better than expected. Our annual report shows broadcasting revenues of $12 million.[2] No one believed that we would be able to achieve this figure in our first year.

Some of you will recall that there[3] was considerable concern when we purchased four television stations from the Albany Corporation.[4] Some people felt that regular television had reached its peak and that the future was in cable television.[5] Fortunately, we were able to overcome the opposition, and our success shows that our efforts have[6] been justified.

In a few days I will issue a report on the progress of our four new stations. C. R. Brown[7]

334

Dear Mr. Doyle: I have discussed a possible change in our radio broadcasting format with our program[8] director, Miss Jane Royal. She and I agree that our listening audience might be increased appreciably[9] if we adopt a person-to-person programming format for at least one-half of our broadcast day.

Studies have[10] indicated that this format has gained wide acceptance all over the country. At this time our local listening[11] audience is exposed to this concept only one hour per day on a competing station. Our federal[12] license permits us to alter our programming format if we desire to do so.

Please consider our suggestions[13] and let us know if you agree with our plans for this change. Because you are the principal owner of the station,[14] Mr. Doyle, we want to have your support before we proceed with any action. Very sincerely yours,[15]

335

Dear Friend: We would like to recommend a radio for your consideration—the Air Master. We think this[16] radio is an outstanding value. It is portable and operates either on batteries or electric[17] current.

Prove to yourself that the Air Master is the finest radio on the market today. Just fill in and[18] mail the enclosed postage-paid card. When we receive it, we will send you the Air Master for a ten-day free home trial.[19] If the radio fails to meet your expectations, just return it to us; you will be under no obligation.[20]

If you decide to keep the Air Master, you will be getting a fine value at $69, which[21] is a reduction of almost 50 percent from its regular price. You may, of course, charge it to your account[22] and pay for it when you receive your monthly statement.

Mail the card today and enjoy the Air Master. Yours truly,[23] [460]

Reading and Writing Practice

336

Transcribe: July 15

an·ten·na

built-in

heavy-gauge *hyphenated before noun*

nonr

al·to·geth·er

con·sis·tent

par

um

conj

if

per·son·al·ly

nc

Transcribe: 6 p.m.

[138]

337

as

passed

de·liv·ered

intro

ex·pired

bro·chure

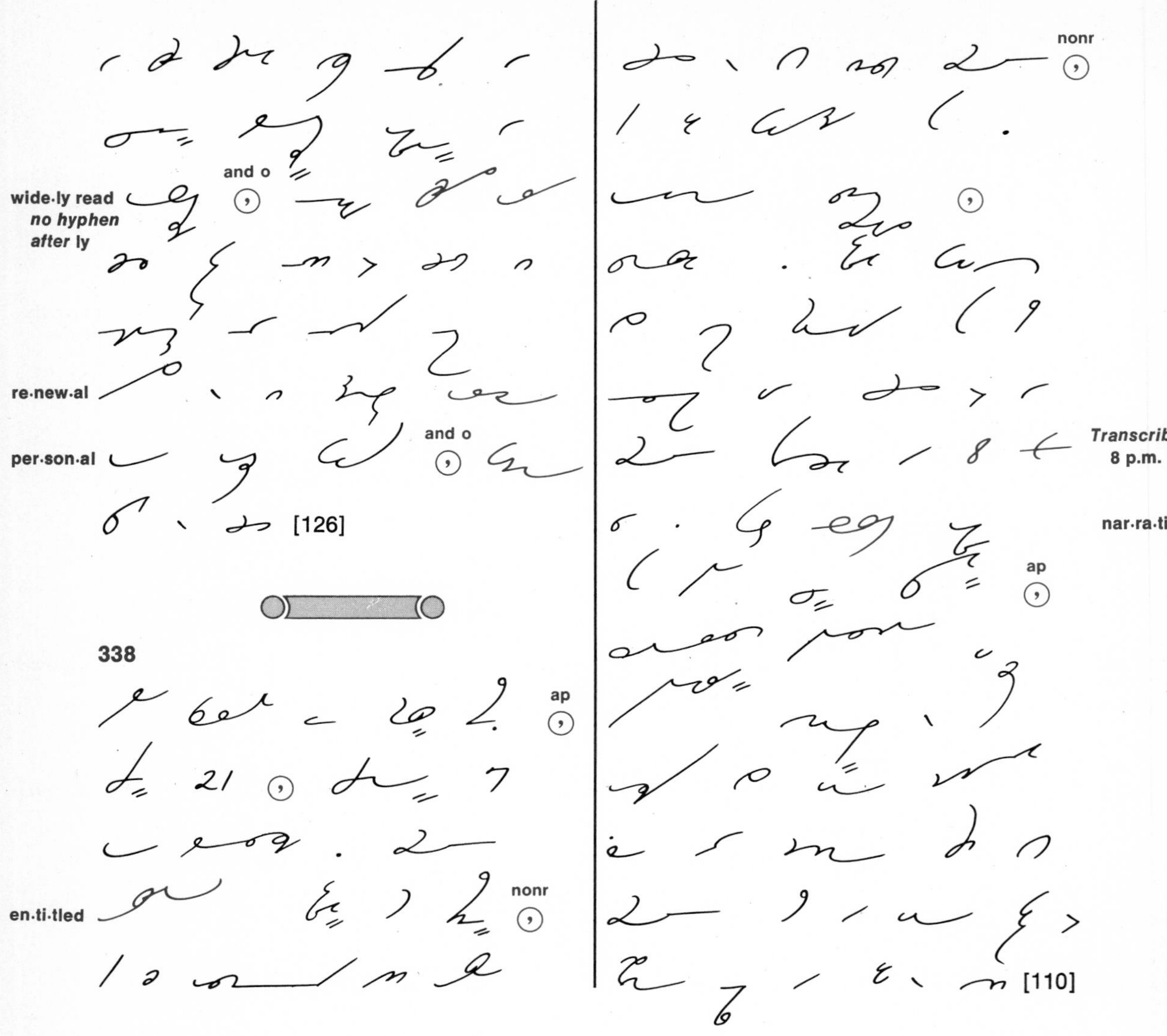

Secretaries who hold long personal conversations on the telephone are a problem in any business office. Whether an executive is in an office alone or in conference, he or she appreciates the secretary's maintaining "phone silence" unless the phone calls are truly necessary.

Developing Shorthand Writing Power

339 WORD FAMILIES

-rer

1

-rt

2

1. *Wearer, bearer, nearer, dearer, fairer, clearer.*
2. *Expert, convert, revert, shirt, alert, insert.*

340 FREQUENTLY USED NAMES

Last Names

1

Men's First Names

2

1. *Hart, Howell, Humphrey, Hunt, Hunter, Irwin.*
2. *Geoffrey, Harry, Harvey, Henry, Herman, Hugh, Irving.*

Building Transcription Skills

341 Business Vocabulary Builder

scholars Learned persons; those who have studied in a special field.

inspired *(verb)* Influenced; spurred on; encouraged.

unconditional Not limited; without restrictions.

Writing Practice

342 PREVIEW

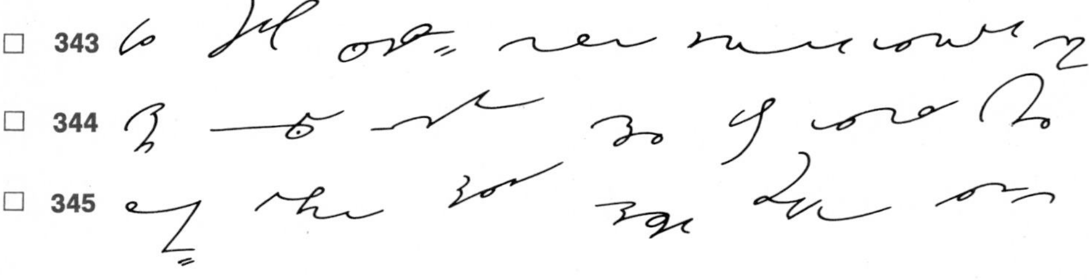

343 *Pity, videotape, Einstein, clearer, scholars, recorders, coupon.*

344 *Thank you for your, miniature, unconditional, consequently, whatever, regret, difficulty.*

345 *Elgin, treasurer, substituted, newscasts, versatility, technical.*

LETTERS

343

Dear Ms. Hart: It is a pity that Wilson videotape was not available in Einstein's day. Einstein could[1] have used videotape to make his ideas clearer to those who work so hard to understand them. Even more[2] important, scholars today could still be inspired by the real-life sight and sound of that great person.

Wilson introduced[3] its first videotape recorder in 1956. Since then we have added 25 models to our[4] line. We are constantly striving to improve the quality of our recorders. No recorder on the market[5] today has a brighter, clearer picture than the Wilson.

A Wilson system can do many things for a company[6] such as yours. If you will give us the opportunity, we can show you how this system can add interest to[7] your training sessions and help you sell your products more effectively. Just return the enclosed coupon. Yours truly,[8]

344

Dear Mr. Irwin: Thank you for your letter asking for information about service on the miniature[9] radio you purchased in June.

Since you purchased it three months ago, it is covered by our unconditional[10] guarantee. Consequently, there will be no charge for either parts or labor. Please send it back to us so that we[11] can make whatever repairs are necessary.

We regret that you have had difficulty with the set. We are[12] confident that after the repairs have been made, it will provide you with many years of fine service. Yours truly,[13]

345

Dear Mr. Irving: I am pleased to recommend Mr. Herman Jennings for a position on your staff at[14] radio station KTX.

Mr. Jennings worked for our station here in Elgin, Illinois, for nearly three years.[15] During that time he served as treasurer and chief accountant. On two or three occasions he actually substituted[16] as an announcer on our newscasts. His versatility made him a valuable member of our staff.[17] Needless to say, we were disappointed when we lost him to a larger station in Chicago.

In addition[18] to his technical skills, Mr. Jennings' pleasant personality made him a favorite of our entire staff.[19] We would be happy to rehire him if he ever decided to return to Elgin. Very sincerely yours,[20] [400]

● Reading and Writing Practice

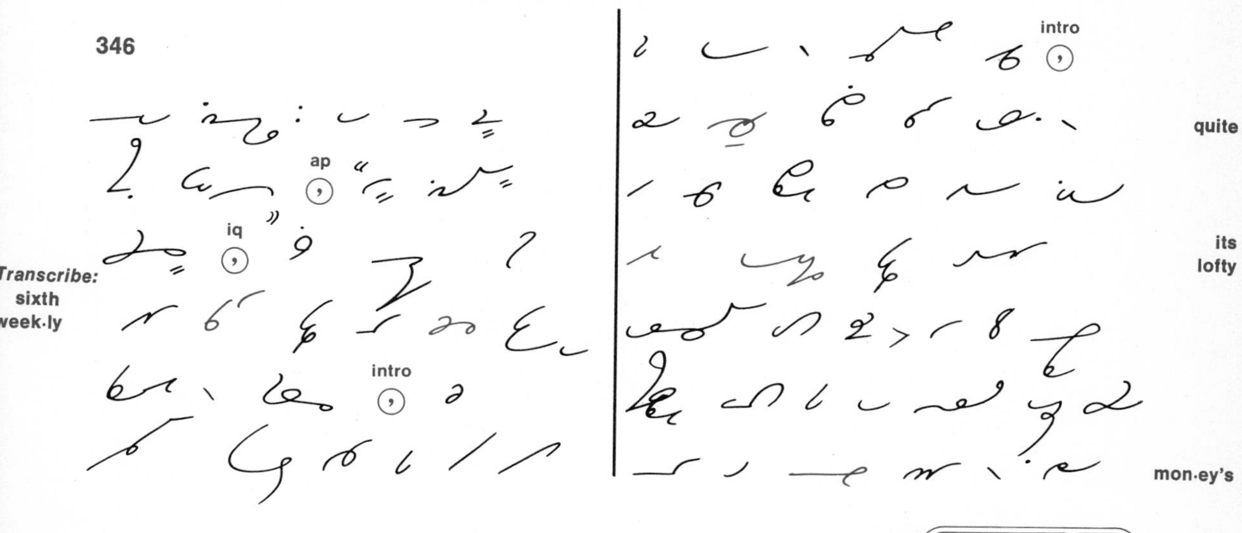

neigh·bor·hood

un·rea·son·able

conj

fair·er

if

[214]

347

intro

ex·pert

Transcribe:
11 percent

nc

un·for·tu·nate
re·al·ly

er·ror

ser

too-fre·quent
hyphenated before noun

thought-pro·vok·ing
hyphenated before noun

and o

intro

va·ri·ety

conj

[166]

348

ste·reo

ap

fre·quent·ly asked
no hyphen after ly

if

its

555-4982 [103]

349

Transcribe:
50 cents
news·stand

50

if

week's

15

car·ri·er

[93]

LESSON 39

Developing Shorthand Writing Power

350 FREQUENTLY USED PHRASES

Omission of Words

1 

Omission of A

2 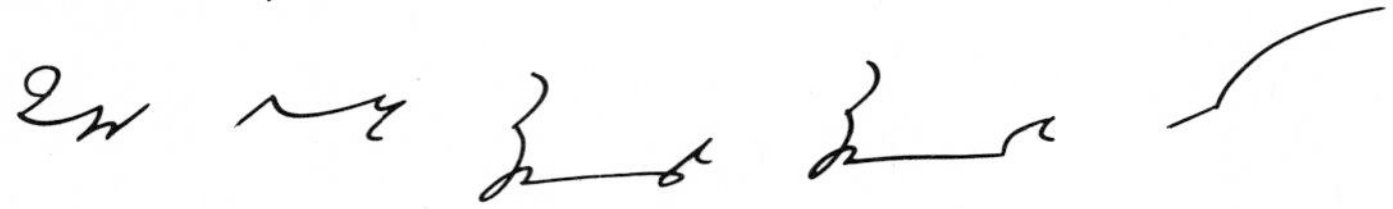

1. *Glad to say, glad to see, one of the, one of the best, one of our, one or two, three or four.*
2. *As a result, at a loss, for a few minutes, for a few months, at a time.*

351 GEOGRAPHICAL EXPRESSIONS

New-

1 

States

2 

Foreign Cities and Countries

3

1. *New York, New Orleans, New London, New Bedford, New Britain, Newark.*
2. *Oregon, New Jersey, Connecticut, Illinois, Tennessee, Massachusetts, Alaska.*
3. *Glasgow, Wales, Ireland, Belfast, Dublin, Birmingham.*

Building Transcription Skills

352 Business Vocabulary Builder

closed-circuit television A system whereby television signals are sent to selected receivers.

soliciting Requesting; seeking.

emphasize To point out; to stress.

● Writing Practice

353 PREVIEW

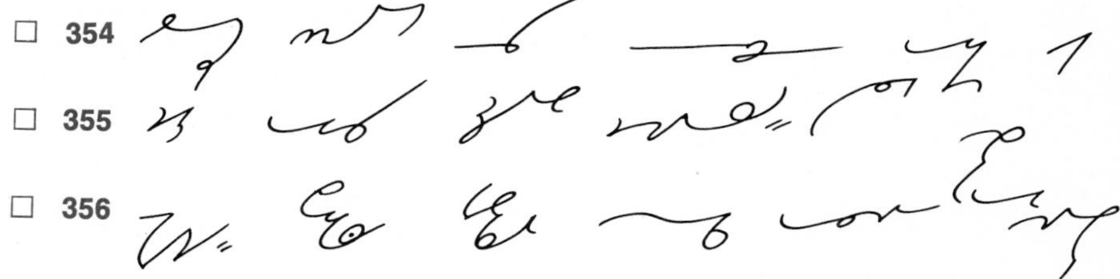

354 *Television, wonderful, medium, men and women, logic, touch.*
355 *Stations, located, subsidiaries, Scotland, dimension, capabilities.*
356 *New Bedford, appropriate, participants, glad to say, lecture, contribution.*

LETTERS

354

Dear Mr. Sims: Television is, of course, a wonderful medium of entertainment. It can also be[1] a wonderful medium for teaching and learning.

Through television, students can see and hear great men and women[2] of the past and the present. They can explore foreign lands. They can follow the logic of a difficult problem[3] in math.

If you do not have a closed-circuit television system in your school, get in touch with the New York[4] Television Company. We will be glad to survey your school, recommend a suitable system, and give you[5] an estimate on the cost of installation. All this will be done without any obligation on your part.[6] Just return the enclosed postage-paid card for more information; you will be glad you did. Very cordially yours,[7]

355

To the Staff: On January 2, we will become the owners of three television stations located in[8] Newark, New Orleans, and New York. The stations will become subsidiaries of the International Broadcasting[9] Company. As a result of this purchase, our company will now own stations in the United States as[10] well as in Scotland, Wales, and Ireland.

We are indeed fortunate to be able to purchase these stations, each of[11] which is an acknowledged leader in its market area. Our operation of these stations adds a great new[12] dimension to our capabilities for serving the general public with information, education,[13] and entertainment.

We are very excited at the prospects of this new venture in broadcasting. A. R. Brown[14]

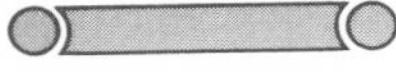

356

Dear Dr. Overman: The National Association of Broadcasting Executives will hold its annual[15] convention in New Bedford, Connecticut, from October 30 to November 2. We are preparing a[16] program that we think will be appropriate for the needs of our participants. We are glad to say that we expect[17] the largest turnout in the history of the association.

Because you are one of the country's leading[18] television news producers, we would like you to present a one-hour lecture on current issues in[19] television broadcasting. We feel that your contribution would be an outstanding one and would represent a highlight[20] of our program. The specific day we have open is Thursday, October 31, but we can arrange[21] another time if you wish.

Will you please let us know by July 1 if you can speak at our meeting. Yours truly,[22] [440]

● Reading and Writing Practice

357

dra·ma

geo

·com·plish

intro

en·u·ine

ate's

intro

ace·ment

anscribe:
ten

r·range·ments

if

coun·sel·ors

nc

Transcribe:
8 a.m.

wo

[190]

358

li·cense

conj

so·lic·it·ing

if

em·pha·size

enu

chan·nels

conj

an·ten·na

Transcribe:
$9

[186]

359

rev·e·nue

Transcribe:
15 perce

year

as

day·tim

intro

intro

[164]

LESSON 40

Developing Shorthand Writing Power

360 WORD BEGINNINGS

Trans-

1 

Dis-

2 

Inter-

3 

---

1. *Transmit, transfer, transcribe, transcription, transport, transportation, transpose, transit.*
2. *Disappointed, distressed, disaster, disappear, disband, dislocate.*
3. *Interstate, intercity, interboro, interject, interdependent, intermittent.*

Building Transcription Skills

---

361 Business Vocabulary Builder

justify To support or warrant an action.

expectations Hopes; forecasts.

niche A suitable place or position.

Progressive Speed Builder (80-120)

362 PREVIEW

363

364

365

366

367

363 As you know, sponsoring, series, ball-point, slightly, I suggest.
364 Gentlemen, discontinue, while, enough, justify, regret.
365 Canceled, contract, seriously, discussed, trial, New York.
366 Outline, assistant, transfer, represents, $4,000, personally, appointment.
367 Complete, results, exceeded, expectations, another, additional, finance.

LETTERS

363

[1 minute at 80]

Mr. Washington: As you know, since January we have been sponsoring a series of television spots/ on station KYZ advertising our new line of ball-point pens. While this advertising has increased our sales//slightly, I do not feel television is the medium through which to advertise this product.

I suggest, therefore,///that we do not renew our present contract and use our money in other, more productive ways. J. C. Bates [1]

364

[1 minute at 90]

Gentlemen: At a recent meeting our advertising department decided to discontinue our spot television/advertising on Channel 13 in which we advertised our ball-point pens.

While we have experienced a slight increase in sales//of our ball-point pens, we do not feel that the increase has been large enough for us to justify continuing this form of///advertising during the coming year.

It is with regret, therefore, that we are not renewing our contract with you. Sincerely, [2]

365

[1 minute at 100]

Mr. Washington: Now that we have canceled our contract with television Channel 13, do you have any definite plans for other/types of advertising for our ball-point pens? If you do not, may I suggest that you seriously consider advertising them on//radio station KYF. I discussed this matter with our president, Mr. Johnson, and he feels that we should give this medium a trial.///

Please stop in to see me on your next visit to New York, and let us discuss the matter. I will be in the office all next week. J. C. Bates [3]

366

[1 minute at 110]

Mr. Bates: Attached is an outline of a plan that my assistant and I put together to transfer our advertising from television to radio./The plan will cost $8,000, which represents a saving of $4,000 over the cost of television advertising.

Personally,//I have some doubts about the value of radio advertising for this particular product. I am, however, willing to give it///a six-month trial.

I have an appointment with one of the KYF programmers who will help us arrange a schedule for our spots. Harry Washington [4]

367

[1 minute at 120]

Mr. Bates: Enclosed is a complete report on the results of the six-month trial advertising of our ball-point pens over radio station KYF. I am happy/to say that our results from this advertising have exceeded our best expectations. Our sales of ball-point pens have increased 20 percent since July.

On the basis//of this trial, I recommend that we continue our radio advertising for another year. In order to do this, we will need an additional advertising///appropriation of $10,000. I am sure that we will have little difficulty getting this amount from the finance committee. Harry Washington [5] [500]

Reading and Writing Practice

368

iq

Chil·dren's

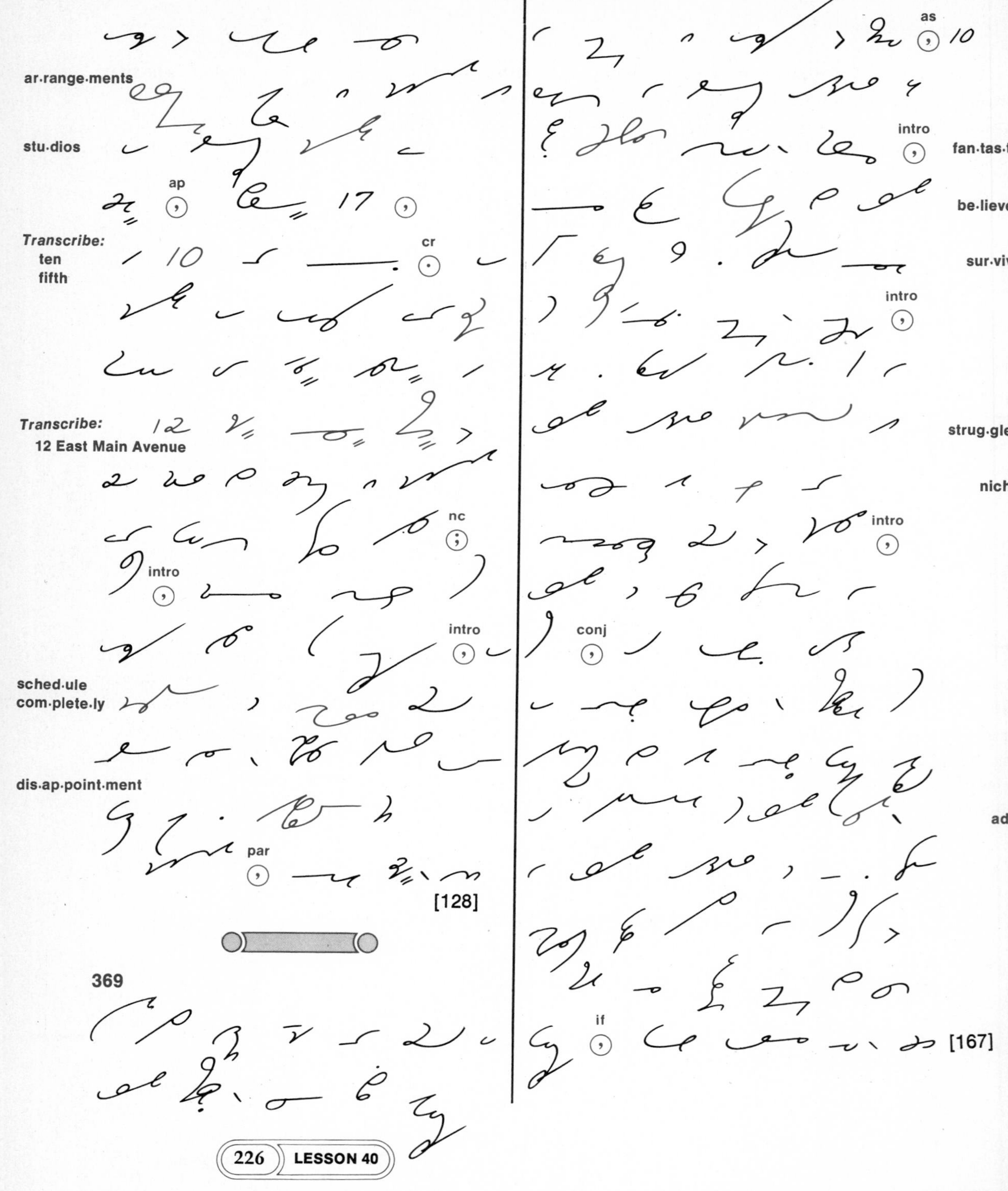

ar·range·ments
stu·dios
ap
17
Transcribe:
ten
fifth
10
cr
Transcribe:
12 East Main Avenue
12
nc
intro
intro
sched·ule
com·plete·ly
dis·ap·point·ment
par
[128]
369
as
10
intro
fan·tas·tic
be·lieved
sur·vive
intro
strug·gled
niche
intro
conj
ads
if
[167]

PART

Devising Shorthand Shortcuts for Your Job

Sometimes students make the assumption that all they have to do to increase their shorthand speed is to learn a great many shortcuts. However, this assumption is not valid. Shortcuts are not the answer to shorthand speed. Shortcuts can be of value to you only if the words they represent occur very frequently in your dictation. If they do not, the shortcuts will be more of a hindrance than a help in the development of your shorthand speed. If the words do not occur frequently, you will not have an opportunity to use the shortcuts often enough to be able to write them without thinking. The instant that any shortcut causes you to hesitate for even a fraction of a second, it is a hindrance. You will do far better to write the expression in full.

While you are in school, you should stay away from shortcuts almost entirely and write everything in accordance with the word-building principles of Gregg Shorthand. You will have time enough to devise shortcuts when you are on the job.

Even on the job, you should think carefully about any shortcut that you adopt. Before you adopt it, decide whether the shortcut meets the following essential requirements:

1 Is the full outline so long or difficult to execute that you cannot write it in full rapidly? Consider this question carefully. There are relatively few outlines in Gregg Shorthand that cannot be written rapidly according to the word-building principles of the system.

2 Does the word occur in your dictation enough to justify the time it will take you to learn the shortcut?

3 Is the shortcut distinctive enough to cause you no difficulty when you transcribe?

If the answer to these three questions is yes, then the adoption of the shortcut may be worthwhile.

As a rule, it is best to use only shortcuts that you are able to devise after careful thought. There is one situation, however, in which you would be justified in forming a new shortcut during dictation. This is when a very long, difficult word or phrase is used repeatedly and you have good reason to believe that it will be used many more times in the dictation.

For example, a stenographer was taking dictation in which the expression "one-class service" recurred. The first three times the secretary wrote the expression in full, but when it occurred the fourth time, the secretary wrote *oo-k*-intersected *s*.

After the dictation, the stenographer took the precaution of making a note of the shortcut used for "one-class service" so that the notes would be easy to read, even several days later.

Although shortcuts have their limited place in taking dictation, you will be wise to follow the advice of an experienced reporter who said, "When in doubt, write it out!"

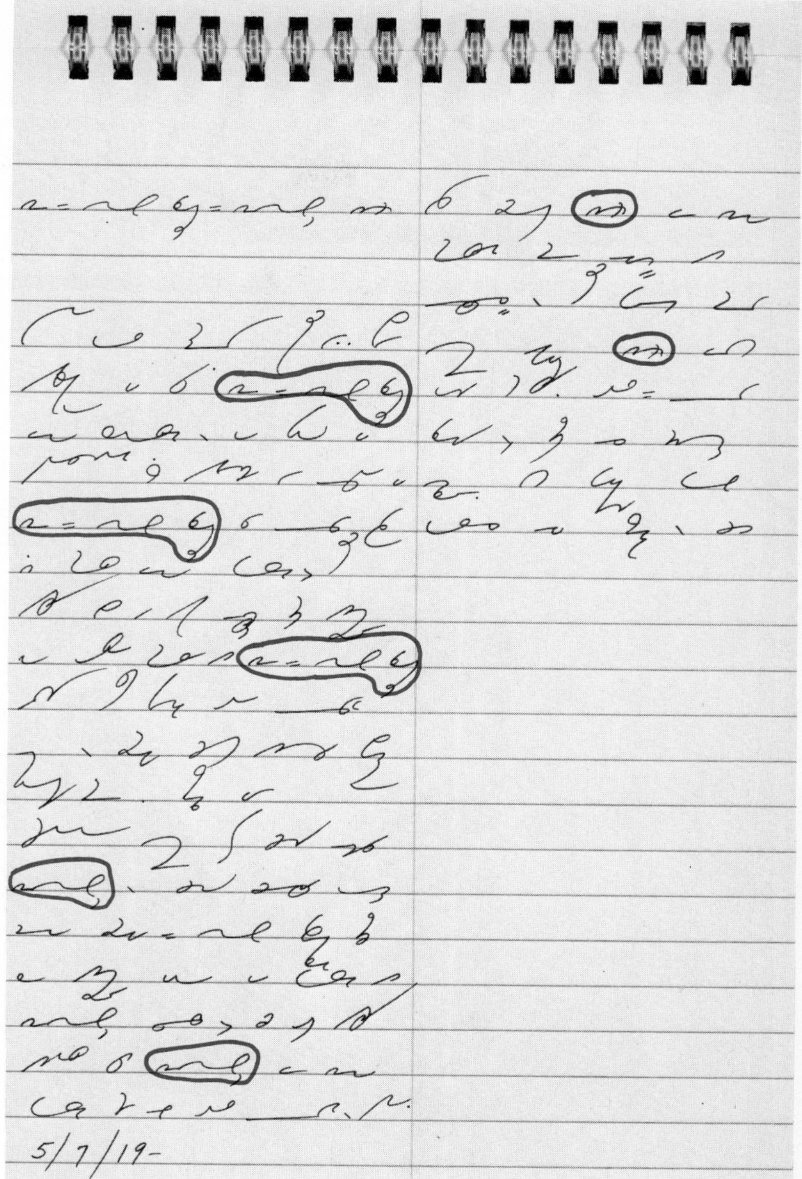

Illustration of shortcuts devised during dictation

CHAPTER 9 Communication

Developing Shorthand Writing Power

370 OUTLINE CONSTRUCTION

Word Endings -tract, -trict, -truct The vowel is omitted in the word endings *-tract, -trict, -truct.*

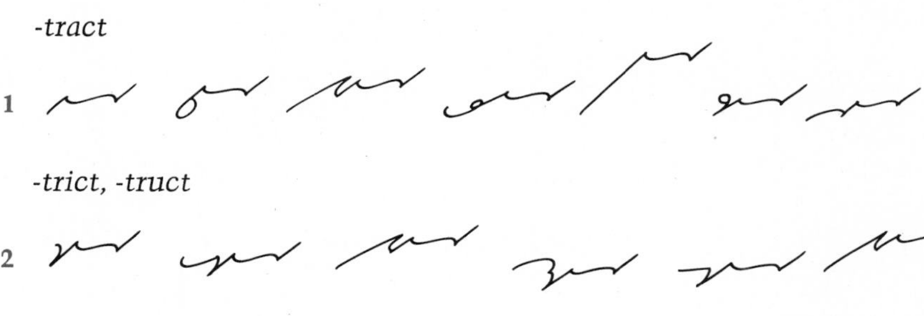

1. *Tract, attract, distract, retract, detract, extract, contract.*
2. *Strict, restrict, district, construct, instruct, destruction.*

Building Transcription Skills

371 SIMILAR-WORDS DRILL right, write

right Correct; opposite of left.

This is the right *thing to do.*
Please sit on the right *side, not the left.*

write Draw; trace; inscribe.

I will **write** *the letter.*

● Reading and Writing Practice

372 Communications

It was

1876

It is

[260]

373 LETTERS

it

col·lege

writ·ten

writ·ing

enu

right

mem·o·ran·dums

intro

con·struct·ing

ser

de·scrib·ing

de·vel·op

com·plete

if

ap

com·pe·tent

yours

em·ploy·ees'

[212]

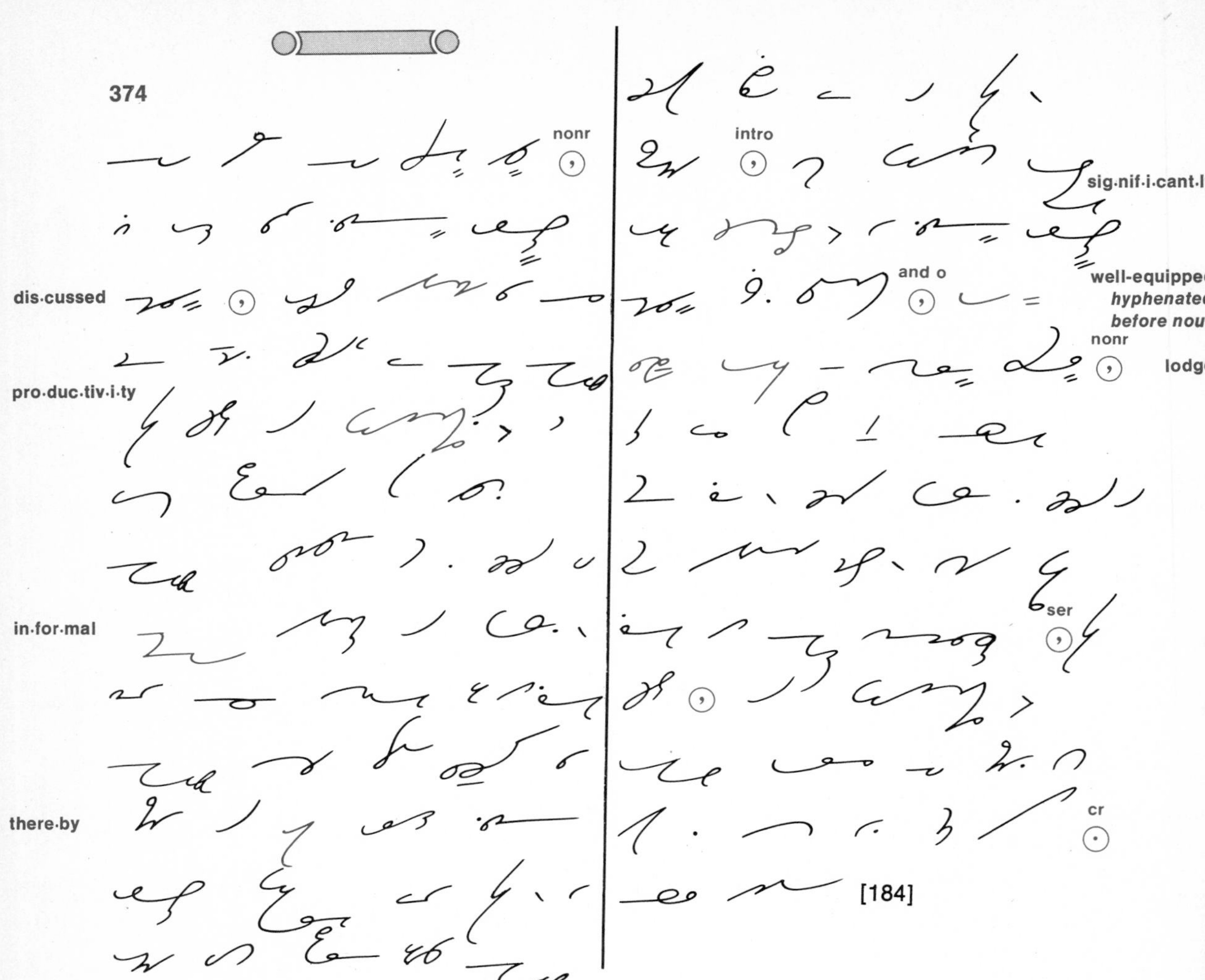

An attractive letter signifies more than a responsible secretary; it becomes a sample of the taste and character of the company. No letter that a secretary mails should ever be less than perfect.

Developing Shorthand Writing Power

375 RECALL DRILL m

In this drill you will review the different uses of the alphabetic stroke *m*.

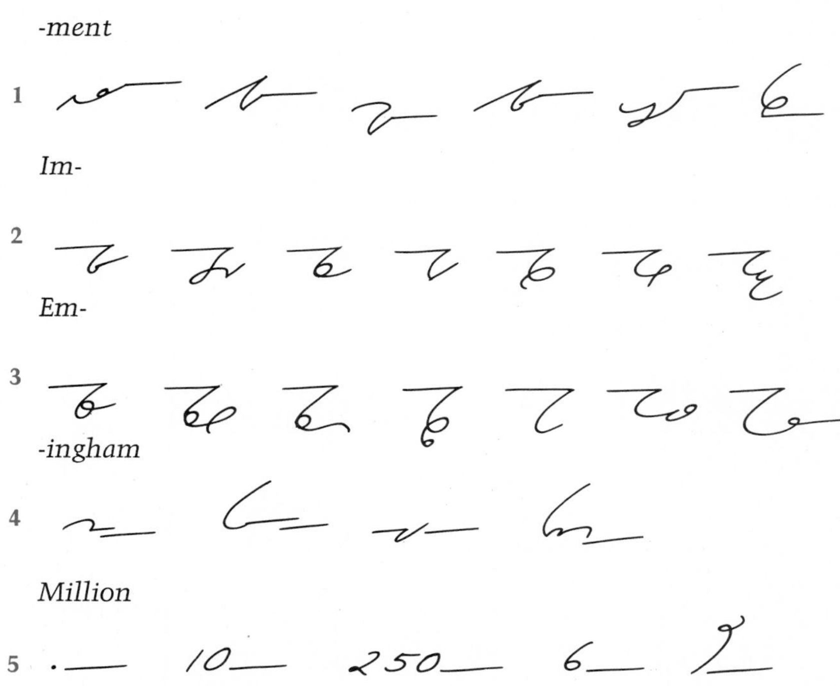

---

1. Treatment, department, compartment, deportment, resentment, basement.
2. Import, impact, impair, impart, impasse, impression, improper.

3. *Empire, embarrass, embark, embassy, ember, employ, emblem.*
4. *Cunningham, Birmingham, Nottingham, Buckingham.*
5. *A million, 10 million, 250 million, 6 million, several million.*

Building Transcription Skills

376 ACCURACY PRACTICE

In this lesson you will study the correct joining of circles in the body of a word.

1. *Rate, raid; writ, read; late, laid.*
2. *Main, name; deck, dig; take, tag.*
3. *Care, gale; rack, lake; pave, beef.*

● Writing Practice

377 PREVIEW

☐ **378**

☐ **379**

☐ **380**

378 *Telephoned, Cunningham, answered, courteous, image, encourage, techniques.*
379 *Encountered, records, consultant, successful, bottom, authority, properly.*
380 *Delivered, elements, communications, effective, listener, impressed.*

LETTERS

378

To All Employees: Yesterday I was away from the office and telephoned our sales department for information[1] about a particular order on which our company is working. Miss Grace Cunningham, the secretary[2] who answered the telephone, so impressed me with her courteous but helpful response that I wanted to[3] tell you about it.

Many people do business with our company only by telephone. Their image of us[4] is formed by the oral responses they receive from our employees.

May I encourage each of you to take just[5] a few moments to examine your own particular telephone techniques. If you are honestly striving to[6] convey the best image of our company possible, I extend my thanks for the extra effort you are making.[7] If you are not, why not try making a change. I believe your efforts will be rewarded many times. Jane Smith[8]

379

Ms. Buckingham: Due to the many problems we have encountered with our new records management system, we have[9] hired Mr. Bob Green of the Empire Company to work with us as a consultant.

Mr. Green has been successful[10] in solving problems such as those we have experienced, and we believe that he will be able to get to[11] the bottom of our troubles very quickly. Mr. Green has authority to examine all documents[12] pertaining to the system, to interview anyone he needs to see, and to implement those changes he feels are[13] necessary to make our system work properly.

If you have any questions, please contact me. J. L. Forest[14]

380

Dear Mr. Grant: Recently a well-known speaker, Dr. Janice Cunningham of Pennsylvania State College,[15] delivered a lecture to the student body on the key elements of communications in business. I was[16] fortunate to be in the audience.

The title of the speech was "Effective Listening." Dr. Cunningham stated[17] that in order for effective communication to occur, the listener must concentrate with the same[18] intensity as the speaker. I was so impressed with Dr. Cunningham's comments that I contacted her concerning[19] the possibility of her speaking at the annual meeting of our association next June. She[20] accepted my invitation, and I have scheduled her for two sessions on the second day of the meeting.

Please plan[21] to introduce Dr. Cunningham at each of the sessions. I will appreciate your assistance. Yours truly,[22] [440]

Reading and Writing Practice

381

ban·quet

high·lights

buf·fet

intro

na·tion·al·ly known
no hyphen after ly

brief

coun·try's
fore·most

intro

nonr

mil·lion

par

hon·o·rar·i·um

ap

18

Transcribe:
7 p.m.

cr

[203]

382

com·pa·ny's
po·ten·tial

yours

me·dia

across

Transcribe: 10 million

ob·li·ga·tion

intro

rep·re·sen·ta·tives

[141]

383

long-dis·tance

geo

conj

intro

nev·er·the·less

conj

conj

here·af·ter

intro

if

if

[217]

Secretarial Tip
Typing Quotations in Business Letters

Sometimes your employer will insert a quote from a book, magazine, or other source in a letter. The dictator may read the quotation to you or may simply mark it in the source document and tell you to copy it in the proper place.

Here are a few points you should keep in mind when you type quotations.

1 Copy a quotation exactly as it appears in the original—even the errors. If you find an error (perhaps a misspelled word or an incorrect capitalization), type it exactly as it is in the original, but immediately after the error type *(sic)* in parentheses.

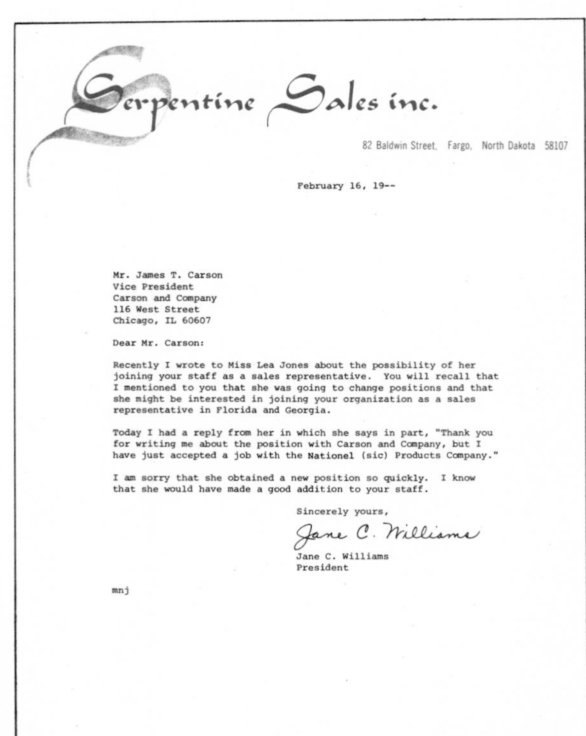

Serpentine Sales inc.

82 Baldwin Street, Fargo, North Dakota 58107

February 16, 19--

Mr. James T. Carson
Vice President
Carson and Company
116 West Street
Chicago, IL 60607

Dear Mr. Carson:

Recently I wrote to Miss Lea Jones about the possibility of her joining your staff as a sales representative. You will recall that I mentioned to you that she was going to change positions and that she might be interested in joining your organization as a sales representative in Florida and Georgia.

Today I had a reply from her in which she says in part, "Thank you for writing me about the position with Carson and Company, but I have just accepted a job with the Nationel (sic) Products Company."

I am sorry that she obtained a new position so quickly. I know that she would have made a good addition to your staff.

Sincerely yours,

Jane C. Williams

Jane C. Williams
President

mnj

Figure 1: (a) Copy a quotation exactly as it appears in the original. (b) Run a short quotation in with the text matter that introduces the quotation, enclosing it in quotation marks.

The expression *sic* is Latin for *thus*. It is used to indicate that an expression is reproduced as it is in the original, even though it may be incorrect. (See Figure 1.)

2 If the quotation is a short one (fewer than four lines), run it in with the text matter that introduces the quotation. Be sure, of course, to enclose it in quotation marks. (See Figure 1.)

3 If the quotation is a long one (four lines or more), indent it from both margins *without* quotation marks (See Figure 2.)

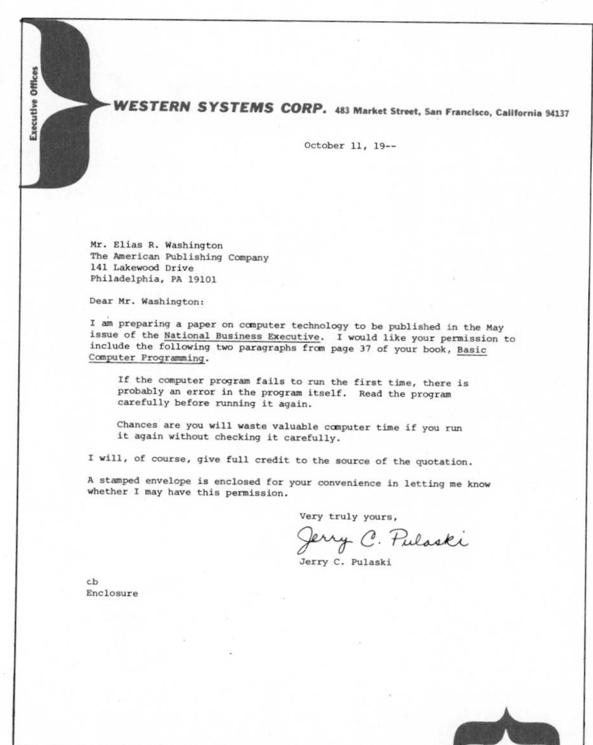

Executive Offices

WESTERN SYSTEMS CORP. 483 Market Street, San Francisco, California 94137

October 11, 19--

Mr. Elias R. Washington
The American Publishing Company
141 Lakewood Drive
Philadelphia, PA 19101

Dear Mr. Washington:

I am preparing a paper on computer technology to be published in the May issue of the National Business Executive. I would like your permission to include the following two paragraphs from page 37 of your book, Basic Computer Programming.

> If the computer program fails to run the first time, there is probably an error in the program itself. Read the program carefully before running it again.
>
> Chances are you will waste valuable computer time if you run it again without checking it carefully.

I will, of course, give full credit to the source of the quotation.

A stamped envelope is enclosed for your convenience in letting me know whether I may have this permission.

Very truly yours,

Jerry C. Pulaski

Jerry C. Pulaski

cb
Enclosure

Figure 2: Indent a long quotation from both margins without quotation marks.

Developing Shorthand Writing Power

384 WORD FAMILIES

-way

1

-rous

2

1. *Halfway, byway, parkway, passageway, highway.*
2. *Prosperous, dangerous, numerous, generous, vigorous, humorous.*

385 FREQUENTLY USED NAMES

Last Names

1

Women's First Names

2

1. *Jackson, Jefferson, Jenkins, Jennings, Johnson, Jones.*
2. *Emily, Emma, Eve, Frances, Gail, Gloria, Grace.*

Building Transcription Skills

386 Business Vocabulary Builder

citizens' band radio A radio equipped with channels for private communications.

directory Telephone book; a listing.

Writing Practice

387 PREVIEW

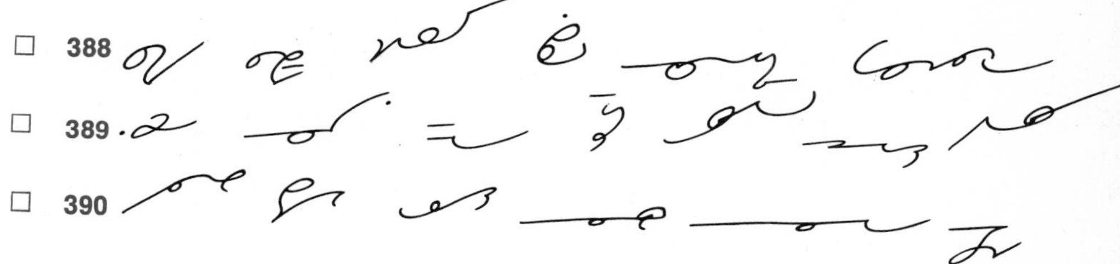

388 *Accompanied, equipped, stranded, hazard, microphone, practicality.*
389 *Aware, maintaining, internal, interoffice, entitled, numerous, delighted.*
390 *Decrease, assistance, reduce, minimize, minimal, impact.*

LETTERS

388

Ms. Grace: Last week I accompanied a friend on a drive in the desert near Ridgeway, Arizona. The car in[1] which we were riding was equipped with a citizens' band radio.

We were stopped by a stranded motorist whose[2] car was stalled on the highway, creating a dangerous traffic hazard. We pushed the car off the highway. Then[3] my friend picked up the microphone of the CB radio in our car and issued a call. Within a few minutes'[4] time a tow truck was on the way.

I was impressed with the practicality of the CB radio. I[5] believe we could improve our operations if we installed them in our fleet of trucks. Will you please contact a local[6] dealer and get an estimate on the cost of installing CB radios in our trucks. Robert Jackson[7]

389

Dear Mr. Jefferson: Most business executives are aware of the importance of maintaining good[8] communications with their customers. However, they sometimes forget the importance of internal communications[9] in their organizations. They take great care with correspondence that goes out of the building, but they often[10] neglect inter-office memorandums.

It is for businesses such as these that we have prepared a new book[11] entitled *Internal Office Communications.* We feel that it is by far the best book of its type on the market[12] today. The book was written in an interesting, informative style by Dr. Gloria Jenkins of Ridgeway[13] State College. It is filled with numerous suggestions on ways to improve office communications. It is[14] available to you at the low price of only $10.

If you would like to receive an examination[15] copy, just fill out, sign, and return the enclosed card. When you receive the book, we feel sure you will want to keep[16] it. If you are not delighted with it, however, you may return it within ten days. Very cordially yours,[17]

390

To the Staff: Beginning July 1, the local telephone company will charge 10 cents for information[18] services in this area. The objective is to decrease telephone customers' dependence on assistance[19] from operators. This would, of course, reduce the telephone company's salary expenses. However, it[20] could increase our telephone charges significantly.

There are numerous things we could do to minimize the[21] financial impact of this action on our company. Here are just three:

1. Whenever possible, check the local[22] directory before you call.
2. Keep a record of all numbers you must obtain from the telephone[23] operator.
3. Keep a booklet of frequently used numbers next to your telephone where it will be handy.

Your[24] concern and awareness of the new policy will ensure a minimal financial impact on us. Gail Jones[25] [500]

● Reading and Writing Practice

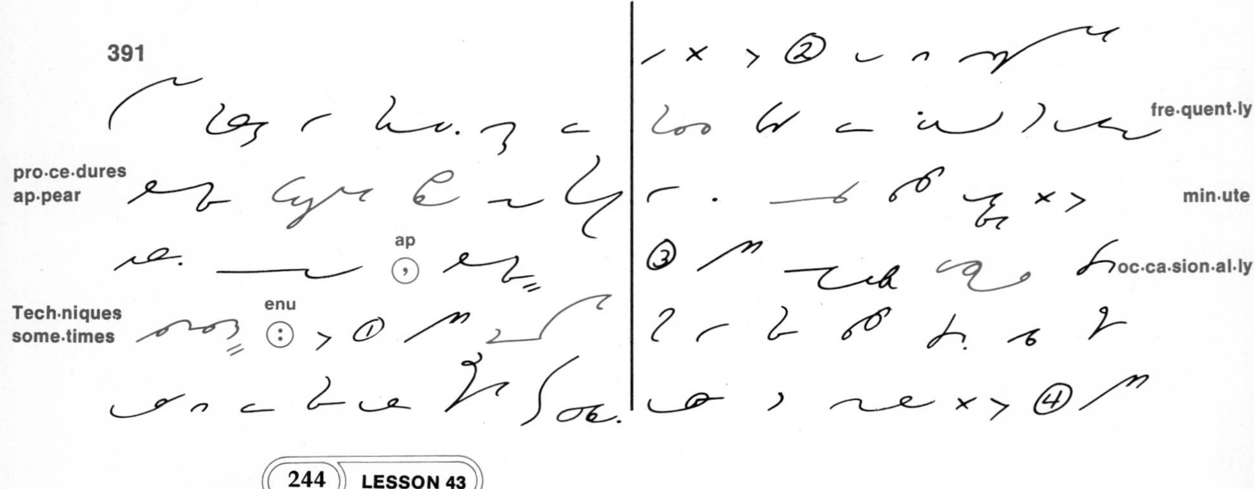

nu·mer·ous

iden·ti·fy

Transcribe:
421 Eastern Parkway

nc

com·pli·ments

[161]

392

Ex·ec·u·tive

when

ex·ten·sion

ne·ces·si·ty

trans·fer
in·com·ing

ser

con·fer·ence

nc

ser

Transcribe:
5
20
500

if

ob·li·ga·tion-free
hyphenated before noun

[151]

Developing Shorthand Writing Power

393 FREQUENTLY USED PHRASES

Words Omitted

1

Several

2

1. *Will you please, one or two, two or three, three or four, men and women, once or twice.*
2. *Several days, several days ago, several months, several months ago, several minutes.*

394 GEOGRAPHICAL EXPRESSIONS

-ville

1

States

2

Foreign Cities

3 

1. *Nashville, Knoxville, Brownsville, Asheville, Louisville, Danville, Jacksonville, Crawfordsville.*
2. *Iowa, Indiana, Minnesota, Ohio, Pennsylvania, Alabama, Illinois, Texas.*
3. *Bordeaux, Copenhagen, Marseilles, Cherbourg, Madrid, Lisbon.*

Building Transcription Skills

395 Business Vocabulary Builder

conspicuous Visible; obvious.

productivity The amount of work completed.

flat rate A set amount that is charged for a service regardless of usage.

● Writing Practice

396 PREVIEW

☐ **397**
☐ **398**
☐ **399**

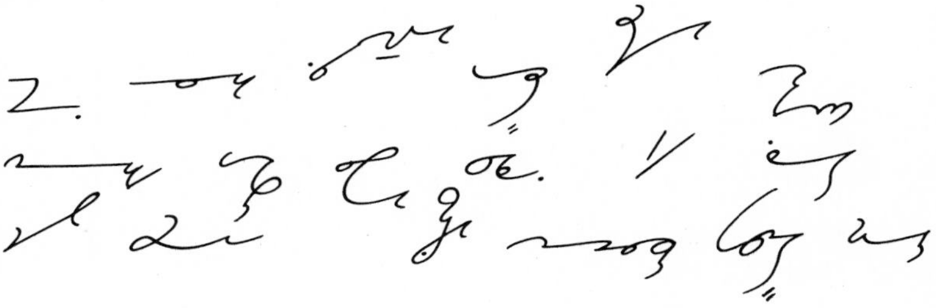

397 Informing, memorandums, headquarters, Louisville, several times, conspicuous.
398 One of the most, occupations, enables, answering, $1, helpful.
399 Studies, failure, associates, communications, Brownsville, solutions.

LETTERS

397

To All Department Heads: In the past, company policy for informing district employees of important[1] management decisions has been to send memorandums from our headquarters in Louisville to division heads[2] with instructions to transmit the information to their personnel. Unfortunately, several times we have[3] had problems with this procedure. Some of our employees claim they are never informed about important matters.[4]

The new policy, therefore, will be to send two copies of all memorandums to each division head. You should[5] keep one copy and post the other in a conspicuous place—such as a bulletin board.

This procedure should[6] provide for better communication. Will you please see that it is instituted immediately. Frank James[7]

398

Dear Mr. Martin: One of the most important recent inventions for business people in service occupations[8] is the General Signal Phone. This little device enables your customers to contact you wherever[9] you may be during the day. Here is how it works.

When a customer calls your number, our answering service receives[10] the call and immediately sends a signal to the small pocket receiver that you carry at all times.[11] You call the answering service as soon as possible, and you are given the caller's name and number. This[12] enables you to call back within a few minutes.

At the present time the service is available in New York,[13] Pennsylvania, and Ohio. However, we expect that the service will be available throughout the entire[14] nation within a year.

The cost of this service is $1 a day. The General Signal Phone can mean[15] increased earnings every day. Call us soon and discover the advantages of this helpful device. Yours truly,[16]

399

Dear Mr. Norton: Studies show that time and again the major cause of failure on the job is not lack of[17] technical skills. The major reason for failure is the inability to get along with one's associates.[18] In most cases the problems people experience could be eliminated if communications were[19] improved.

The Brownsville Publishing Company has just placed on the market a new book entitled *Improving*[20] *Communications.* It offers many solutions to job-related problems. It could be just what you need to make[21] your business a more enjoyable place in which to work. At the same time it could help you to improve the[22] productivity of your staff.

If you want to receive an examination copy of the book, simply return your[23] check for $15.95 and we will send it to you. If you are not satisfied with the book after[24] you have examined it carefully for ten days, you may return it for a full refund. Very truly yours,[25] [500]

Reading and Writing Practice

400

se·ri·ous

long-dis·tance

nc ;

intro ,

un·au·tho·rized

per·son·nel

par ,

,

nonr ,

re·ceive

cr .

com·plete

co·op·er·a·tion

[159]

401

intro ,

heard

ap·pears

de·ci·sions

cr .

en·cour·age

ini·tial

[115]

402

ap·prox·i·mate·ly

Transcribe: 50 percent

conj

de·crease

intro

over·seas

agree·ment

ser

un·lim·it·ed

and o

intro

nonr

uti·lize

[157]

Developing Shorthand Writing Power

403 WORD BEGINNINGS AND ENDINGS

-ful

1

Com-

2

Be-

3

1. *Hopeful, handful, wonderful, meaningful, helpful, grateful, beautiful.*
2. *Compare, complete, combination, combine, companion, competent, continue.*
3. *Become, begin, became, believe, belief, belong.*

Building Transcription Skills

404 Business Vocabulary Builder

recruit *(verb)* To enlist; to seek to obtain.

flying colors Complete success.

full-scale Total; complete.

Progressive Speed Builder (90-125)

The letters in this Progressive Speed Builder begin at 90 words a minute and run to 125 words a minute.

405 **PREVIEW**

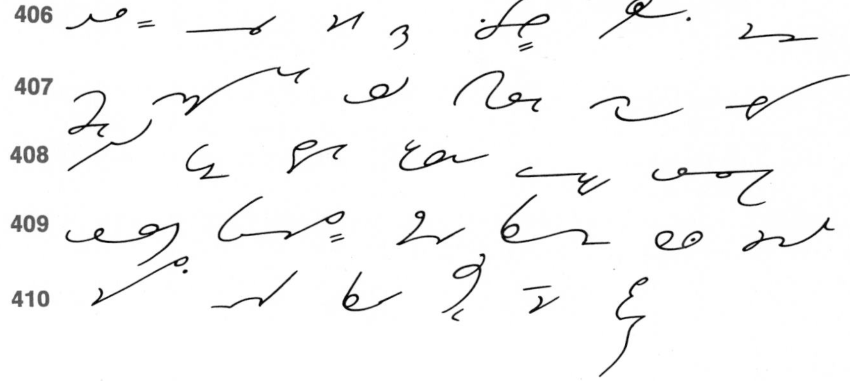

406 *Three-minute, station, yourself, Bahamas, dialing, someone.*
407 *Convince, customers, rather, difference, quality, next time.*
408 *Wouldn't, person, assistance, operator, almost, remember.*
409 *Relative, Bermuda, effect, bargain, area, seconds.*
410 *Studying, enclosed, chart, savings, interstate, expensive.*

LETTERS

406

[1 minute at 90]

Dear Mr. Gates: Just $2.25 is the rate for a three-minute, station-to-station call that you dial yourself/from New York to the Bahamas. This low rate is in effect Monday through Friday between 7 p.m. and 7 a.m.//The rate is even lower on Saturday and Sunday.

It is as easy as dialing any other call. When you need to///talk to someone in the Bahamas, just pick up the telephone. It is the next best thing to being there in person. Sincerely, [1]

407

[1 minute at 100]

Dear Mr. Gates: For several years we have been trying to convince our customers to dial their own interstate long-distance calls direct/rather than call person-to-person. Why? When you dial your own calls, you save both time and money. There is no difference in the quality//of the call. What makes the difference in time and cost is the fact that you are not involving our operator.

The next time you wish to make///a long-distance call, dial it yourself. Examples of the savings you can make by doing so are shown on the enclosed chart. Cordially yours, [2]

408

[1 minute at 110]

Dear Mr. Gates: Wouldn't you like to make two long-distance calls for the price of one? You can do this if you dial your long-distance calls yourself instead of/calling person-to-person.

During business hours, a three-minute, coast-to-coast call costs $3.30 if you call person-to-person. However,//if you make that call station-to-station and dial it yourself without the assistance of the telephone operator, the cost is only/// $1.35. You save almost 60 percent.

Remember, dial your long-distance calls yourself and get two for the price of one. Very sincerely yours, [3]

409

[1 minute at 120]

Dear Mr. Gates: Do you have a relative or friend you would like to call in Bermuda? Now it is easier and cheaper than ever. You can dial any number/in Bermuda station-to-station and talk for three minutes for as little as $3. This low rate is in effect every day from 9 p.m. to 7 a.m.//

All you have to do is dial the call yourself to take advantage of this bargain. You just dial the area code and the person's telephone number. You can reach///your party in a matter of a few seconds.

This is just another example of our efforts to bring you the best service at the lowest cost. Very truly yours, [4]

410

[1 minute at 125]

Dear Mr. Gates: As you will see by studying the enclosed rate chart, you can save money on your long-distance calls if you dial them yourself. If you compare the rate for/person-to-person calls with the rate for calls that you dial yourself, you will see a great difference. If you dial station-to-station when you call, your savings can be large.

Rates are//lower on interstate calls that you dial yourself because they cost much less to handle. Often person-to-person calls take two or three minutes of an operator's time, and///this is very expensive. When you dial your own calls, no operator is needed.

When you make a long-distance call, why not dial it yourself and save. Yours very truly, [5]
[545]

Reading and Writing Practice

411

Week·ly
com·pet·ing
as
ap·pli·ca·tion
full-scale
hyphenated before noun
be·lieve
when
its
help·ful
ser
intro

as·sess
qual·i·ty
self-ad·dressed
if
coun·ty's

[210]

412

intro
rep·re·sen·ta·tive
tech·niques

plan·ning

par

two-hour *hyphenated before noun*

ap

12

ser

role-play·ing

nonr

intro

im·ple·ment·ed

ar·range·ments

[180]

413

thank-you *hyphenated before noun*

par

intro

par

[110]

CHAPTER

Finance

Developing Shorthand Writing Power

414 OUTLINE CONSTRUCTION

Omission of Unaccented Vowel In -en, -an, -on When the endings *-en, -an, -on* are unaccented, the vowel may be omitted, thus making it possible to obtain fluent, easily readable outlines.

1. *Garden, olden, golden, even, burden, harden, Stephen.*
2. *Sudden, wooden, threaten, written, straighten, frighten, brighten.*
3. *Toughen, roughen, hyphen, darken, fallen, woolen, sharpen.*
4. *Urban, suburban, slogan, orphan, organ.*
5. *Person, comparison, mason, season, prison, pardon.*

Building Transcription Skills

415 SIMILAR-WORDS DRILL expand, expend

expand To enlarge; to spread out.

If we expand *our operations, we will need additional capital.*

expend To use up; to spend.

We must expend *our total budget if the project is to succeed.*

Reading and Writing Practice

416 The Need for Money

The American

Metals

1368, [173]

417 LETTERS

[100]

if

pay·roll

so·lu·tion

intro

amount

sal·a·ry

nc

real

boon

to·day's

nc

418

rec·om·mend·ed

intro

con·sid·er·able

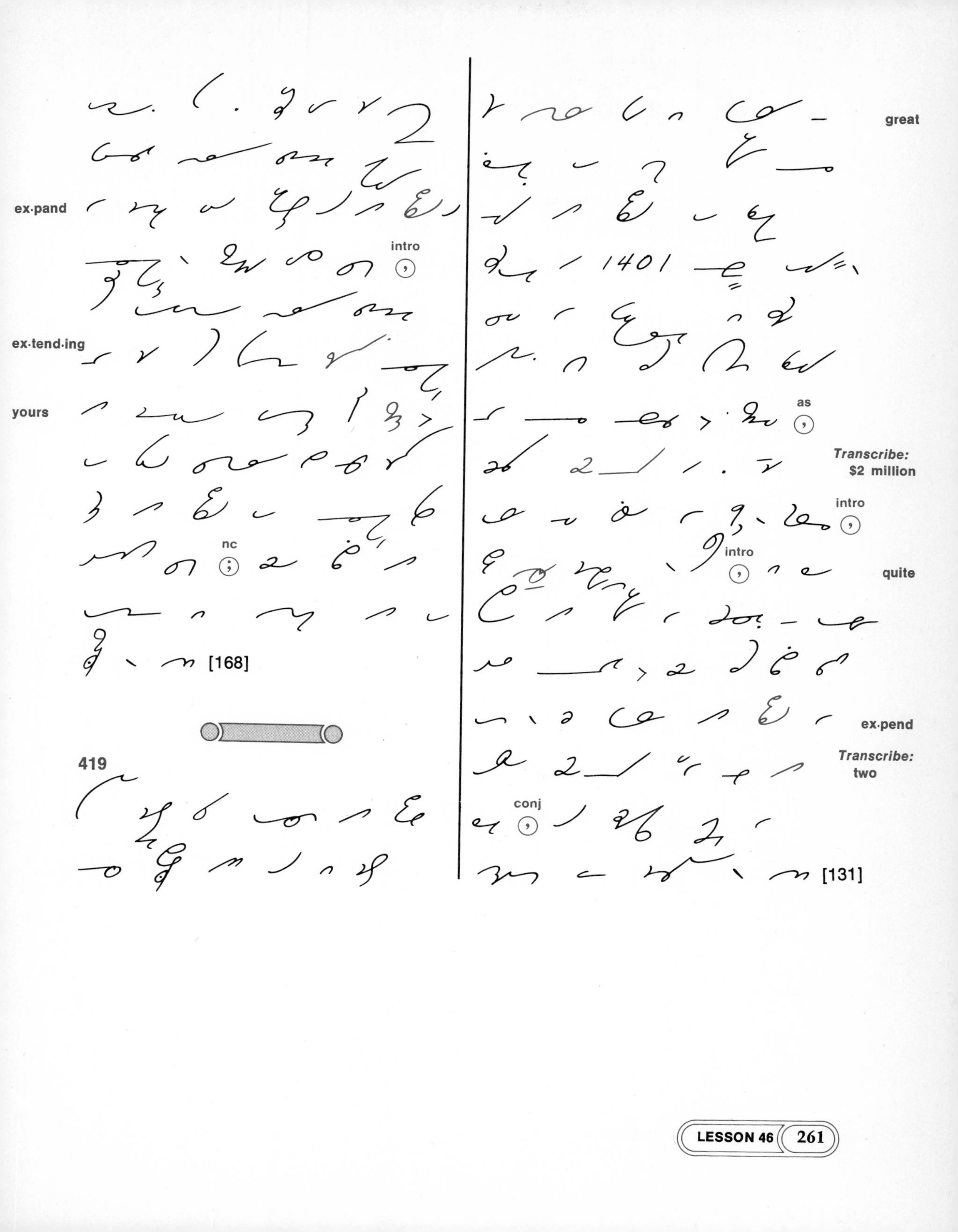

ex·pand

intro

ex·tend·ing

yours

nc

[168]

419

great

1401

as

Transcribe: $2 million

intro

intro

quite

ex·pend

Transcribe: two

conj

[131]

Developing Shorthand Writing Power

420 RECALL DRILL r

In this drill you will review the situations in which the alphabetic stroke *r* is used.

R

1

Re-

2

-er, -or

3

-rity

4

-ure

5

1. *Rate, far, mere, nearly, prime, pride, relate.*
2. *Repair, refinish, refurnish, review, refuse, repel, repeat, refer.*
3. *Reader, meter, voter, leader, motor, factor.*

4. *Integrity, sincerity, charity, similarity, prosperity, minority, majority.*
5. *Feature, future, creature, mature, overture, nature, natural.*

Building Transcription Skills

421 **ACCURACY PRACTICE**

In this drill you will practice the joining of circles outside angles.

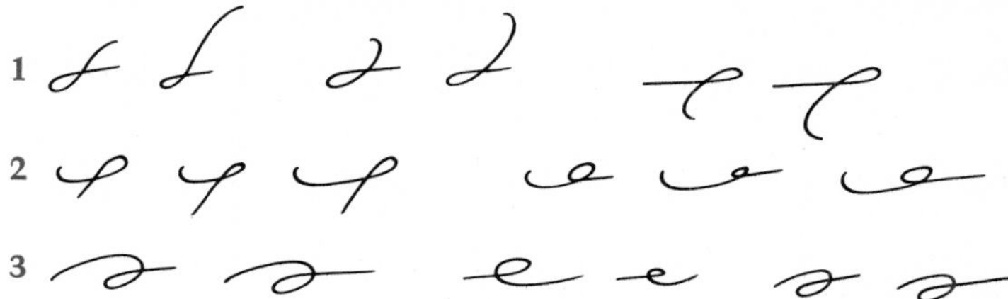

1. Pain, been; fan, vain; map, maybe.
2. *Rash, reach, latch; rain, lean, lame.*
3. *Gain, game; nail, near; cane, came.*

● Writing Practice

422 **PREVIEW**

□ 423

□ 424

□ 425

423 *Retire, everyone, beyond, appealing, conveniently, security, family.*
424 *Fortunes, sluggish, seized, economically, utilization, bargains.*
425 *Union, majority, automatically, beneficiary, institutions, possible.*

LETTERS

423

Dear Mr. Peters: How would you like to retire at age 65 or 70 with $100,000[1] in your bank account? Almost everyone would like that kind of retirement fund, but most people feel that[2] such a lofty goal is far beyond their reach. Your goal of complete financial security at retirement[3] is much easier to achieve than you might imagine.

The First Savings and Loan Association pays the highest[4] interest allowed by law, and your savings are protected by an agency of the federal government.[5] If you are 35 years of age and can save $100 a month, you will have more than $100,000[6] when you reach retirement age. If this sounds appealing to you, we will be happy to show you how[7] a First Savings and Loan retirement program can help you.

Drop in at one of our seven conveniently[8] located offices any weekday and let one of our experienced staff members show you what we can do to[9] help you realize complete financial security for you and your family when you retire. Yours truly,[10]

424

Dear Mr. Park: Some of America's greatest fortunes were begun by people who saw opportunity in[11] a time when business was sluggish. These people seized the opportunity to buy real estate when others were selling[12] at low prices. It takes nerve and insight to invest in real estate when business is economically depressed.[13] It also requires utilization of every financial resource at one's command.

As you know, the[14] condition of the real estate market is not particularly good at this time. This means that now is the time to[15] buy; there are many real bargains on the market. If you would like to invest in real estate but do not have the[16] financial resources, why not come to the State National Bank and discuss the matter with one of our[17] representatives. Start on the road to future financial security by investing wisely now. Sincerely yours,[18]

425

Dear Mr. Tate: Two important features of our credit union are often forgotten by the majority[19] of our members. These are:

1. All credit union loans are insured. If a member dies while the loan is in effect,[20] the loan is paid automatically.

2. Deposits up to $2,000 are doubled and remitted to[21] the beneficiary upon the death of the member.

These services can be purchased at other financial[22] institutions for an extra fee, but they are just part of the package when you borrow from or make deposits[23] with us. We pay the highest interest rate allowed by law on all deposits, and we charge the lowest interest[24] rate possible on all loans that we make.

Why not use the services of your credit union soon. Sincerely yours,[25] [500]

Reading and Writing Practice

426

div·i·dend

Transcribe:
4 percent
eighth

as

con·sec·u·tive

its

intro

ded·i·cat·ed

nc

for·ward

[137]

427

re·cent

amount

intro

Transcribe:
$315

ex·pressed
an·nu·al

as

if

nc

prin·ci·pal

fur·ther

if

[194]

428

an·nounce

nonr

ma·jor

intro

Stone's

acquaint·ed

[121]

429

Transcribe: $86

86

intro

over·drawn

if

else·where

[90]

Developing Shorthand Writing Power

430 WORD FAMILIES

-coming

1

-line

2

1. *Coming, incoming, becoming, unbecoming, welcoming, overcoming.*
2. *Line, outline, dateline, deadline, headline, align.*

431 FREQUENTLY USED NAMES

Last Names

1

Men's First Names

2

1. *Jordan, Kaplan, Katz, Kelly, Kennedy, King, Kirk.*
2. *Jack, James, Jerry, Jim, John, Jose, Joseph, Kenneth.*

Building Transcription Skills

432 Business Vocabulary Builder

consolidation The process of uniting or combining.

offshore *(adj.)* Located at a distance from the shore.

appraised value The estimated worth of something.

Writing Practice

433 PREVIEW

☐ 434

☐ 435

☐ 436

434 *Experienced, depression, tragedy, devising, prosper, streamline.*
435 *Themselves, obligations, burdensome, consolidation, yellow.*
436 *Continuous, investment, capable, trust, individual, convenient.*

LETTERS

434

Dear Mr. Jordan: Perhaps you are too young to have experienced the financial panic of an economic[1] depression. A depression is a time of tragedy for people all over the world.

In 1929,[2] when the world experienced one of the worst depressions of all time, the founders of our organization,[3] the American National Bank, began devising unique financing methods to help businesses grow and[4] prosper. Since that time we have been providing financial knowledge and financial backing to American[5] businesses in both good times and bad.

No matter how big or small your company is, we are in a position to[6] help you streamline and modernize your financial operation. Won't you give us an opportunity to tell[7] you how we can help you. We will be glad to have a representative visit you to outline a program[8] specifically for your company. Just tell us on the enclosed card when it will be convenient for you. Yours truly,[9]

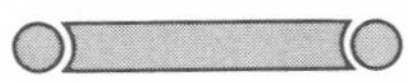

435

Mr. Kirk: At one time or another, we think most people find themselves in a difficult financial situation.[10] Their fixed monthly financial obligations leave little room to provide for emergencies.

If your monthly[11] financial obligations are becoming too burdensome for you to handle, may we suggest that you contact[12] your local Consumer Finance Corporation office and make arrangements for a consolidation loan.[13] One of our well-trained representatives will outline a plan that can help you solve almost any financial problem.[14] Of course, there is no charge for coming in and listening to one of our representatives explain how our[15] organization operates.

The locations of our offices are listed in the yellow pages. Yours truly,[16]

436

Dear Mrs. James: The proper management of substantial sums of money requires continuous effort by people[17] with judgment and skill in investment, tax, and estate planning. It is a very complicated matter.

Life[18] becomes less complicated when you place your financial affairs in the capable hands of the trust department[19] of the Westport Bank. Our representatives can review your current holdings and outline a program that will suit[20] your individual needs.

Why not let us have the opportunity to show you just how we can help you keep[21] your finances from becoming too complicated. Stop in when it is convenient for you. Very truly yours,[22] [440]

Reading and Writing Practice

437

con·do·min·i·um

Transcribe: 40 percent

par

ap·praised

if

ex·plain

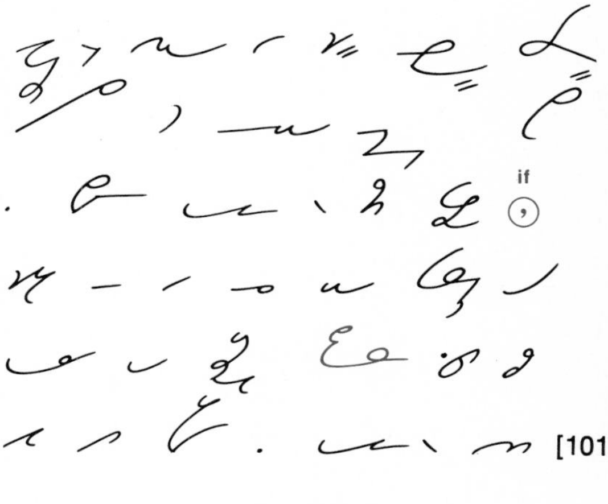

[101]

438

re·spon·si·bil·i·ty
forth·com·ing
ex·pan·sion

as

cap·i·tal

off·shore

sites

Transcribe: $100 million

be·com·ing
in·volved

if

[121]

439

if

long-play·ing *hyphenated before noun*

149

20

and o

world's

best-loved *hyphenated before noun*

intro

conj

[113]

440

tale

ini·tia·tive

1950

above-ground hyphenated before noun

nonr

its

conj

conj

if

nc

[175]

441

week's

ac·cept

ap

ex·plains

ser

ref·er·ence

li·brary

coun·sel

ad·vice

if

[147]

Secretarial Tip
Your Typewriter

In your transcription course you are probably doing all your transcribing on one typewriter. Consequently, you are probably thoroughly familiar with its touch, its service mechanisms, and any special characters it may have. The more at home you are with your typewriter, the more rapidly you will be able to transcribe.

Of course, when you report for that first office job, you may not find the same make and model typewriter as the one you use in school. If that is the case, you will have to spend a day or two getting used to the new machine. In all probability, the machine that you will use on your first job will be an electric typewriter.

Some of the service mechanisms, such as the tabulator and the backspacer, are located at different points on various machines. On some machines the number 1 is located on the top row of the keyboard; on others the lower case *l* is used for the figure 1. In addition, there may be keys for special characters such as the plus sign, the equal sign, and the division sign.

In some offices you will find typewriters that have self-correcting devices. This will aid you greatly in correcting any typographical errors you may make. Still other offices may have editing typewriters that use magnetic tape to record your typing.

You can actually see what you are typing on a device similar to a television screen. After you have finished typing a "page" of correspondence, you can check it for errors or rearrange the copy before having the work actually printed on paper.

Of course, after you have typed on your office machine for some time, you will become as familiar with it as you are with your present machine. But until you become adjusted to it, your production rate may suffer a bit. You can shorten the period of adjustment, however, by making an effort, while you are still in school, to become familiar with as many makes and models of typewriters as possible.

In the various offices of your school there are probably several different makes of machines, and you may be able to obtain permission to examine them and even type on them. If you can arrange to visit a business office or two in your city, you will probably find several models in use that you can study.

Remember, the sooner you adjust to the working conditions that prevail in your employer's office, the sooner will you become a productive worker—and your office typewriter is an important piece of equipment to which you will have to adjust!

Developing Shorthand Writing Power

442 FREQUENTLY USED PHRASES

To

1

Contractions

2

1. *To be, to see, to say, to have, to vote, to prepare, to point, to bring, to buy.*
2. *Don't, isn't, aren't, haven't, weren't, hasn't, couldn't, shouldn't.*

443 GEOGRAPHICAL EXPRESSIONS

-ton

1

States

2

Foreign Cities

3

1. *Charleston, Galveston, Brockton, Cranston, Trenton.*
2. *Colorado, Idaho, New Mexico, Georgia, South Carolina, Arkansas, Kansas.*
3. *Berlin, Hamburg, Leipzig, Nuremberg, Munich.*

Building Transcription Skills

444 Business Vocabulary Builder

overdrawn *(verb)* To have written checks for more money than there is in an account.

insufficient Not enough; lacking.

balance *(noun)* The amount left after deductions have been made.

Writing Practice

445 PREVIEW

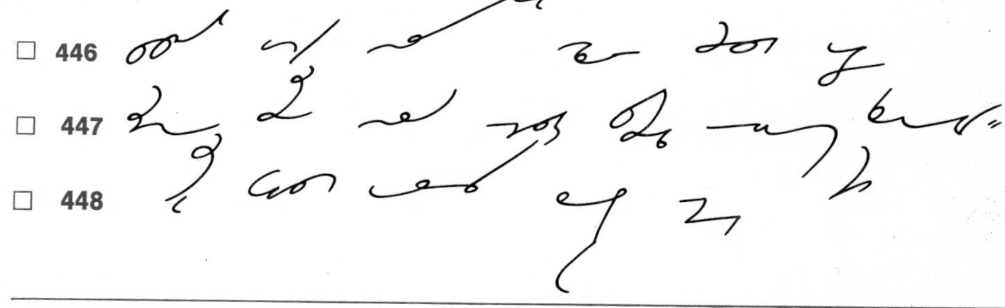

446 *Accounts, awkward, creditors, concern, financial, repayment.*
447 *Fiscal, severe, current, institutions, adversely, mortgage, Charleston.*
448 *Savings, protection, limited, eligible, information, very truly yours.*

LETTERS

446

Dear Mr. Adams: The Trenton Furniture Company has over 2,000 active accounts receivable.[1] At a given time, the balance of these accounts is usually more than $250,000. Of[2] course, most of our customers pay their bills on time. If they do not, we are placed in an awkward position; we cannot[3] pay our own creditors on time.

Your failure to make regular payments on your account is causing us a[4] great deal of concern. We have written you three times, but you have not even acknowledged our letters. If we do not[5] hear from you by June 10 regarding your past-due balance of $758, we will be forced[6] to take legal action.

As you know, we have always been willing to work with our customers. If you are having[7] financial difficulty, please tell us. I am sure that we could work out a repayment schedule that you could meet.[8] Don't wait any longer; contact us immediately to make arrangements to pay your account. Sincerely yours,[9]

447

Dear Mr. Houston: As you probably know, federal fiscal policies have placed severe strains on the current[10] money supply. Most lending institutions have been adversely affected by these policies; South Carolina[11] Savings Association is no exception. We are now unable to secure any additional[12] mortgage money for the remainder of this year. Therefore, we will not be able to provide financing for the[13] development of your subdivision in Charleston.

There are a few mortgage loan companies in the area[14] that now have funds to finance major projects, but their interest rates are somewhat higher than what you indicated[15] you can pay.

If you don't obtain financing before the first of next year, please call us again. Very truly yours,[16]

448

Dear Mr. Hunt: More and more people are buying low-cost savings bank life insurance for these reasons:

1. It is[17] sold directly to you at a savings bank or by mail; no agent comes to your home.
2. It is the ideal way[18] to secure sound protection on a limited budget.
3. It offers all standard forms of life insurance for[19] men, women, and children.

If you live or work in Colorado, you are eligible to buy savings bank life[20] insurance. Thousands of people in Colorado have bought life insurance protection from the Mutual Savings[21] Bank of Denver. They get high-quality protection at low prices. They gain the advantages of doing[22] business with a large savings bank, and they get the friendly, helpful service of local people.

Don't wait; come in to[23] the Mutual Savings Bank and let one of our officers give you complete information. Very truly yours,[24] [480]

Reading and Writing Practice

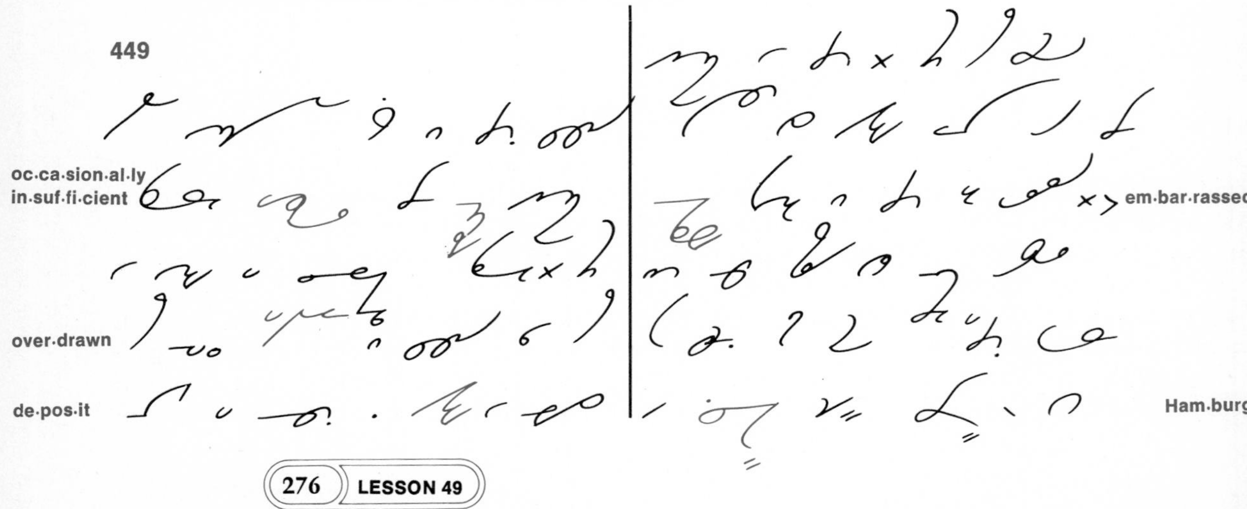

Transcribe: $100

ser

hon·ored

conj

qual·i·fy

intro

at·tached

its

shouldn't

[177]

450

for·ward

de·ci·sion
com·mit·tee

ap

[92]

451

conj

conj

intro

fi·nan·cial
as·sis·tance

[79]

Developing Shorthand Writing Power

452 WORD ENDINGS

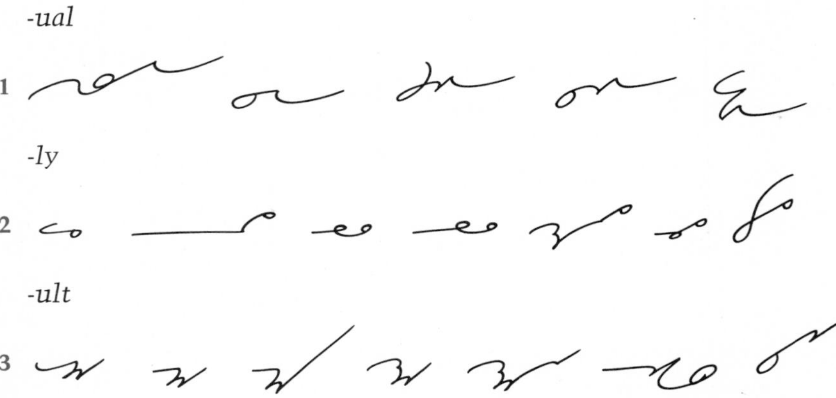

1. *Gradual, annual, factual, actual, perpetual.*
2. *Only, monthly, nearly, merely, constantly, neatly, badly.*
3. *Result, insult, insulted, consult, consultant, multiply, adult.*

Building Transcription Skills

453 Business Vocabulary Builder

lecturers Speakers.

demand deposits Funds that can be withdrawn by a depositor immediately and without advance notice.

Progressive Speed Builder (90-125)

454 PREVIEW

455 *Yesterday, club, discussed, whether, payroll, deductions, subscribe.*
456 *Coincidence, inquiries, start, indicates, excellent, investment.*
457 *Promised, several days ago, accountant, outline, appreciate.*
458 *Finance, proposal, impressed, instituted, responsibility, memorandum.*
459 *Inquired, approved, details, attached, voluntary.*

LETTERS

455

[1 minute at 90]

Mrs. Davis: Yesterday I attended a meeting of the Employees' Club. The major topic discussed at the meeting was/whether employees of the National Investment Company could purchase company stock and pay for it through monthly payroll//deductions. On an informal vote, 90 of the 100 people present indicated that they would subscribe to such///a plan if it were available.

I wonder whether we shouldn't discuss this matter at our next monthly meeting. Bill Smith [1]

456

[1 minute at 100]

Mr. Smith: By a strange coincidence, I had four inquiries last week from employees asking whether we had a stock purchase plan or whether/we were going to start one. I think this is a good sign because it indicates that our employees feel that the stock of our organization//represents an excellent investment.

I will discuss this matter with the finance committee when it meets next month and see what would///be involved in setting up such a plan. As soon as I have anything definite to report, I will get in touch with you. Ellen Davis [2]

457

[1 minute at 110]

Mr. Smith: As I promised you several days ago, I took up with the finance committee the matter of a stock purchase plan in which employees of/ our organization could pay for their stock through monthly payroll deductions. All the members of the committee are in favor of some kind of plan. I//have, therefore, asked our accountant, Ms. James, to outline a plan and submit it at the June 18 meeting of the finance committee.

Ms. James will wish to///discuss the plan with you. I would appreciate it if you would give her all the help you can. Will you please call her soon to arrange a meeting. Ellen Davis [3]

458

[1 minute at 120]

Mr. Smith: Mr. Jones, who chairs the finance committee, presented the proposal you and Ms. James made regarding an employee stock plan to the board of directors/at its August 15 meeting. The members of the board were very well impressed with the plan, and one of the members wondered why we had not instituted a plan years//ago.

We must now take steps to put the plan into operation. The first thing to do is to inform the employees of our plan and invite them to take part in///it.

Will you please be good enough to take the responsibility for preparing a memorandum outlining the procedures that should be followed. Ellen Davis [4]

459

[1 minute at 125]

To All Employees of the National Investment Company: Many of you have inquired whether the company had a stock purchase plan and, if so, how you could take part in it./

Yesterday the board of directors approved a stock purchase plan under which all employees may purchase company stock and pay for it through monthly payroll deductions. All the// details of the plan are outlined in the booklet that is attached.

Please understand that this is a purely voluntary plan. If after having studied the plan you decide you///would like to subscribe to it, fill out the forms in the back of the booklet. If you want more information, call Ms. Mary Green on Extension 7576. Bill Smith [5] [545]

Reading and Writing Practice

460

con·fer·ence

geo

in·clude

key·note

fi·nan·cial con·sul·tant

ap

par

year's

com·plet·ing

self-ad·dressed

[139]

461

intro

suf·fi·cient

par

be·yond

safe·ty

ex·cess

par

Transcribe: $1,000

yield

par

length

when

ex·cel·lent

cap·i·tal

intro

great·er

[177]

462

ads

isq

intro

pru·dent

ul·ti·mate·ly

re·al

intro

anal·y·sis

intro

conj

[219]

Motor Vehicles

Developing Shorthand Writing Power

463 OUTLINE CONSTRUCTION

Omission of Short E Between P and K The omission of short *e* between *p* and *k* in words of more than one syllable results in outlines that are both fluent and legible.

Respect, expect, prospect, suspect, speculation, picture, picnic.

Omission of Short E In -fect, -ject The omission of short *e* in the combinations *-fect, -ject* results in outlines that are easy to write and to read.

-fect

1

-ject

2

1. *Affect, effect, effective, perfect, infect, defect, defective.*
2. *Project, inject, reject, adjective, dejected, conjecture.*

Building Transcription Skills

464 SIMILAR-WORDS DRILL council, counsel

council An assembly; a group; an elected body.

The City Council *will meet tomorrow.*

counsel *(noun)* Advice; lawyer.

I need your counsel *in this matter.*
Mr. Jacobs is my legal counsel.

counsel *(verb)* To advise.

Please counsel *me on just what I should do.*

Reading and Writing Practice

465 Auto Safety

1. Observe

3. Even though

[233]

466 LETTERS

ap

coun·sel

it

al·leged
breach

de·fec·tive

com·pre·hen·sive

one-year
hyphenated before noun

nc

com·pa·ny's

sum·mons

intro

nc

[149]

467

ap

cit·ed

mile·age

intro

ex·haust
emis·sion

Coun·cil

par

conj

emit·ting
ex·cess
pol·lu·tion

conj

mis·led

ve·hi·cle

ap

14

Transcribe:
3 p.m.

cr

555-7518

[164]

Developing Shorthand Writing Power

468 RECALL DRILL t, d

In this drill you will review the different uses of the alphabetic strokes *t* and *d*.

Trans-

1

Past Tense

2

De-, Di-

3

-ward, -hood

4

---

1. *Transfer, transmit, transact, transcribe, transcription, transmittal.*
2. *Based, traced, pressed, tripped, stimulated, distributed, initialed.*
3. *Depend, decide, department, direct, diploma.*
4. *Inward, outward, backward, neighborhood, motherhood, brotherhood, sisterhood.*

Building Transcription Skills

469 ACCURACY PRACTICE

In this Accuracy Practice you will drill on a number of the fluent, graceful blends of Gregg Shorthand.

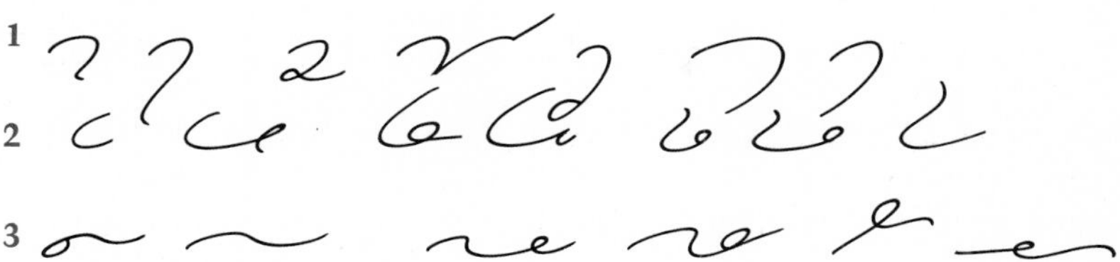

1. *Company, can be; confer, confident, convey; govern, can have.*
2. *Present, please; brain, below; free, flee, value.*
3. *Acre, glad; clear, great; dark, milk.*

● Writing Practice

470 PREVIEW

☐ 471

☐ 472

☐ 473

471 *Satisfied, vehicles, excellent, sedan, overhaul, valves.*
472 *Scraping, windshield, frustrating, magnets, available, neighborhood.*
473 *Compacts, warranty, Thanksgiving, plump, absolutely.*

LETTERS

471

Dear Mr. Edwards: As you know, I have purchased my new automobiles from your company for the past ten years.[1] I have always been satisfied with the vehicles, and your service has always been excellent. However, the[2] new sedan I purchased recently has not proved satisfactory.

In seven months I have driven it only[3] 6,000 miles. During this time I have had to overhaul the transmission, reline the brakes, and replace two[4] valves. Obviously, this amount of service on a new automobile indicates that something is wrong.

Frankly,[5] I am tired of bringing the car to your service department every two or three weeks for repairs. Therefore, I have[6] decided to trade the car in on a new one. If you would like to discuss accepting this car as a substantial[7] trade-in on a new model, please get in touch with me immediately to set up a meeting. Yours truly,[8]

472

Dear Mr. Green: Scraping snow and ice off your windshield is a frustrating job. Defrosting your windshield with the heater[9] in your car is a time-consuming, expensive process.

A simpler idea for handling ice and snow in the[10] winter is to cover your windshield with a Morris plastic windshield cover. This cover has powerful magnets[11] on the edges that adhere to the roof and hood of your car to provide a snug fit so that snow does not get to[12] the windshield. You simply place the cover over your windshield on a cold, snowy night and pull it off the next morning.[13] You are ready to drive.

The Morris plastic windshield cover costs only $15; it is available[14] from your neighborhood auto supply store. If you prefer, you can order one directly from us. Yours truly,[15]

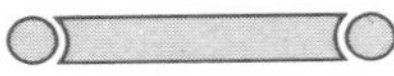

473

Dear Mr. Brown: We have just received a shipment of 150 General automobiles. The new[16] vehicles include two- and four-door models, station wagons, and compacts. All our vehicles are backed by a one-year[17] warranty, which we believe is the best in the industry.

With Thanksgiving approaching, we would like to give you[18] a plump, delicious turkey for your dinner table absolutely free. All you need to do is come into our[19] showroom and take a drive in one of our outstanding new automobiles. You will be thrilled at the fine quality[20] that characterizes all General vehicles. Our cars have the style and speed of sports cars, yet they give you[21] economical transportation.

Come in today, and don't forget to pick up your Thanksgiving turkey! Yours truly,[22] [440]

● Reading and Writing Practice

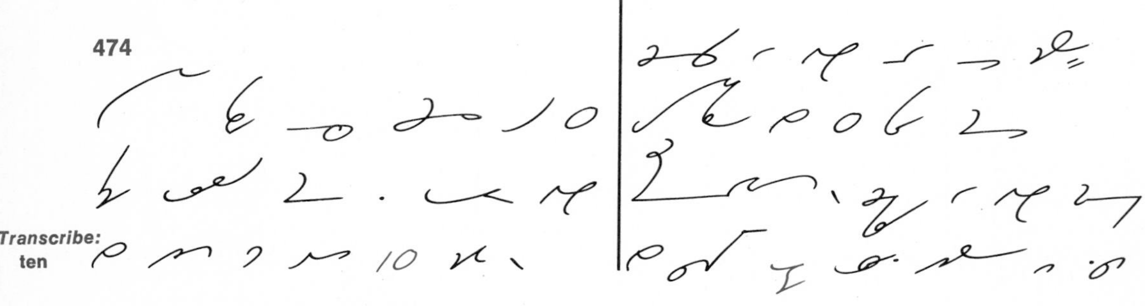

intro ,

Transcribe: 10,000

conj ,

moment's dis·com·fort

care·ful

ex·cel·lent

min·i·mum

re·pair·ing

intro ,

[166]

475

conj ,

So·ci·ety

against

en·coun·ter

if ,

com·pa·nies

nc ;

as·sis·tance

if ,

if ,

law·yer

[180]

High Fashion

Developing Shorthand Writing Power

476 WORD FAMILIES

-sity, -city

1

-ically

2

1. *Varsity, university, capacity, scarcity, publicity, simplicity.*
2. *Politically, economically, ethically, physically, technically, medically.*

477 FREQUENTLY USED NAMES

Last Names

1

Women's First Names

2

1. *Knight, Knox, Lamb, Lane, Larson, Lee, Levine, Lewis.*
2. *Helen, Irene, Jane, Juanita, Janice, Judy, Kathleen, Laura.*

Building Transcription Skills

478 **considerate** Kind; thoughtful.

Business Vocabulary Builder
necessitated Required; made necessary.
literally Actually; really.

Writing Practice

479 PREVIEW

480 Eagle, engine, guaranteed, 50,000, warranty, internal, maintenance.
481 University, informed, specifically, afternoon, considerate, economically.
482 Publicity, transportation, authorized, legislature, appropriated, congestion.

LETTERS

480

Dear Mr. Smith: We build the Eagle car to last a long time. The Eagle is one of the few cars on the market[1] with an engine that is guaranteed for 50,000 miles.

Our warranty comes with all cars sold and serviced[2] in the United States. Basically, it states that the engine block and internal parts will remain free of defects[3] with normal use and maintenance for 50,000 miles. If any defect appears before the warranty[4] expires, we will repair it free.

How can we offer such a warranty? First, our engine is simpler than a[5] regular engine. Because there are fewer moving parts, fewer things can go wrong. Second, the engine has proved its[6] dependability in over 5 million miles of road testing.

Make your next car an Eagle. Yours truly,[7]

481

Dear Mr. Knox: Last week I had my car tuned at the University Service Center. I left the vehicle[8] there early in the morning on my way to work. At 10 a.m. I received a call from your service manager,[9] Mr. Paul Smith, who informed me that I had a few problems with my car of which I was unaware. He told me[10] specifically what the repairs would cost, and I gave him permission to go ahead with the work.

In the afternoon,[11] I stopped by to get my car and was most impressed by the responsible, considerate treatment I received.[12] The car was ready when I arrived, and the cost of the repairs was actually less than the quoted price. My car[13] now runs more smoothly and economically than it has for a long time.

You may consider me a regular[14] customer in the future, and I will recommend your services to my associates as well. Yours truly,[15]

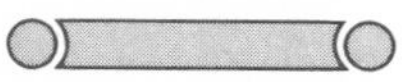

482

Dear Neighbor: During the past few months your local newspaper has given considerable publicity to[16] our new public transportation service system here in Lee County. This low-cost transportation service was authorized[17] and funded by the last state legislature, which appropriated a large sum of money to ensure its[18] operation for two years.

The system will be successful, however, only if you and your neighbors discover[19] for yourselves the many advantages of riding the bus. In the first place, it is cheaper than driving your own[20] car, and you don't have to worry about finding a parking space. In addition, it is more convenient than driving,[21] and you can ride to within a block or two of any destination in the uptown area. Driving[22] your own car, on the other hand, adds to the traffic congestion problem and increases pollution.

If these reasons[23] make sense to you, why don't you give our public transportation system a trial soon. Very cordially yours,[24] [480]

• Reading and Writing Practice

483

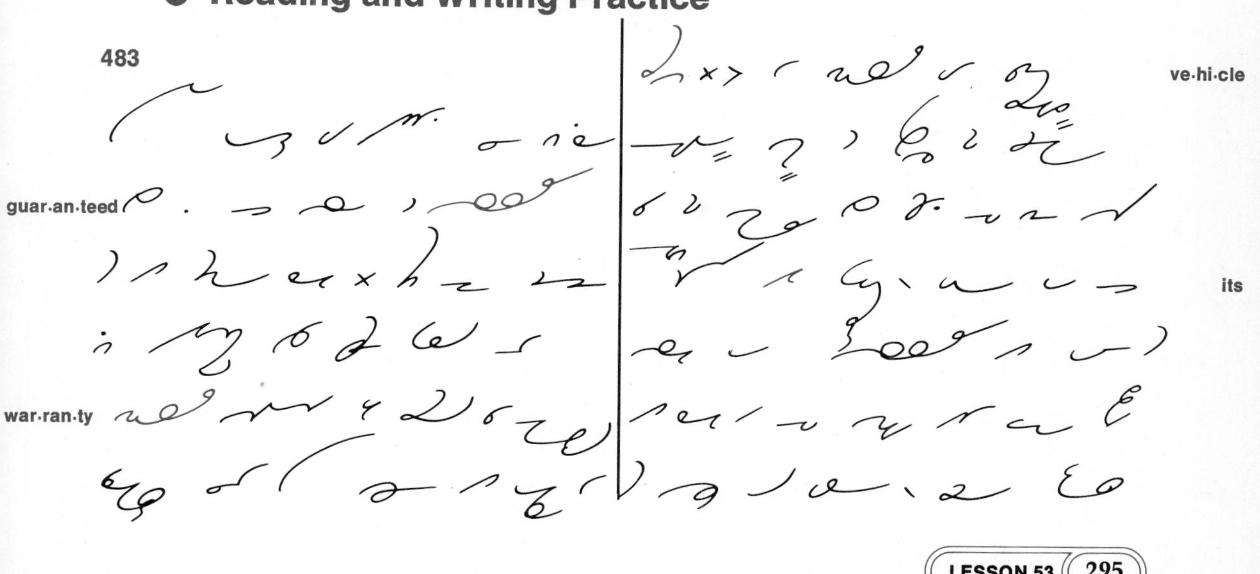

ex·clu·sion

par

ne·ces·si·tat·ed
mis·use

Isn't

suf·fi·cient

par

be·lieve

nc

[172]

484

par

bud·get

dis·cov·er·ing

pe·ri·od·i·cal·ly

tune-up

ser

knowl·edge

self-con·fi·dence

ap

Main·te·nance

Transcribe:
$3.95

3^{95}

[133]

485

if

ser

drive·way

intro

intro

when

ba·si·cal·ly

if

yours

hard-earned
hyphenated
before noun

thor·ough·ly

cont

if

[184]

486

when

intro

an·noy·ance

conj

trou·ble-free

nc

[111]

Developing Shorthand Writing Power

487 FREQUENTLY USED PHRASES

In Order

1

As You

2

1. *In order, in order that, in order to see, in order to be, in order to have, in order to prevent, in order to obtain.*
2. *As you know, as you can, as you may, as you say, as you will, as you are, as you would.*

488 GEOGRAPHICAL EXPRESSIONS

-boro

1

States

2

Foreign Cities

3

1. *Greensboro, Jonesboro, Murfreesboro, Hillsboro, Attleboro, Marlborough.*
2. *Oklahoma, Kansas, Montana, Nebraska, North Dakota, South Dakota, Maryland.*
3. *Naples, Rome, Budapest, Vienna, Salzburg, Prague.*

Building Transcription Skills

489 Business Vocabulary Builder

conceivable Imaginable.
vibration Shaking; trembling.
acceleration The act of moving faster.

Writing Practice

490 PREVIEW

491 *According, magazine, selected, economy, aware, entitled, in order.*
492 *International, sharp, attractive, Europe, determined, vehicle, driveway.*
493 *Tulsa, window, attendants, guarded, reasonable, outstanding.*

LETTERS

491

Dear Mr. Johnson: Congratulations on your purchase of a new Road King automobile. According to *Motor*[1] *View* magazine, you have selected an automobile that ranks first in its class in engineering excellence,[2] comfort and convenience of operation, and fuel economy.

As you are aware, the service your car[3] receives will determine how well it performs. Therefore, we intend to do everything in our power to guarantee[4] you the service to which you are entitled.

Our repair center, which is located at 426[5] Hillsboro Drive, is open daily from 6:30 a.m. until 10 p.m. Our well-trained mechanics will efficiently[6] take care of all your needs. In order for us to do our job, however, you must bring your car in for its[7] scheduled maintenance. Please check your owner's manual and call us when it's time for your first checkup. Cordially yours,[8]

492

Dear Mr. Green: At the International Car Rental Company, we like to keep our cars looking sharp. Back in[9] the days when we were a small company, we learned that people enjoyed driving good-looking cars. We gave them attractive[10] autos, and they gave us their business. In fact, they gave us so much business that today we are renting more cars[11] than any other company in the world.

Wherever you travel in the United States you will find an[12] International agency. If your travel takes you to Europe, you will also find an International agent in[13] Rome and Naples.

No matter where in the world you rent one of our cars, we are determined to rent you a vehicle[14] that you would be happy to park in your own driveway.

In order to reserve a car, call our toll-free number,[15] (800) 555-9207; one of our courteous agents will be glad to help you. Yours truly,[16]

493

Gentlemen: We have just opened a new public parking building near your offices in Tulsa, Oklahoma.[17] Most of our present customers say that in their opinion, our parking service is the finest in the city.[18]

In order to park in our new building, you purchase a one-month permit, which you display on your window. You leave[19] your car in our large ground-floor receiving area, and one of our attendants parks it in your reserved parking[20] space. Your car is locked and guarded during the day. When you stop by for it after working hours, you are behind[21] the wheel within three minutes' time.

In order to see our new parking service in operation, stop in at the[22] corner of Fifth and Vine Streets. You will be pleased with the reasonable cost of our outstanding service. Yours truly,[23] [460]

Reading and Writing Practice

nc wo

[128]

495

re·turned

intro

dif·fi·cul·ties

ap

en·coun·tered enu

conj

intro

45

when

vi·bra·tion

4

as

imag·ine

intro

par·tial

cr

[167]

496

when

test-drive

intro

de·ci·sion

when

nonr

spe·cif·i·cal·ly

al·most

con·ceiv·able

ac·cel·er·a·tion

ser

brak·ing

and o

through

conj

intro

[178]

497

fac·to·ry-trained *hyphenated before noun*

as

pre·ven·tive

intro

isq

iq

555-3623

[127]

Secretarial Tip
Dictation Don'ts

Don't report for dictation without first being sure that you have plenty of pens—at least two—and sufficient paper in your shorthand notebook. It is disturbing to your employer if you must interrupt the dictation to return to your desk to get another pen or a new notebook.

Don't disturb anything on your employer's desk when you get ready to take dictation. If you usually write with your notebook on the ledge of the desk but find a stack of papers on the ledge, don't move them; write with your notebook on your knee.

Don't stare at your employer or look bored as he or she is concentrating or groping for a word. Keep your eyes on your notebook. If the pause is long enough, you might even "patch up" an outline or two that you did not write accurately and that might cause you difficulty in transcribing later.

Don't suggest a word for which your employer may be reaching unless you are encouraged to do so.

Don't let your employer's dictation get too far ahead of you. If you are getting further and further behind, by all means interrupt. It is no disgrace to fall behind; even the fastest, most experienced stenographer will occasionally find the dictation too fast.

Don't hesitate to ask your employer to repeat an unfamiliar or unusual word.

Don't linger at the dictator's desk if a visitor interrupts who obviously will remain for some time. Return to your desk and begin transcribing. When you see the visitor leave, return and, without being asked, read back the last sentence or two.

Don't excuse yourself, when taking dictation, to answer a telephone call. Your employer's time is valuable. Arrange to have someone answer your phone and take messages while you are taking dictation.

Developing Shorthand Writing Power

498 WORD BEGINNINGS AND ENDINGS

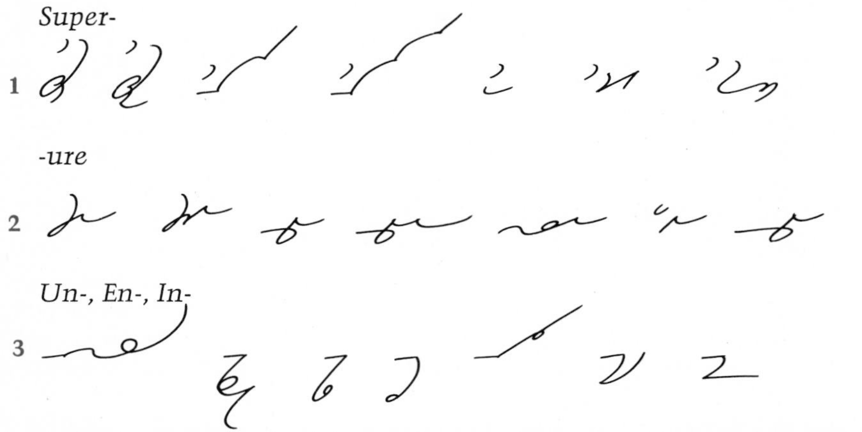

1. *Supervise, supervisor, superintend, superintendent, superior, superstition, superfluous.*
2. *Feature, future, nature, natural, creature, overture, mature.*
3. *Unclaimed, unbearable, enjoy, envy, indeed, infant, inform.*

Building Transcription Skills

499 Business Vocabulary Builder

dispose of To get rid of.

fleet A group of vehicles operated as one unit.

patents Legal rights granted for the exclusive making, use, and sale of an invention.

Progressive Speed Builder (100-130)

You didn't have difficulty writing at a speed of 125 words a minute for one minute in the previous Progressive Speed Builder, did you? Do you think you can squeeze into one minute just 5 words more? The last letter in this Progressive Speed Builder is counted at 130 words a minute. If you can get something down for every word in the 130-words-a-minute letter, you are indeed making progress!

500 PREVIEW

501

502

503

504

505

501 *Haven't, wondered, leasing, without, commitment, transaction.*
502 *Provides, something, within, facilities, maintenance, decision.*
503 *Shouldn't, executives, professionals, anywhere, dispose, let us, details.*
504 *Rather, counsel, of course, services, obligation, appointment.*
505 *Already, because, release, invested, capital, outlays, letterhead.*

LETTERS

501

[1 minute at 100]

Dear Mr. Trent: Haven't you often wondered whether you could save money by leasing your trucks instead of owning your own? Now you can find out/without any risk or commitment.

Under our three-month trial leasing plan, you can test the advantages of leasing. If the plan doesn't//appeal to you after three months, you simply tell us, and that will be the end of the transaction.

Let us tell you all about this plan. Simply/// indicate on the enclosed card when our representative may call. You will, of course, be under no obligation. Very cordially yours, [1]

502

[1 minute at 110]

Dear Mr. Trent: The National Leasing Company does more than lease you the trucks you need; it provides total service. If something goes wrong with one of the/trucks, no matter where or at what time, we will have one of our service units there within an hour.

We operate more than 1,000 service facilities// throughout the country. When you lease your trucks from us, we take care of everything, including maintenance, fuel, and road service.

Before you make a///decision to purchase trucks of any kind, let us tell you about our leasing service and how it can save you thousands of dollars every year. Sincerely yours, [2]

503

[1 minute at 120]

Dear Mr. Trent: The car you use for your business shouldn't be yours; it should be ours.

For business executives like you there are people like us whose business is leasing cars/to business. We are a national organization of leasing professionals who can deliver and service cars almost anywhere in the country. We can write// you a lease, handle your insurance, and dispose of the car you are now using.

Let us give you more details about our leasing plans. Invite one of our representatives///to tell you about each of them. We will be happy to send a representative if you will tell us when it will be most convenient for you. Very truly yours, [3]

504

[1 minute at 125]

Dear Mr. Trent: Perhaps you may have wondered at what point in your business life it would pay you to lease a truck or a car rather than buy it. The chances are it would pay you/to do so right now. If you want to find out, talk to our representatives. We are the leaders in the leasing field and have the experience to give you wise counsel.

We will,//of course, be honest with you. If we feel that it would be better for you to buy a car or a truck, we will tell you so. If we feel you will save money by leasing, we will tell///you all about our leasing services. We will do this without placing you under any obligation.

Why not call us for an appointment today. Very cordially yours, [4]

505

[1 minute at 130]

Dear Mr. Trent: Perhaps the best time to lease a fleet of trucks is when you already own a fleet of trucks. Why? Because we will buy your trucks at a fair price and then lease them back to you./

This will release the capital you have invested in them. It will free you from the possibility of further capital outlays. It will also free you from the problems involved//in keeping all the records necessary to operate a fleet of trucks.

When you lease from us, we take care of your maintenance needs, your repairs, and many other services.

Are///you interested? If you are, call us at the number at the top of this letterhead. We will get in touch with you to arrange an appointment at your convenience. Very sincerely yours, [5] [585]

Reading and Writing Practice

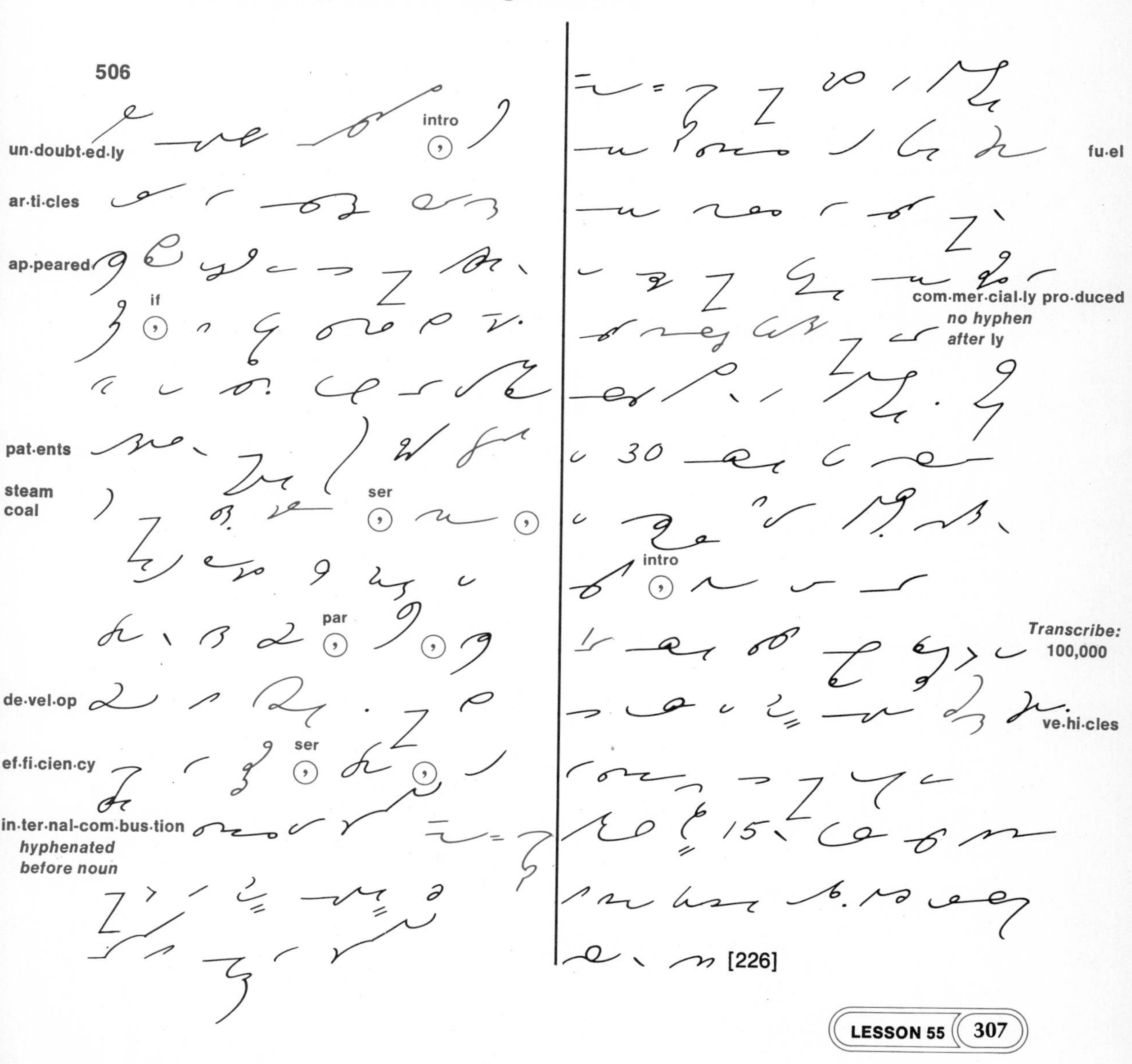

507

Olym·pic

nc

too

pres·tige
its

de·cades

intro

ex·clu·sive

pos·sess

world's

intro

above-av·er·age
hyphenated before noun

if

[144]

508

when

if

if

[106]

CHAPTER 12

Automation and Data Processing

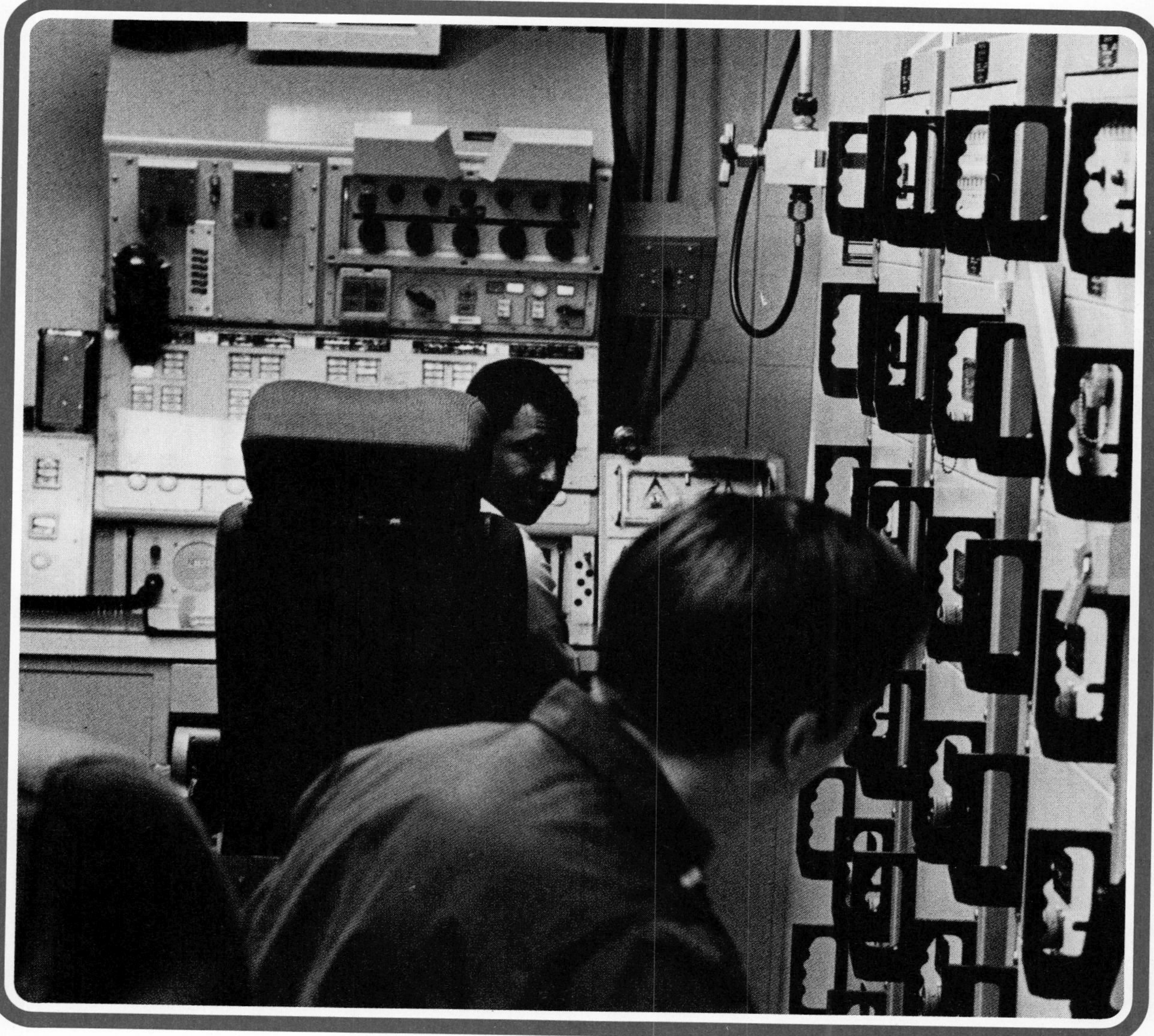

Developing Shorthand Writing Power

509 OUTLINE CONSTRUCTION

Omission of Vowel In -vent, -vention The vowel is omitted in the combinations *-vent, -vention*

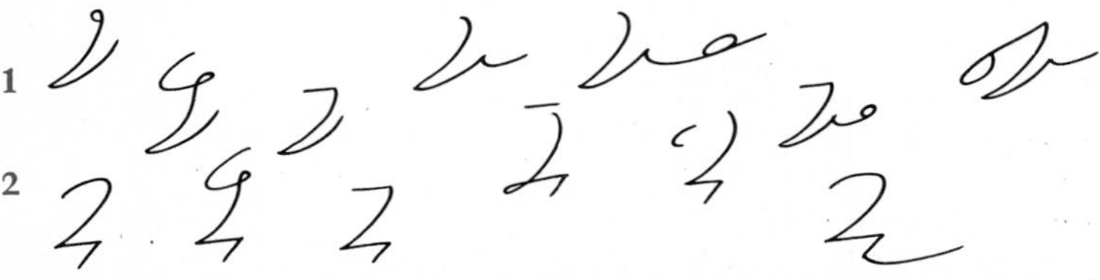

1. *Event, prevent, invent, venture, ventilate, inventory, adventure.*
2. *Convention, prevention, invention, intervention, circumvention, conventional.*

Omission of Vowel In -sive The vowel is omitted in the ending *-sive.*

Massive, comprehensive, apprehensive, offensive, expensive, defensive, excessive.

Building Transcription Skills

510 SIMILAR-WORDS DRILL device, devise

device (*noun*) Something that has been constructed or invented for a particular purpose; a plan or scheme.

He has invented a device *that will make computer programming easier.*

devise *(verb)* To invent; to make up.

If we can devise *the right computer program, our output should double.*

Reading and Writing Practice

511 The Computer

The input

[245]

512 LETTERS

when

ben·e·fit

enu

de·crease

and o

de·tailed

fis·cal

cred·i·tor

par

ap·peal

[140]

513

intro

con·sid·er·able

ser

pro·ce·dures

intro

de·vised

as

ev·er·y day

intro

its

max·i·mum

com·pre·hen·sive

and o

conj

ef·fi·cient·ly

if

[179]

514

intro

conj

be·lieve

na·tion·wide

ad·min·is·tra·tive

if

par

[152]

Developing Shorthand Writing Power

515 RECALL DRILL I

In this lesson you will review the situations in which the alphabetic stroke for *l* is used.

L

1

Will

2

Well

3

-lity

4

-lty

5

---

1. *Lee, lead, lay, relay, clay, play, player.*
2. *Will, willing, unwilling, willingly, unwillingly, willed.*

3. *Well, wells, welfare, welcome, welcoming, farewell.*
4. *Ability, facility, reliability, durability, stability, utility.*
5. *Faculty, penalty, realty, loyalty, royalty, novelty.*

Building Transcription Skills

516 ACCURACY PRACTICE

The subject of your practice in this drill is the letter *o*. Remember to keep the *o* hook deep and narrow.

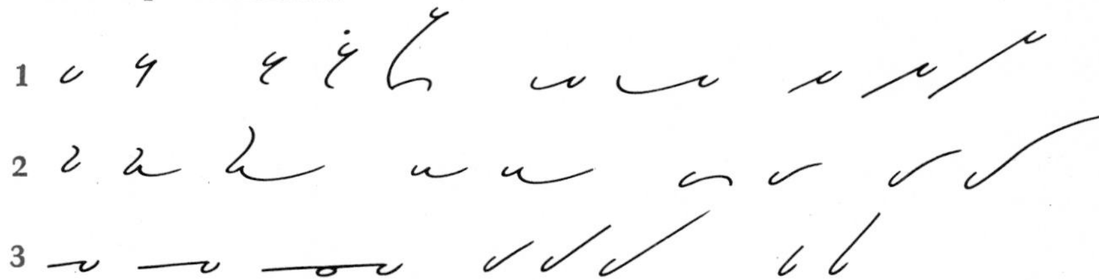

1. *Of, ocean; was, hope, object; row, low; toe, dough, ditto.*
2. *So, sore, fall; or, all; of course, of the; ordinary, autumn.*
3. *No, mow, memorandum; what, order, audit; show, jaw.*

Writing Practice

517 PREVIEW

☐ 518

☐ 519

☐ 520

518 *Authorized, Seattle, faculty, comprehensive, facilities, estimate.*
519 *Significant, volume, services, justify, welcome, discussing.*
520 *Programmer, qualifications, engineering, technical, willingly.*

518

Dear Mr. Hall: Last week our board of education approved my proposal to install two computer terminals[1] in the math department of the local high school this fall. We have been authorized to rent telephone lines to[2] a central computer in Seattle, Washington. Our faculty members have prepared a comprehensive plan[3] for the use of these facilities, and we welcome this opportunity to provide basic computer training[4] for our students.

I have been given the responsibility of making contacts with firms such as yours to[5] receive bids for the rental of the equipment we will need. Enclosed is the complete proposal for our program.[6] If you are interested, please study our data and give us an estimate before June 15.

For further[7] information, call me at 555-3327 during regular school hours. Very cordially yours,[8]

519

Dear Mr. Turner: Because of a significant increase in our volume of business last year, we find that we[9] are no longer able to process effectively the amount of work now facing us.

Last year when your[10] representative, Ms. Rosa Lopez, discussed the possibility of using your computer services, we felt[11] that it would probably be at least three years before we could justify the added expense of such a change. Now,[12] however, we are ready to enter into a contract with a private firm to handle some of our work, and[13] we would welcome the opportunity of again discussing this matter with Ms. Lopez.

Would she or another[14] of your representatives be free to meet with us? Please call my office for an appointment. Cordially yours, [15]

520

Dear Mr. Lewis: I read your advertisement in the local newspaper for a computer programmer at[16] your Jacksonville, Florida, plant. Will you please consider me an applicant for this position.

I am enclosing[17] a data sheet that lists in detail my qualifications for this position. As you will note, I have worked[18] as a programmer for more than eight years with two well-known engineering firms in the South. I have had experience[19] with a wide variety of technical assignments, and I am eager to apply my skills to the projects[20] you describe in your advertisement. I am also enclosing a list of both character and business[21] references. Each of the people on the list can attest to my dependability, character, and reliability.[22]

I would willingly fly to Jacksonville for an interview at your convenience. If you are interested,[23] please call me at (809) 555-6749 in Miami any weekday after 6 p.m.[24] If you prefer to correspond with me, please use the address shown at the top of this letter. Yours very truly,[25] [500]

Reading and Writing Practice

521

tech·nol·o·gy

conj

well known *no noun, no hyphen*

best-known *hyphenated before noun*

and o

[134]

522

uti·lize

spon·sor·ing
sem·i·nar

ap

Transcribe: 10 a.m.

first·hand

par

intro

com·pli·men·ta·ry

par

wel·come

in·crease
its

prof·its

nc

for·ward

[164]

523

rec·om·mend·ed

mu·tu·al

ap

stream·line

ap

as·sis·tant

cr

555-0620

[87]

524

intro

dis·cov·ered

intro

conj

cr

[84]

Developing Shorthand Writing Power

525 WORD FAMILIES

Ind-

1

-pression

2

1. *Industry, industrious, independent, indispensable, indicate, indication.*
2. *Impression, depression, expression, compression, oppression.*

526 FREQUENTLY USED NAMES

Last Names

1

Men's First Names

2

Women's First Names

3

1. *Lindsey, Logan, Lopez, Lynch, Marshall, Martin.*
2. *Larry, Leonard, Manuel, Mario, Matthew, Michael.*
3. *Linda, Lisa, Lois, Lorraine, Louise, Lydia, Madeline.*

Building Transcription Skills

527 Business Vocabulary Builder

untapped *(adjective)* Not used.
channeling Directing through or into a desired course.
consumption The act of using up something.

Writing Practice

528 PREVIEW

☐ 529

☐ 530

☐ 531

529 *Congratulate, decision, install, union, overhead, potential, acknowledged.*
530 *Previous, ourselves, slight, analysts, endeavor, untapped.*
531 *International, reliable, programmer, impression, replacement.*

LETTERS

529

Dear Mr. Lindsey: We wish to congratulate you on your decision to install one of our on-line computer[1] terminals for your credit union office. The Independent Computer Company has been adding at[2] least one new company to our list of clients each week during the past two years.

Businesses such as yours have found[3] their operations to be greatly simplified with an on-line computer terminal. We know you will be able[4] to provide better, quicker service to your customers with lower overhead expenses than you now have.[5] We know, too, that your business will grow rapidly because potential customers will become aware of the[6] efficient way their transactions can be handled.

To assist you and your staff in learning to operate the new[7] equipment, we are sending Miss Lisa Marshall, a member of our staff, to your office for five days. She is an[8] acknowledged expert in the field, and we are confident that within a week you and your staff will be thoroughly[9] familiar with your new on-line computer terminal.

We look forward to working with you. Very cordially yours,[10]

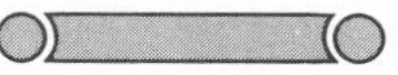

530

To the Staff: Enclosed is a copy of our sales production figures for the past year. The figures indicate that[11] despite a small increase over the previous year's sales figures, we fell far below the goals we set for ourselves[12] last January. Even though the nation is experiencing a slight economic depression, I am[13] convinced that the market potential for our new line of computers is much greater than these figures indicate.[14]

Business analysts are constantly discovering both direct and indirect applications for computer[15] use in almost every field of endeavor. Our major challenge, therefore, is to sell our customers on these untapped[16] uses of our products.

One of our staff writers, Mr. Leonard Martin, is presently preparing a[17] circular based on all current research data. We will give each of you a copy of this circular as soon as[18] it is available for your use in making future contacts with our customers. Manuel Martinez[19]

531

Dear Mr. Miles: The new computer that your company installed here at International Industries has[20] been malfunctioning recently. We are unable to get the reliable output we must have for our daily[21] operations. One of your service representatives has been to our offices on four occasions during[22] the past month. However, our computer is still not working properly.

Our chief programmer, Miss Mary Lynch,[23] is under the impression that we received a faulty computer. She has suggested that we ask for an[24] immediate replacement. Before we take this action, however, I think you should come to our office to discuss[25] the problem personally, Mr. Miles.

Please call me to let me know when we may expect you. Sincerely yours,[26] [520]

● Reading and Writing Practice

532

plan·ning

geo

de·vel·oped

unique

yours

au·to·ma·tion

as

quan·ti·ty

nonr

uti·lizes
ex·cess
chan·nel·ing

con·sump·tion

intro

win·ter

nc

wo

elim·i·nat·ed

ef·fect

ar·chi·tect

ef·fi·cient

and o

[171]

533

chief

when

com·pli·cat·ed

par

in·clined

Smith's

past

nonr

25,

ab·sent

im·pres·sion

par

dis·cussed

oc·ca·sions

con·sis·tent·ly

isq

iq

intro

ob·served

at·ten·dance

par

[193]

534

intro

Transcribe: 8 percent

fis·cal

intro

di·vi·sion's

ser

nonr

month's

[147]

Developing Shorthand Writing Power

535 FREQUENTLY USED PHRASES

Words Omitted

1

In Addition

2

1. *Some of our, some of the, many of the, one of the, in the future, about the matter, in the world, on the subject.*
2. *In addition, in addition to the, in addition to this, in addition to that, in addition to them, in addition to these.*

536 GEOGRAPHICAL EXPRESSIONS

St.

1

States

2

1. *St. Louis, St. Paul, St. Charles, St. John, St. Augustine.*
2. *Alabama, Alaska, Arizona, California, Colorado, Connecticut.*

Building Transcription Skills

537 Business Vocabulary Builder

voucher An authorization for payment.

orientation The introduction to an unfamiliar situation.

unfounded Not based on fact; groundless.

Writing Practice

538 PREVIEW

☐ 539

☐ 540

☐ 541

539 Significant, output, decades, technological, utilizing, Alabama.
540 Vocational, to provide, procedures, facilities, voucher, materials.
541 Businesses, failure, modern, unfounded, demonstration.

LETTERS

539

Dear Mr. Reed: You are probably aware that most significant gains in industrial output during the[1] past several decades have resulted from technological advances. We believe that the computer has[2] been the single most important influence on business productivity.

If you are not fully utilizing[3] all the advantages of computer technology in your business, perhaps now is the time to discuss[4] this with one of our consultants. We believe we can show you how you can increase your production while keeping your[5] expenses near their present level.

If you are interested in receiving further information about our[6] services, just drop by our office at 426 Alabama Avenue between 9:30 a.m.[7] and 5:30 p.m. Monday through Friday. There will be no obligation on your part, of course. Sincerely yours,[8]

540

Dear Mr. James: Our vice principal in charge of vocational programs here at St. Thomas School has approved my[9] request to provide a week of data processing training for our office procedures students. Your offer to[10] allow us to use your excellent facilities at Arizona Technical College is very generous.[11]

We plan to bring our students to your center each day from 10 a.m. to 12 noon during the week of April[12] 4. We are very excited about this fine opportunity for our students to participate in ten[13] hours of orientation training in the practical applications of data processing. I know the[14] students will profit greatly from the experience, and I am sure that many of them will elect to seek further[15] training at your institution.

I have sent a voucher to the board of education to cover the cost[16] of the materials the students will use during this program; you will receive a check shortly. Cordially yours,[17]

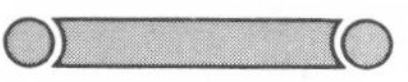

541

Dear Ms. Johnson: Most small businesses in America today are doing their office work the way they did ten[18] years ago. Their failure to use modern, up-to-date computer technology may be one of the reasons they[19] are still small businesses.

If you have been concerned that your business expenses would be greatly increased if you were[20] to switch some of your work to a computer, let me assure you that your fears are unfounded.

The St. Louis[21] Computer Company can help you streamline your operations. In addition, we can show you how to decrease your[22] costs. Let us explain how our organization has done just this for hundreds of businesses in this area.[23] Call 555-6219 for an appointment so that we may give you a demonstration. Cordially yours,[24] [480]

Reading and Writing Practice

542

tre·men·dous·ly

conj

use·less

per·son·nel

al·most

ap·ti·tude

well-pay·ing
hyphenated before noun

if

well-trained
hyphenated before noun

and o

[170]

543

yours

ap

your·self

intro

ac·cess

Transcribe:
1,000

intro

enu

up-to-the-min·ute *hyphenated before noun*

intro

first·hand

[274]

544

intro

ad·mit

skep·ti·cal

par

intro

ben·e·fits

fis·cal

vol·ume

25,

intro

cont

20,

as·sure

main·stay

[140]

Secretarial Tip
Special Care

ALWAYS BE VERY CAREFUL:

When you transcribe names. A person's name is important. Anyone's pride is wounded on receiving correspondence in which his or her name is misspelled. A person feels unimportant in the eyes of the writer who makes such an error. When there is the slightest doubt in your mind about the correct spelling of a name, check the files or some other source.

When you type dates. When your employer says "Friday, April 10," be sure that Friday is the tenth and not the ninth or the eleventh.

When you type figures. If you should type "$5,000" instead of "$4,000," you have made only one typing error—but that error could cost your company $1,000. It might even cost you your job!

When you type a member of a pair of "similar words." Be sure that you type the correct member. You would put yourself in a very bad light indeed if you type "I will have your report in a *weak*."

When your employer is enclosing something. When your employer says, "I am enclosing a booklet," this means that *you* must enclose it. Always place enclosures in the envelope before you submit letters for signature and indicate on the carbon that the enclosures were made.

When you cannot read an outline in your notes. If you cannot read an outline that obviously affects the sense of a sentence, don't guess at it and submit the letter for signature. If your guess is wrong and your employer discovers the error, you won't enhance your reputation as an efficient secretary. Your employer should be consulted when you can't read an outline.

Developing Shorthand Writing Power

545 WORD BEGINNINGS AND ENDINGS

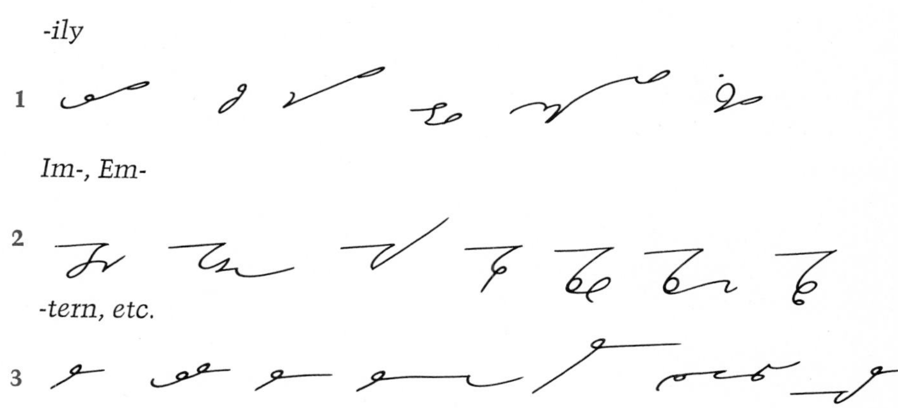

1. *Readily, easily, steadily, necessarily, customarily, hastily.*
2. *Impact, impersonal, imparted, impeach, embarrass, embargo, embassy.*
3. *Turn, return, term, terminal, determine, thermometer, modern.*

Building Transcription Skills

546 Business Vocabulary Builder

obsolete Out-of-date.

peculiar Distinctive; different from the usual.

primarily Chiefly.

Progressive Speed Builder (100-130)

The letters in this Progressive Speed Builder begin at 100 words a minute and run to 130 words a minute.

547 **PREVIEW**

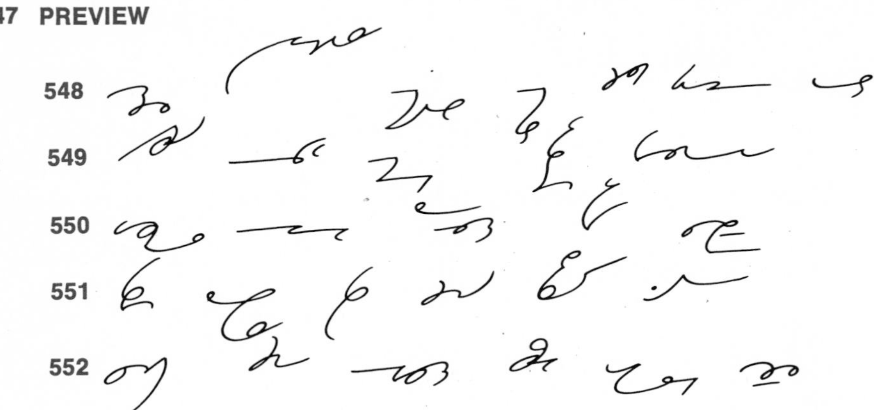

548 Consequently, demonstrate, inventories, invoices, situation, showroom, let us.
549 Designed, many things, information, specific, peculiar.
550 Occasionally, moments, electronics, obtain, equipment.
551 Basic, elaborate, payable, second, expanded, handle.
552 Active, fewer, mistakes, assigns, replenish, quickly.

LETTERS

548

[1 minute at 100]

Dear Mr. Green: Most of our customers are first-rate buyers of a computer. Consequently, the first thing we do is demonstrate how easy/it is to operate a Johnson 118.

Then we point out how useful it is. A Johnson 118 turns out instant information//on inventories. It does invoices and sales reports. It performs many other vital accounting functions. It gives fast and accurate///control of your whole financial situation.

Stop in at our showroom and let us demonstrate a Johnson 118 for you. Yours truly, [1]

549

[1 minute at 110]

Dear Mr. Green: The Johnson 118 computer works for a living. It was designed to do many things, including recording information, storing/ it, and organizing it.

The 118 will do all the general accounting jobs that are common to every business. In addition, it will do//the specific jobs that are peculiar to your business.

The 118 does many different jobs concurrently and makes results immediately///available to you.

Mail the enclosed card for full information about the 118 or call us at (212) 555-3136. Sincerely, [2]

550

[1 minute at 120]

Dear Mr. Green: Even the best computers will occasionally have their bad moments. When this happens to your computer, you, of course, want your computer company/to repair it immediately.

That is why the Johnson Electronics Company has field service centers you can call at any time of the day and any day//of the week. Each service center has spare parts on hand. If it does not happen to have the spare part your computer needs, it can obtain the part quickly from another service///center.

When you are in the market for computers or electronic equipment of any kind, come to the Johnson Electronics Company. Very truly yours, [3]

551

[1 minute at 125]

Dear Mr. Green: If your business is like most, your first computer will be a basic computer. We hope it will be a Johnson Model 118, which is fast and easy/to operate.

By the time you are ready for a second computer, you will probably want something more elaborate. You will want something that can do your accounts payable,//your payroll, and your billing.

And that is what is so nice about a Johnson 118. With this equipment, you will not need a second computer. Your Johnson 118///can be expanded to handle all the jobs just mentioned and many more.

When your business is ready for its first computer, make it a Johnson 118. Very truly yours, [4]

552

[1 minute at 130]

Dear Mr. Green: May I take this opportunity to tell you how pleased we are with our installation of a Johnson 118 computer.

Taking care of our 1,000 active/accounts used to be a full-time job for three people. Now the 118 handles these accounts in only a few seconds a day and makes fewer mistakes. As soon as the orders//come in each morning, the computer assigns merchandise to each customer. If we have the item in stock, it is shipped the same day.

That is not all the 118 does for us. It provides///us with a weekly sales report on each item so that we can replenish our stock quickly when our supply gets low.

We are delighted with our Johnson 118. Cordially yours, [5] [585]

Reading and Writing Practice

553

in·quir·ing
mer·its

leas·ing

ap

pri·mar·i·ly

mod·el
ob·so·lete

cont

when

intro

par

wheth·er

conj

qual·i·fied

[184]

554

quite
crit·i·cal

enu

im·prove·ment

[97]

PART

Improving Your Spelling and Vocabulary

It is impossible for everyone to know the spelling and meaning of every word. The English language is much too vast for one person to know everything. During your study of shorthand and transcription, you have done a great deal of work to improve your spelling and your vocabulary. You may soon be working in an office, and you must be responsible for continuing the improvement of your spelling and vocabulary.

There are two main problems in the improvement of your spelling and vocabulary, and there are two directions in which to pursue this improvement. The first problem is the general improvement of your spelling and vocabulary—improvement that every person should continue throughout life. The other problem is the improvement of your spelling and vocabulary for your specific job. Your success as a secretary will depend heavily on your ability to understand and to spell the words that are dictated in the course of the day's work. If you are not familiar with a word, it is seldom possible to spell it. In your own transcription work you have perhaps made some errors because you did not know the meaning of a word.

Each type of business has its own characteristic vocabulary and each person within the business has a unique vocabulary. This simplifies the problem of the new secretary. It is not necessary to know and to be able to spell every word in the language. It is necessary to know and be able to spell only the relatively small vocabulary used in the office where you work.

There is a right way and a wrong way to do this. The wrong way is to wait until you make a mistake and have to rewrite a letter.

There is a much better way,

however. Usually you will have a few days' notice before you report to work on a new job. If you do, try to obtain any printed matter, price lists, or catalogs issued by the company for which you are going to work. Study these carefully for new words. Look up the new words in a dictionary to learn their meanings and how to spell them. Make lists of the most difficult ones so that you will have them available when you begin your new job. When you begin work, ask permission to read some of the correspondence from the files and compile lists of words from the correspondence. When you notice that any word or phrase occurs very frequently, devise a shorthand shortcut for it, but be very sparing with the shortcuts. You should be able to hold down the list of worthwhile shortcuts to ten or twelve.

After working with this plan for a week or two, you may find that there are a few words that still bother you. Make a list of these words on an index card and keep them on your desk as you transcribe. This way you can check the spelling of any one of these words in a second by glancing at the card.

The improvement of your general ability in spelling and vocabulary is a more difficult task. It involves a great deal of reading and a constant awareness of the necessity for remembering the spelling and meaning of words that you see.

Whether you are attempting to improve your general ability or your ability to spell and recognize the words peculiar to your job, remember that your best friend and most patient helper is a good dictionary.

Merchandising

Developing Shorthand Writing Power

555 OUTLINE CONSTRUCTION

Double Consonants It is unnecessary to repeat the double consonant sound in compound words like *bookkeeper.*

Bookkeeper, bookkeeping, roommate, earrings, nighttime, newsstand, storeroom.

Ness After Words Ending In N or M The word ending *-ness* is joined to *n* or *m* with a jog.

1. *Firmness, grimness, dimness, slimness, calmness.*
2. *Evenness, sternness, thinness, plainness, suddenness, openness.*

Building Transcription Skills

556 SIMILAR-WORDS DRILL plane, plain

plane An airplane; an aircraft.

The plane *was due to arrive two hours ago.*

plain *(noun)* Level, treeless land; a broad strip of flat land.

Crossing the vast plain *was a great trial for the people.*

plain Clear; obvious.

Your intentions regarding your overdue payment are plain.

Reading and Writing Practice

557 Wanted!

A person

[196]

558 LETTERS

book·keep·er

25

plane

par

when

plain

as

ap 25

if

sup·pli·ers

nc

intro

past

con·se·quent·ly

intro

[144]

559

intro

de·luxe

Amer·i·ca's

func·tions

ser

di·a·ry

fi·nan·cial

intro

al·most

ser

prin·ci·pal

re·cip·i·ent

if

con·ve·nience

intro

[178]

560

intro

geo

and o

rea·son·able

ser

mer·chan·dise

an·ni·ver·sa·ry

intro

ser

al·ready

[133]

Developing Shorthand Writing Power

561 RECALL DRILL ten blend

In this drill you will review the various combinations represented by the *ten* blend.

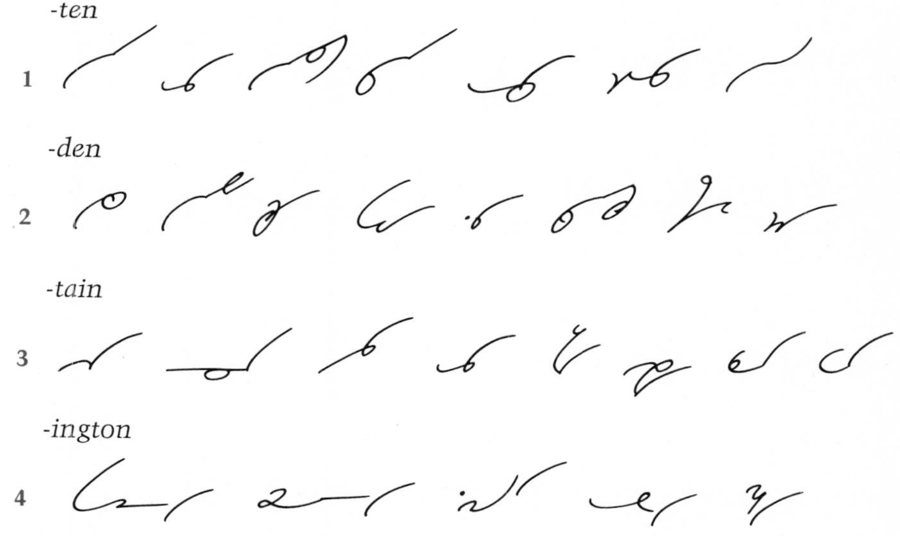

1. *Tend, written, tentative, attend, lighten, straighten, tenant.*
2. *Deny, dentist, widen, broaden, hidden, identify, evidence. sudden.*
3. *Contain, maintain, detain, retain, obtain, captain, certain, pertain.*
4. *Bloomington, Wilmington, Huntington, Lexington, Washington.*

Building Transcription Skills

562 ACCURACY PRACTICE

In this drill you will practice the various joinings of the *oo* hook. Keep the *oo* hook deep and narrow.

1

2

3

4

1. *You, world, you can; yours truly, you would, other; wood, woman.*
2. *New, none, numb; nut, mood.*
3. *Shoe, chew; one, whom; you want, you are, you will.*
4. *Cool, gull; us, you have; rubber, group, up.*

Writing Practice

563 PREVIEW

☐ 564

☐ 565

☐ 566

564 *To make, actually, merchandise, statistical, population, sculptures, prestigious.*
565 *Recycling, Lexington, interchange, modern, United States, neighborhood, within.*
566 *Utilities, instituting, in which, quantities, insulator, savings, self-addressed, records.*

LETTERS

564

Dear Mr. Huntley: In response to your inquiry concerning the marketing of high-priced art works, your best approach in my opinion[1] would be to make direct contact with those people who actually deal in this merchandise.

Statistical[2] evidence shows that only about

[147]

569

fairs

ser

up-to-date hyphenated before noun

its

pic·ture

intro

if

[135]

570

as

worth·while

phase

if

[95]

Developing Shorthand Writing Power

571 WORD FAMILIES

-minal

1

Coat

2

1. *Nominal, terminal, criminal, abdominal.*
2. *Coat, coated, overcoat, undercoat, topcoat, raincoat.*

572 FREQUENTLY USED NAMES

Last Names

1

Women's First Names

2

1. *Mason, Maxwell, McConnell, McCoy, Mendez.*
2. *Martha, Maria, Marilyn, Marsha, Mildred.*

Building Transcription Skills

573 **Business Vocabulary Builder**

recoup To recover; to regain.

liquidation The converting of assets into cash.

allegations Statements made without proof.

Writing Practice

574 PREVIEW

☐ **575**

☐ **576**

☐ **577**

575 *Developed, dryers, techniques, seminar, acknowledged, stylist, incentive, we hope to see.*

576 *Processing, shortly, terminal, we have been, distributing, hardware, union, to make.*

577 *Warehouse, partially, minimize, liquidators, Washington, liquidation.*

LETTERS

575

Dear Mrs. Mason: The National Beauty Products Company has just developed a new line of blow dryers[1] that your customers are sure to enjoy. These dryers also make possible some important timesaving changes[2] in the techniques your operators currently use. We are conducting a seminar on Wednesday evening at[3] 7 p.m. at the Palm Beach Beauty School. We would like to demonstrate our new line to as many of your[4] operators as possible.

Miss Martha Mendez, acknowledged as a leading West Coast hair stylist, will conduct the[5] seminar and demonstrate our new techniques. As an incentive to your operators to attend our program,[6] we will give each person present a Roberts hair dryer.

The program will last approximately two hours.[7] Refreshments will be served. We hope to see a good representation from your shop, Mrs. Mason. Very truly yours,[8]

576

Dear Mr. McCoy: Thank you for your order of September 27. We are processing the order now,[9] and you will be receiving merchandise shortly from our regional terminal. I am also sending you a[10] catalog listing all our merchandise along with an explanation of our credit policies and terms.

Although[11] we have been distributing hardware supplies for over ten years in every state in the union, we are still[12] happy to make new friends like you. If we can serve your needs in the future by supplying you with a complete range[13] of top-quality hardware merchandise, Mr. McCoy, please do not hesitate to call on us. Cordially yours,[14]

577

Dear Mr. Quincey: We learned this morning through a local newspaper that your clothing warehouse was partially destroyed[15] by fire on March 30. Your immediate concern, of course, is to survey the extent of the damage[16] to your merchandise. You also want to minimize your losses by disposing of your fire- and smoke-damaged[17] stock at nominal prices.

Liquidators Incorporated can guarantee top dollar for your damaged[18] merchandise. We have been in the business of selling damaged stock for ten years and have earned an outstanding reputation[19] for quickly disposing of this type of merchandise through our outlets in Washington and Oregon.

We would[20] like to discuss the matter of helping you recoup as much of your loss as possible. I have asked Mr. Alvin[21] Tate, my assistant, to contact you this weekend. I hope you will give him an opportunity to present[22] our program for the liquidation of your stock. You will find our terms most agreeable. Very cordially yours,[23] [460]

Reading and Writing Practice

578

men's

ser

wear·ing ap·par·el

when

ser

conj

intro

wom·en's

cloth·ing

conj

par

[133]

579

the·ater

ap

re·quest
prompt·ly

conj

intro

Sat·ur·day

cr

fi·nal·ize

[177]

580

Li·cens·ing
au·tho·rized

intro

whole·sale

al·le·ga·tions

if

re·vo·ca·tion

sta·tus

conj

[131]

581

it's

when

nc

par

sim·i·lar·ly

intro

its

nc

par

intro

conj

ef·fect

ap

intro

ours

[171]

Developing Shorthand Writing Power

582 FREQUENTLY USED PHRASES

Or Omitted

1

Intersection

2

1. *One or two, two or three, three or four, day or two, week or two, day or two ago.*
2. *Chamber of Commerce, a.m., p.m., vice versa.*

583 GEOGRAPHICAL EXPRESSIONS

Fort

1

States

2

Foreign Cities

3

1. *Fort Worth, Fort Wayne, Fort Stockton, Fort Myers, Fort Lee, Fort Knox.*
2. *Delaware, Florida, Texas, Illinois, New York, New Jersey, Minnesota.*
3. *Mexico City, Hong Kong, Singapore, Tokyo, Rio de Janeiro, Manila.*

Building Transcription Skills

584 Business Vocabulary Builder

contemplating Considering.

recommendation Advice; suggestion.

retail operations Businesses that sell directly to the consumer.

Writing Practice

585 PREVIEW

☐ 586

☐ 587

☐ 588

586 *Figures, occurred, to me, New Mexico, United States, typically, families, feasibility.*
587 *Word, Minnesota, contemplating, source, more than, executive.*
588 *Initiated, shopper, you want, forward, within, receipt, Christmas, economical.*

LETTERS

586

Dear Mr. Mason: Recently I was studying national production and sales figures in the clothing[1] industry. It occurred to me that our company ought to be developing our markets in Arizona, New[2] Mexico, and Texas because statistics indicate that this section of the United States is one of our[3] fastest growing regions. An area of rapid growth typically includes a large share of young families who[4] represent an ideal market for our infants' clothing.

Please work up figures on the feasibility of our[5] establishing distribution outlets in Arizona, New Mexico, and Texas, and let me hear from you[6] sometime next month. I will present these figures to the board of directors for consideration and final[7] decision.

If you need any further details in order to complete your report, please let me know. Sincerely yours,[8]

587

To All Managers: We have just received word from one of our field representatives in Minnesota that copper[9] prices will rise by 7 cents a pound on June 1.

As you know, we have been contemplating the purchase of[10] a large order of raw copper products sometime during the summer months. If our source is correct, we should place our[11] order immediately so that we can purchase at the existing price. It will cost us more than[12] $25,000 if we wait until the official announcement of a price increase.

I have called a special meeting[13] for Tuesday at 8:30 a.m. in the executive boardroom to consider this matter. Please give the[14] purchase careful consideration and be prepared to make your recommendation at the meeting. Al Davis[15]

588

To the Staff: Recently our purchasing department initiated a program called the Personal Business[16] Shopper. Under this program our employees may buy any item advertised in the enclosed catalog at[17] savings up to 25 percent.

To order any of these items, simply indicate the ones you want on[18] the order blank in the catalog. Then forward it to the Personal Business Shopper on the 40th floor.[19] The items will be shipped within two or three days of receipt of your order.

Use the enclosed catalog to help[20] you with your Christmas shopping; it is an efficient, economical way to buy your presents. J. E. Greenberg[21] [420]

Reading and Writing Practice

589

its

agen·da

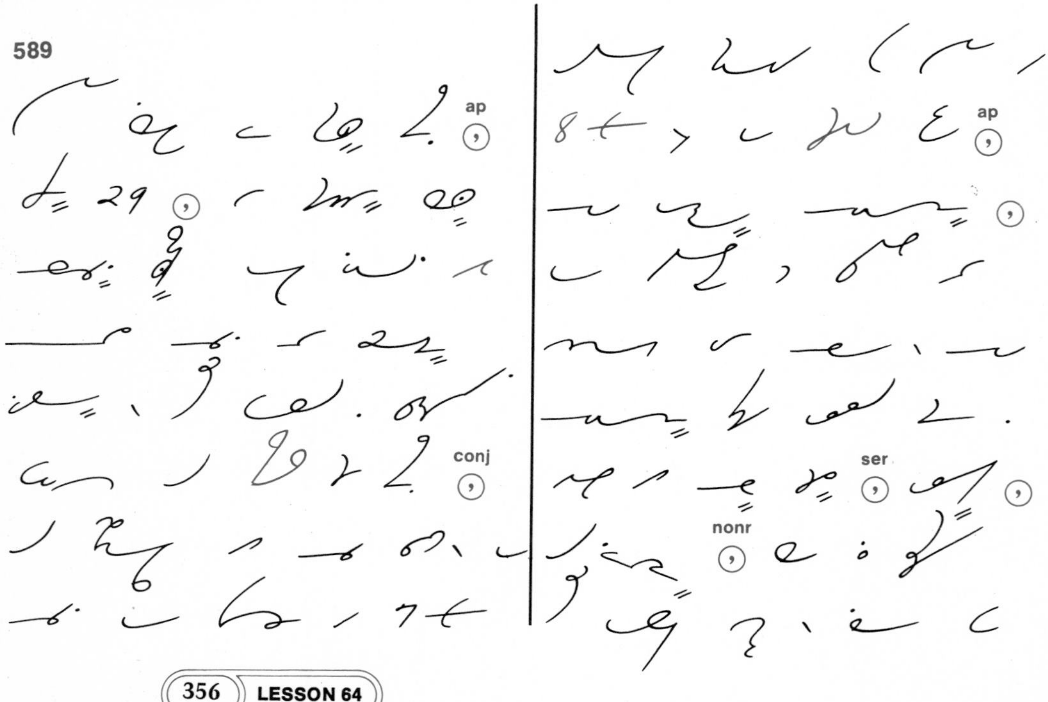

ap

conj

ap

ser

nonr

Transcribe:
8 p.m.
fea·ture

conj

15

ap

555-8351

[180]

590

li·censes

intro

door-to-door *hyphenated before noun*

nonr

intro

coun·cil

[133]

591

intro

wo

poul·try

43
cit·ies
over·seas
intro
[115]

592

intro
fur·ther·more
in·stal·la·tion

busy
intro
be·gin·ning
when
555-
4181
8
6
conj
[158]

Secretarial Tip
Traits

On your first job, your employer will expect you to be able to write shorthand rapidly, to have a command of spelling and punctuation, and to be able to transcribe accurately and rapidly. If you don't have these skills, you probably will not even be considered for a very good job. You should, of course, have much more than these basic skills. You should also have the following qualities.

Tact. Tact is a trait that enables a person to handle what is potentially a disagreeable situation in a way that will leave everyone happy. A secretary is often called upon to exercise tact in dealing with customers, other employees, and executives.

Loyalty. Loyalty is the quality of being faithful to an organization, to its objectives, and to its people. A good secretary is always loyal.

Discretion. The discreet secretary is one who knows when to disclose information about the employer's business to others and when to keep information confidential. The secretary who knows how to use discretion is a valuable employee indeed.

Dependability. A prominent business executive once said, "When I ask my secretary to do something, I know it will be done—and done right. I wish I could say this about all my employees; my job would be far simpler. My secretary will go far in our organization." Will your employer be able to say the same about you?

Poise. Anyone can maintain poise when things are running smoothly. The real measure of a person's poise, however, is conducting oneself properly under trying and difficult situations, which arise all too frequently in the business office. Secretaries who can remain calm when everything seems to go wrong are worth their weight in gold!

Neatness. The thoughtful secretary will not only keep the secretarial work station neat but will also help keep the employer's office attractive. The secretary will see that papers are neatly arranged and that pencils are sharpened. People work better in orderly surroundings.

Developing Shorthand Writing Power

593 WORD BEGINNINGS AND ENDINGS

Circum-

1

Under-

2

-ward

3

1. *Circumstance, circumstances, circumstantial, circumnavigate, circumvent, circumvented.*
2. *Under, underneath, undergo, undergrowth, understate, undertake, understand.*
3. *Inward, outward, backward, backwards, onward, homeward, reward.*

Building Transcription Skills

594 Business Vocabulary Builder

dunning Persistently and urgently demanding payment.

materialize To come into existence; to appear.

distasteful Unpleasant; disagreeable.

Progressive Speed Builder (110-135)

The Progressive Speed Builder in this lesson runs from 110 words a minute to 135 words a minute.

595 PREVIEW

596 Genuine, satisfaction, $600, purchased, considerably, furthermore, we have not had, self-addressed.
597 Dunning, I am sure, to make, creditors, to be able, remainder, we want.
598 Overdue, attorney, eventually, in addition, reputation, probably, by that time, status.
599 Distasteful, to us, undoubtedly, result, relationships, appointment, discuss.
600 Owed, legal, I suggested, period, unpleasantness, resume.

LETTERS

596

[1 minute at 110]

Dear Mr. James: If you are like most people, you thoroughly enjoy doing things for others. It gives you a genuine sense of satisfaction. Here is/your opportunity to do something for us, Mr. James.

Write a check for $600 in payment of the merchandise you purchased from the Smith Clothing//Store last March and place it in the mail. As you know, your account is now considerably overdue. Furthermore, we have written you several times///requesting payment, but we have not had a response to any of our letters.

A self-addressed envelope is enclosed for your convenience. Sincerely, [1]

597

[1 minute at 120]

Dear Mr. James: A dunning letter is never an easy one to write, especially when it is addressed to a customer of long standing like you. But as I am/sure you realize, we must ask all our customers to make payments promptly or we cannot pay our own creditors promptly.

As you know, you owe the Smith Clothing Store//$600. If you cannot make the entire payment at once, at least send us a check for $300 and then tell us when you hope to be able to pay///the remainder.

We want to continue serving your needs in the future as we have in the past, but we can only do so if you pay your account at once. Sincerely yours, [2]

598

[1 minute at 125]

Dear Mr. James: When a creditor refers an overdue account to an attorney, the only one who profits from the purchases you made from the Smith Clothing Store is the/attorney.

You lose because you will eventually have to pay the cost of collection. In addition, you will have a blot on your credit reputation. We lose because//we will probably never again receive another order from you.

You can prevent all this by sending us a check for $600. June 15 is the deadline.///If we have your check by that time, your credit standing will be restored to its original excellent status. If we don't, your account goes to our attorney. Yours truly, [3]

599

[1 minute at 130]

Dear Mr. James: We are about to follow a course of action that is very distasteful to us. We are about to turn your account over to our attorney for collection. This/action will undoubtedly result in the loss of a customer with whom we have had pleasant relationships for many years.

Why are we considering this drastic action?// Simply because you have not paid your overdue account amounting to $600. We have had no answer to our many requests for payment and no explanation.

We have///an appointment to discuss the matter with our attorney on June 15. Your check for $600 before that date will allow us to cancel the appointment. Sincerely, [4]

600

[1 minute at 135]

Dear Mr. James: On June 15 we met with our attorney to discuss the collection of the $600 that you have owed the Smith Clothing Store since last March. He is now in the process/of preparing the necessary legal papers to enforce collection. I suggested, however, that he delay filing these papers for a few days so that I could make one last appeal//to you to send us your check.

Friday, June 25, is the deadline. If we receive your check by that time, all will be well. If we do not, the papers will be filed and both of us will be///in for a period of unpleasantness.

It is up to you. Do we call off our lawyer and resume our former pleasant relationship, or do we tell him to file suit? Sincerely yours, [5] [620]

● Reading and Writing Practice

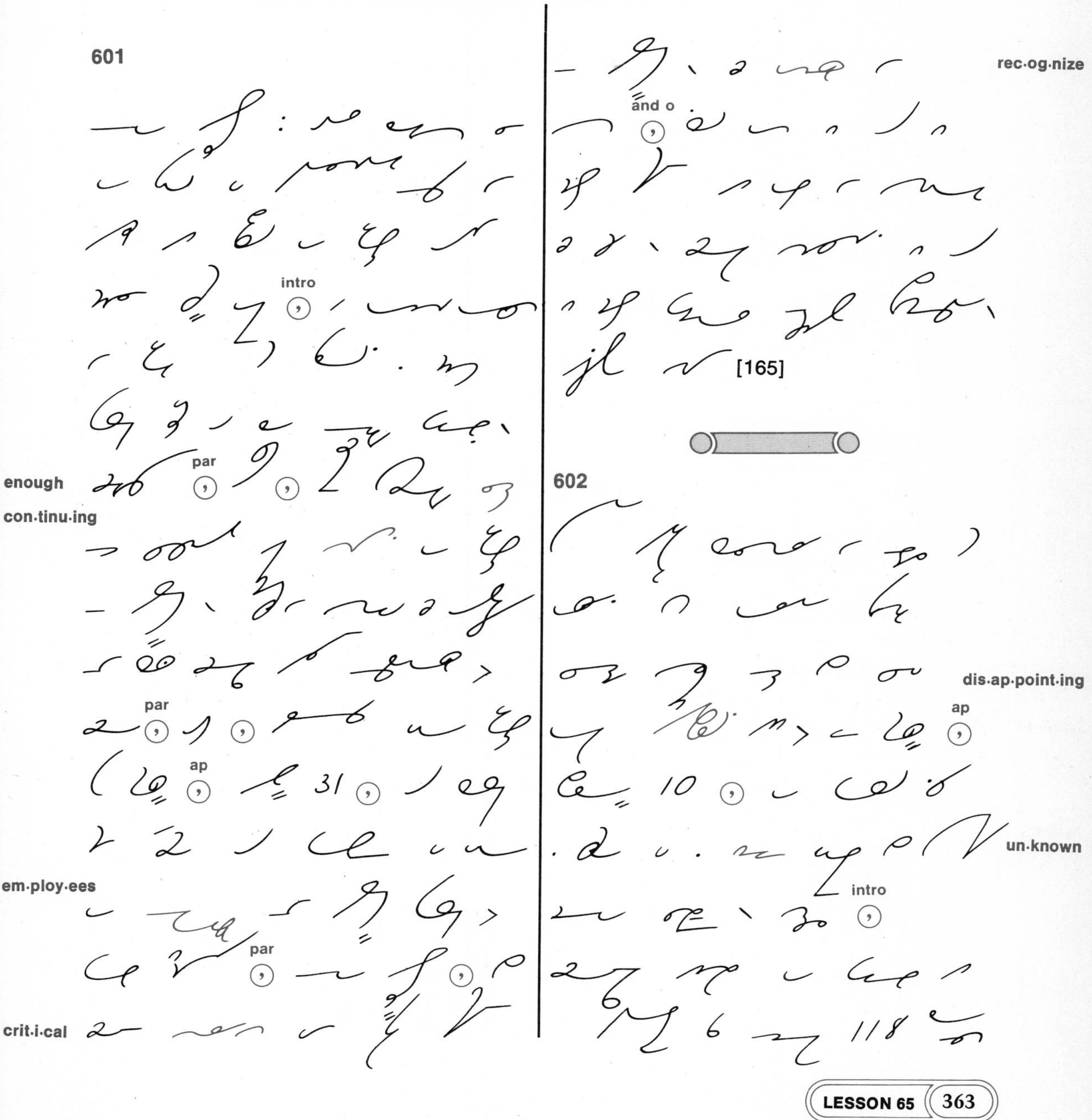

par

delivery
too
inconvenience

[137]

603

factory

ser

thieves
vandals

if

intro

world's
widely used
no hyphen
after ly

if

engineers

nc

there
their

[124]

CHAPTER

14 Publishing

Developing Shorthand Writing Power

604 OUTLINE CONSTRUCTION

Unaccented Diphthong U Omitted Before R and L Omitting the diphthong *u* before *r* and *l* results in fluent outlines for many useful words.

1
2

1. *Accurate, accuracy, inaccuracy, inaccurately, inaugurate.*
2. *Vocabulary, popular, singular, stimulant, ridiculous.*

Building Transcription Skills

605 SIMILAR-WORDS DRILL raising, rising

raising Lifting (by someone or by something); moving upward.

We are raising *the rent next month because of increased overhead costs.*

rising Lifting itself or oneself; moving upward on its own accord.

Because of steadily rising *costs, we are increasing the rent next month.*

Reading and Writing Practice

606 You Can Do It

Today

[188]

607 LETTERS

cont

co·op·er·a·tive
crit·i·cal
in·au·gu·rat·ed

intro

month's

[170]

608

par
re·ceived

cam·paign
par

al·most

ser
smeared

sat·is·fac·to·ry
nc
intro

ap
15
sup·pli·er

[161]

15

609

pre·vi·ous

intro

cop·ies

ap

hard·bound

conj

8 95

months'

conj

al·ready

con·densed

as

pop·u·lar

[159]

610

puz·zle

if

50

it

enough

if

[100]

Developing Shorthand Writing Power

611 RECALL DRILL b

In this drill you will review the various uses of the alphabetic stroke *b*.

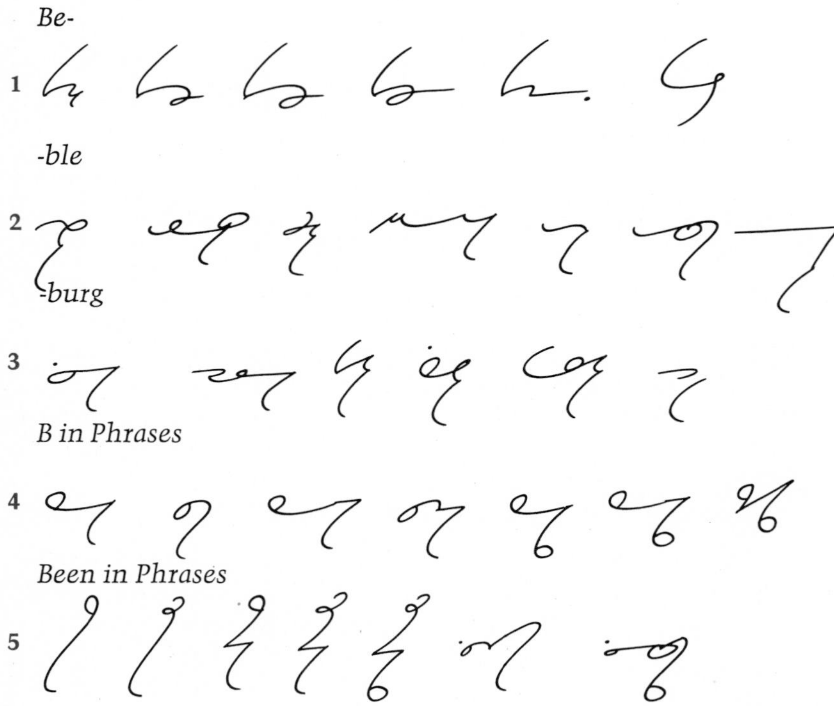

1. *Because, begin, began, became, becoming, believe.*
2. *Capable, reliable, sensible, tolerable, workable, likable, manageable.*
3. *Hamburg, Nuremberg, Pittsburgh, Harrisburg, Plattsburg, Newburgh.*

4. I will be, I can be, I will not be, I cannot be, I will be able, I will not be able, I should be able.
5. I have been, we have been, I have not been, we have not been, we have not been able, he could have been, he might have been able.

Building Transcription Skills

612 ACCURACY PRACTICE

In this drill you will practice the joining of the two forms of *s* to other alphabetic strokes of Gregg Shorthand. Remember to give the *s* a deep curve and to keep it small.

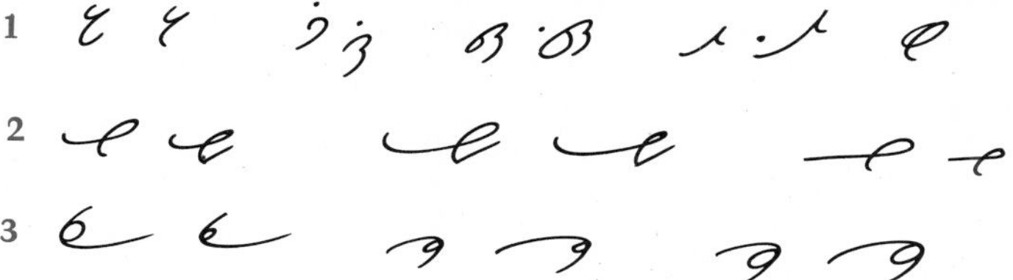

1. *Also, was; whose, who is; use, house; there is, hands; eyes.*
2. *Race, rest; last, least; mass, next.*
3. *Sale, sell; keys, guess; case, gas.*

● Writing Practice

613 PREVIEW

☐ **614**

☐ **615**

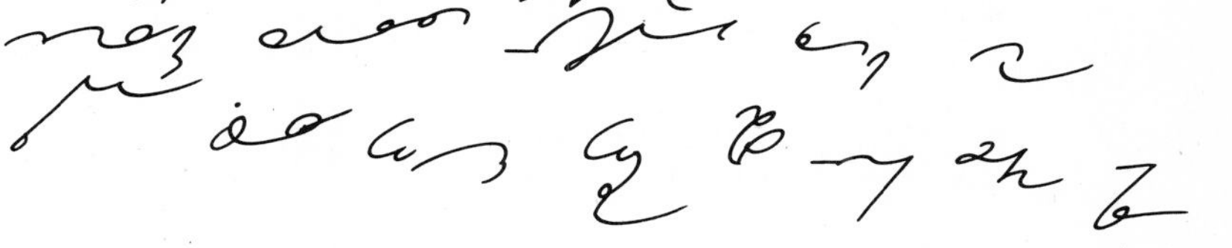

614 *Notified, we wanted, stabilize, adhere, report, approximately, infested, $1 billion, infestation, damage, project, have not been, customers, of course, at least.*

615 *Congratulations, athletic, individuals, circulation, quality, editorial, highlight, programs, professional, we hope that, encourage, we are sure, enjoyment.*

LETTERS

614

Dear Mr. Farmer: Last year when we were forced to increase the price of paper products, we notified all our major[1] customers that we wanted to stabilize prices for as long as possible. You may be sure that we are[2] continuing to do everything possible to adhere to this policy, but we have just received a report[3] that has made us concerned. Surveys indicate that the damage from bark beetles this year is at a record high[4] level. Approximately 13 percent of our trees have been infested, which could represent a $1 billion[5] loss if the infestation is not stopped.

To reduce the damage to our forests from this disease, we are[6] beginning a large-scale spraying project to protect those trees that have not been affected. We are also cutting[7] and burning the dead trees. These actions will cost us a great deal of money. Increased costs may have to be passed along[8] to our customers.

We will, of course, give you at least 60 days' notice of any price changes. Cordially yours,[9]

615

Dear Mr. Kennedy: Congratulations! You have been selected to receive one year's subscription to *American*[10] *Sports,* a new magazine devoted to athletic activities in the West.

By giving free subscriptions[11] to key individuals throughout our circulation area, we hope to spread the word to others[12] regarding the outstanding content and quality of our magazine.

We believe you will be impressed with the[13] editorial staff that we call on for the material in our magazine. Personal-interest stories of[14] events that are close to you will highlight each and every issue. There will be a section devoted to high school[15] athletics, one to college programs, and another to professional sports.

You are under no obligation,[16] of course, but we hope that you will encourage your friends and associates to read *American Sports* if you feel[17] that it is the kind of magazine they would enjoy.

We are sure you will derive many hours of enjoyment from[18] reading this fine magazine. Your first issue is already on its way. Happy reading! Very cordially yours,[19] [380]

Reading and Writing Practice

616

un·til

intro

ap

con·den·sa·tions

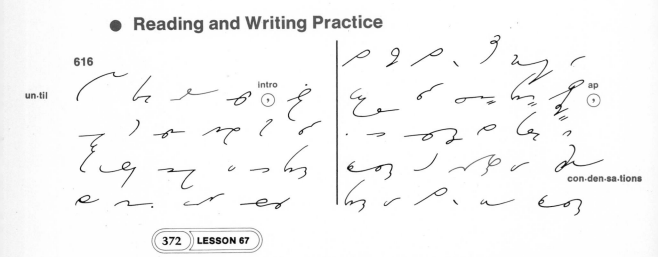

au·thors'

out·stand·ing

intro

if

re·ceive

yours

if

to·tal

nc

[156]

617

hon·or

ap

Har·ris·burg

ap

16

be·gin·ning

7

Transcribe:
7 o'clock

30/

fund-rais·ing
hypenated before noun

nc

30/

Da·vis's

sig·nif·i·cant

nc

at·tend

[151]

618

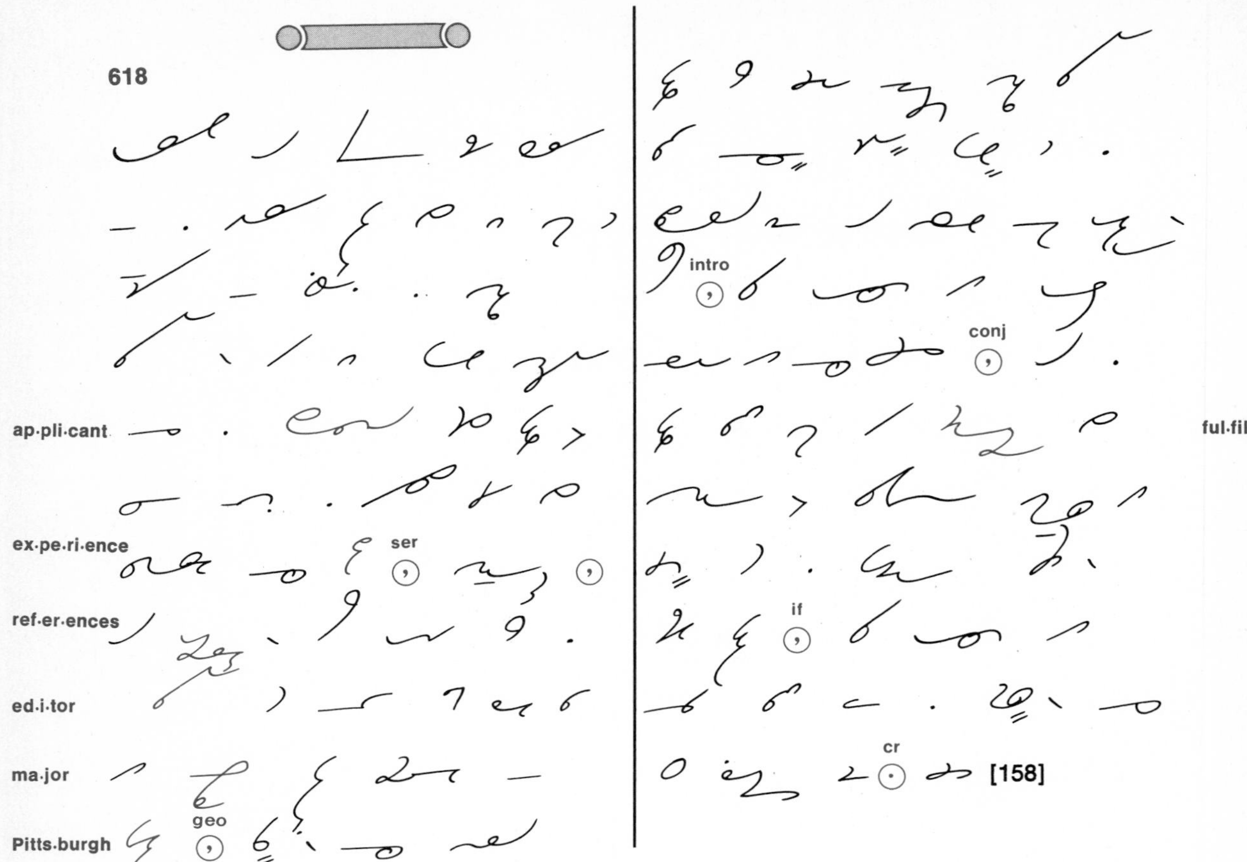

In almost any group of people—offices being no exception—you will find petty annoyances. The idea is to make sure they remain just that—petty.

Developing Shorthand Writing Power

619 WORD FAMILIES

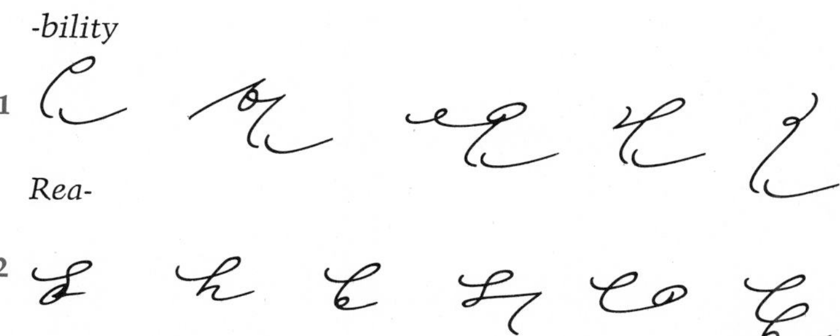

1. *Ability, desirability, reliability, stability, feasibility.*
2. *Reassign, reassure, reappear, reassemble, reapply, reappraisal.*

620 FREQUENTLY USED NAMES

Last Names

1

Men's First Names

2

1. *Miles, Miller, Monroe, Morales, Morgan.*
2. *Milton, Murray, Nathan, Patrick, Paul, Pedro.*

Building Transcription Skills

621 Business Vocabulary Builder

reappraisal A new evaluation.
promotional Relating to advertising.
money order An order for payment (similar to a check) for a specified amount of money.

● Writing Practice

622 PREVIEW

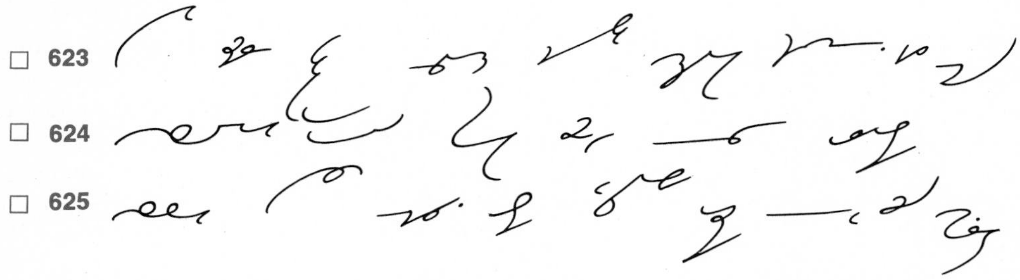

623 *Dear Ms., western, possibility, networks, studios, considerable, forthcoming, shortly, informed.*
624 *Gardener's, wealth, valuable, 2,000, many of them, retrieved.*
625 *Carrier's, to make, instituting, thereafter, self-addressed, received, morning's, we want, comprehensive.*

LETTERS

623

Dear Ms. Miles: We are pleased with the consumer response to your latest novel, *A Great Western Character*.

Before[1] the publication of your book, we discussed the possibility of selling the production rights to one of[2] the major television networks or movie studios. I have discussed your book with several companies,[3] and I am confident that there is considerable interest in making a movie of it.

If sales progress[4] as they have during the past three months, a good offer from a movie or television producer should be[5] forthcoming shortly. I will keep you informed on important developments as they occur. Very cordially yours,[6]

624

Dear Mr. Morgan: If you like to work in your garden and grow things, here is the book for you—*The Gardener's Guide,* by[7] Paul Monroe. This guide contains a wealth of information for plant lovers. It has 320 pages of[8] valuable suggestions and more than 2,000 color illustrations, many of them retrieved from old manuscripts[9] and books rarely seen by people interested in gardening.

Pick up your copy at your local bookstore or use[10] the enclosed order form to obtain one by mail. The cost is only $8.50. Very truly yours,[11]

625

Dear Subscriber: Collection is the most difficult part of your newspaper carrier's business. To make collection[12] easier and more pleasant, we are instituting a new collection policy on the first of April.[13]

On that date and at the beginning of each month thereafter, you will receive a self-addressed envelope with your[14] newspaper. Please send your check or money order for $4.50 to our regional office by the[15] fifth of each month. If we have not received your payment by the seventh, you will be given a reminder with your[16] morning's newspaper. Your subscription will be canceled by the tenth if payment has not been received. This action is[17] necessary because we cannot pay your deserving carrier until you have paid us.

Your cooperation[18] with this policy change will be appreciated. We want to continue delivering to your doorstep[19] a newspaper generally acknowledged as the most comprehensive journal published in the state. Yours truly,[20] [400]

Reading and Writing Practice

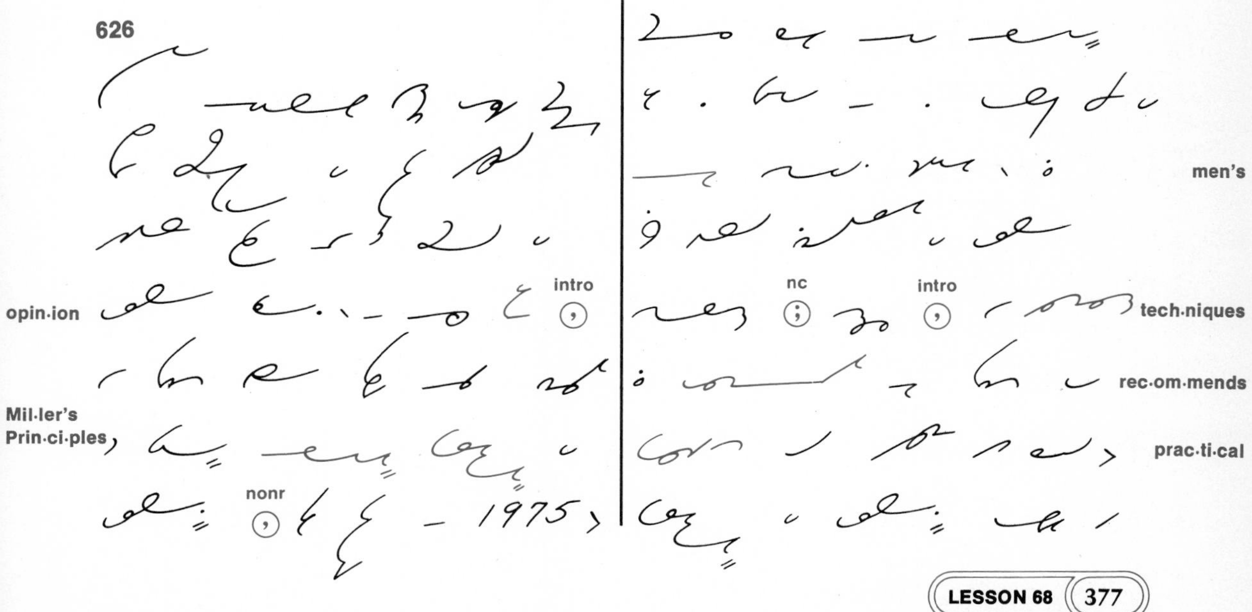

Transcribe:
25 percent

[117]

627

re·sponse

crit·i·cal

intro

it

its

if

uti·lized

com·mer·cial·ly ac·cept·able
no hyphen after ly

and o

ser

de·sign·ers

ad·ver·tis·ing

intro

cam·paign

conj

conj

as

it

if

re·ap·prais·al

[246]

628

moth·er-in-law

when

one-year *hyphenated before noun*

[67]

629

when

as

conj

conj

item-by-item *hyphenated before noun*

nc

conj

two-week *hyphenated before noun*

if

[211]

Developing Shorthand Writing Power

630 FREQUENTLY USED PHRASES

Word Modified in Phrases

1

A Omitted

2

1. *Of course, as soon as, as soon as possible, to do, let us, to us, your order, I hope, we hope.*
2. *For a long time, for a few days, for a day or two, for a few minutes, for a few months, at a time.*

631 GEOGRAPHICAL EXPRESSIONS

-mont

1

States

2

Foreign Cities

3

1. *Dumont, Oakmont, Edgemont, Piedmont.*
2. *Pennsylvania, Tennessee, Utah, Vermont, Washington, West Virginia.*
3. *London, Bristol, Manchester, Plymouth, Edinburgh.*

Building Transcription Skills

632 Business Vocabulary Builder

considerable Significant; fairly large.

limitations Restrictions.

enroll To register; to sign up.

Writing Practice

633 PREVIEW

☐ 634

☐ 635

☐ 636

634 *Thank you for your order, portfolio, you should have, in a few days, subscribers, basic, coupon, initial, to us.*

635 *Returning, commercially, logical, reviewer, limitations, to make, in a few months.*

636 *Congratulations, luggage, sweepstakes, awarding, incidentally, fortune.*

LETTERS

634

Dear Mr. Martin: Thank you for your order for our business executive's portfolio. The order was processed[1] on September 25 and you should have it in a few days.

In the course of a business day, we receive[2] considerable correspondence from subscribers like you asking us to recommend books to help them build a[3] basic business library.

On the enclosed circular are listed five books that we feel should be on every business[4] executive's library shelves. Check the ones you want on the attached coupon, initial the coupon, and return[5] it to us in the enclosed self-addressed envelope. Your new books will arrive shortly. Very cordially yours,[6]

635

Dear Mr. Todd: We are returning your manuscript, "Red Valley," for the following reasons:

1. The manuscript[7] is too long in its present state to be commercially acceptable.
2. The chapter organization does[8] not follow a logical order.
3. The many editing changes make it too difficult for our editors[9] to read.

The reviewer tells me that the manuscript is among the best we have received for several months,[10] but the limitations above prevent us from accepting it at this time. If, however, you would like to make[11] some changes, we would be happy to review it in a few months.

Thank you for considering our company as[12] a prospective publisher of your book. We hope to hear from you again in the near future. Very truly yours,[13]

636

Dear Mrs. Allen: Congratulations, Mrs. Allen! You have won a set of Oakmont luggage in the annual[14] *Home Digest* Sweepstakes Contest. The luggage will be arriving shortly, and we hope you will enjoy the outstanding[15] quality of this fine merchandise.

Each year, as you know, we have the opportunity of awarding more[16] than 2,500 prizes to our regular readers. This year we had over 28,000 contestants,[17] which means that almost 10 percent of them won prizes.

Incidentally, we hope you will tell your friends about[18] your good fortune and encourage them to become subscribers to *Home Digest*. We have enclosed five self-addressed[19] subscription cards for the convenience of your friends who may wish to begin receiving *Home Digest*. Yours very truly,[20] [400]

● Reading and Writing Practice

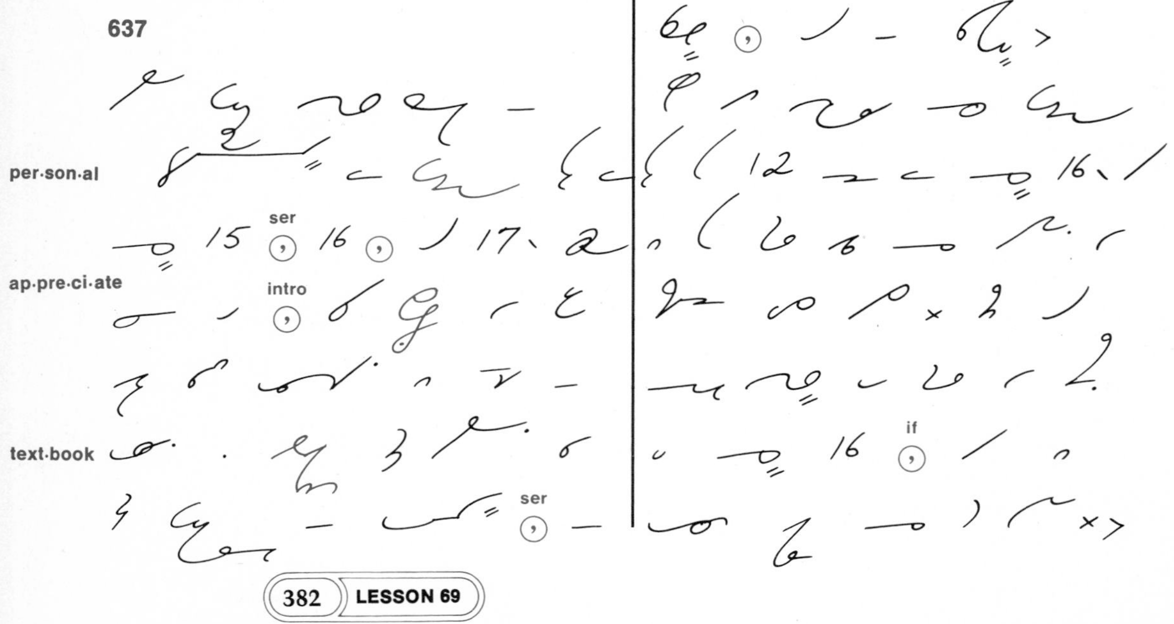

[106]

638

intro

com·pa·ny's

up to date
no noun,
no hyphen

tough

intro

nc

wo

par

en·cour·age

en·roll

[230]

639

ap

pam·phlet

step-by-step
hyphenated
before noun

par

glos·sa·ry

[56]

640

Dix·on's

ap

intro

conj

[104]

641

intro

month's

Transcribe:
75 percent

75,

long-dis·tance

well-writ·ten
hyphenated
before noun

intro

re·course

year's

mon·i·tor

[152]

Secretarial Tip
A Secretary's Duties

What types of duties do secretaries perform most often in the business office today? A study of the work of expert secretaries revealed that the following duties were performed frequently:

1. Taking and transcribing dictation.
2. Filing correspondence and records.
3. Reading and sorting mail.
4. Placing, receiving, and routing telephone calls.
5. Making and keeping records of appointments.
6. Composing letters and reports on own initiative or from oral instructions.
7. Receiving customers and other visitors.
8. Requisitioning supplies.
9. Typing from employer's notes.
10. Making travel reservations.

Of course, secretaries perform many other duties. The nature of these duties depends on the experience of the secretary and the degree of confidence that the employer has in the secretary. Some employers permit their secretaries to sign letters in their absence, supervise clerical help, and assist with personnel problems.

Developing Shorthand Writing Power

642 WORD BEGINNINGS AND ENDINGS

-self, -selves

1

Over-

2

-hood

3

1. *Myself, yourself, himself, herself, yourselves, ourselves, themselves.*
2. *Over, overcome, overcame, overdo, overtake, overpower, overworked.*
3. *Neighborhood, manhood, womanhood, brotherhood, fatherhood, sisterhood.*

Building Transcription Skills

643 Business Vocabulary Builder

utmost *(noun)* The most possible; the best of one's abilities.

revenue Income.

unavoidable Absolutely necessary; inevitable.

Progressive Speed Builder (110-135)

The letters in this Progressive Speed Builder range in speed from 110 words a minute to 135 words a minute.

644 PREVIEW

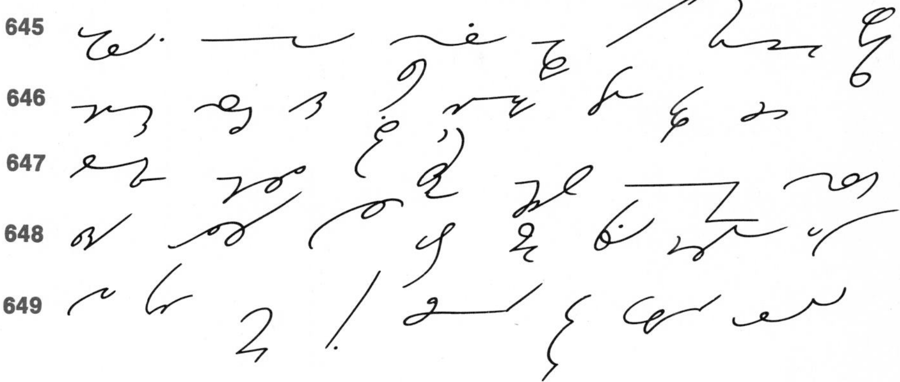

645 Reprinting, manual, glad to hear, in the past, to do, volumes, I hope to be able.
646 Instructions, carefully, to us, however, utmost, better, position, sincerely yours.
647 Telephone, unfortunately, has been, supervisor, in a few days, management, grateful.
648 Used, indicated, to make, whatever, as soon as, behind, schedule, overtime.
649 To know, booth, convention, judging, examined, publication, president, rendered.

LETTERS

645

[1 minute at 110]

Dear Mr. Harper: Our production manager tells me that you are reprinting our new book, the *Smith Correspondence Manual.* I was glad to hear this as/your work has been satisfactory in the past, and I know we can depend on you to do a good job again.

As you know, the *Smith Correspondence*// *Manual* will be issued in two volumes. I am enclosing the first two chapters of the first volume. I hope to be able to send you the remaining/// chapters of the first volume early next week.

As I am sure our production manager told you, we need the first volume by June 15. Sincerely, [1]

646

[1 minute at 120]

Dear Mr. Gray: We have just received your detailed instructions on how we should print your book, the *Smith Correspondence Manual.* I assure you that they will be followed carefully./

The matter of delivery is of considerable concern to us. Our promise to have printed and bound copies in your hands by June 15 was based//on our having all the copy by May 5. Here it is May 15, and we still have not received the copy for the last four chapters. However, we will do our utmost///to get copies to you by June 15.

When we have the complete copy, we will be in a better position to give you a firm delivery date. Sincerely yours, [2]

647

[1 minute at 125]

Dear Mr. Harper: As I told you over the telephone yesterday, we had every hope of getting all the copy of the first volume of the *Smith Correspondence Manual*/to you by May 5. Unfortunately, the company that is setting the type had a strike. The strike has been settled, and the supervisor tells us that all our work will be//completed in a few days.

We realize the difficulties under which you are working. If in spite of those difficulties you are able to get us 100 copies by///June 15 so that we can display them at the Business Management Association meeting in New York, we will be grateful. We know that we can depend on you. Yours truly, [3]

648

[1 minute at 130]

Dear Mr. Harper: I am sending you today by special delivery mail the cover design for the first volume of the *Smith Correspondence Manual*.

The same copy should/be used for the second volume, except for the change I have indicated at the top of the cover design. I am leaving it to you to make whatever dyes are necessary.//Please return the design to us as soon as it has served its purpose.

As we are a little behind schedule (through no fault of yours), we are willing to have your staff work overtime///in order to get the 100 copies we need by June 15. If we don't get those 100 copies, we stand to lose about $100,000 in sales. Sincerely yours, [4]

649

[1 minute at 135]

Dear Mr. Harper: May I thank you sincerely for your efforts in getting 100 copies of the *Smith Correspondence Manual* to us by June 15. You will be interested/to know that the copies arrived on June 14 and were immediately delivered to our booth at the Wilson Hotel where the convention of the Business Management Association//was being held.

Judging by the number of people at the booth who examined the book, we are sure we will sell more than 100,000 copies in the first year of publication. In fact,///we received orders for more than 3,000 copies at the convention.

I am today writing a letter to your president telling him what a fine service you rendered us. Sincerely, [5] [620]

Reading and Writing Practice

650

intro

raise

Transcribe:
$8

par

un·avoid·able

ex·ceed·ing

intro

guar·an·tee
month's

long-stand·ing
hyphenated before noun

[125]

651

intro

chil·dren

fas·ci·nat·ing

par

its

sim·pli·fied

fact-filled
hyphenated before noun

Transcribe:
$9

555-1878 [127]

[90]

653

un·for·tu·nate·ly

intro

intro

geo

geo

[94]

652

Transcribe:
eight

conj

cop·ies

re·cent

rea·son

re·tain

if

im·me·di·ate·ly
de·lete

CHAPTER 15

Insurance

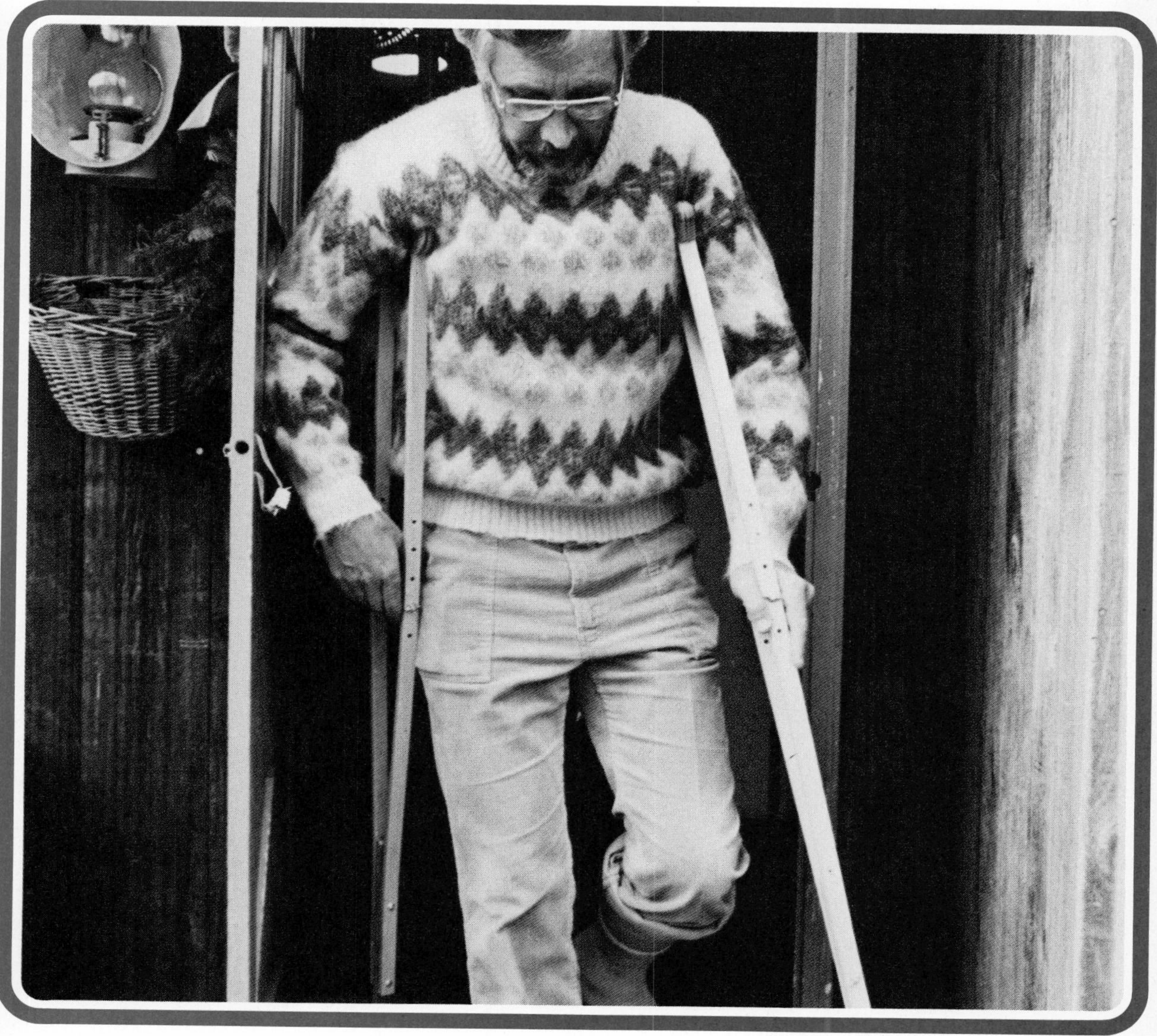

Developing Shorthand Writing Power

654 OUTLINE CONSTRUCTION

Omission of Vowel In -in The vowel in the unaccented word ending *-in* is omitted because its omission gives us a better outline.

1
2
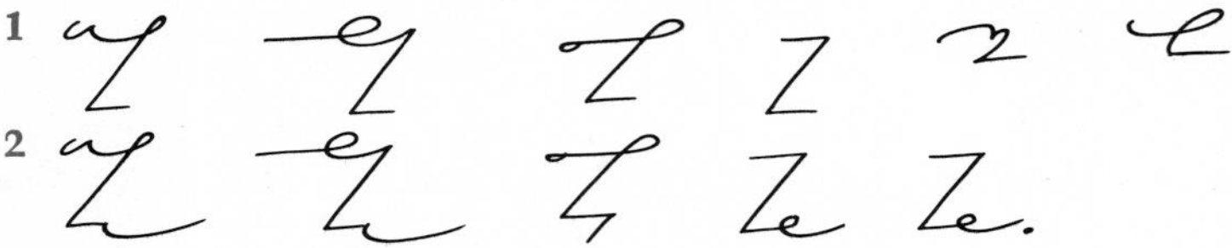

1. *Origin, margin, imagine, engine, cousin, raisin.*
2. *Original, marginal, imagination, engineer, engineering.*

Word Endings -ium, -eum, -dium The word endings *-ium, -eum* are expressed by *em; -dium,* by the *dem* blend.

-ium, -eum

1

-dium

2
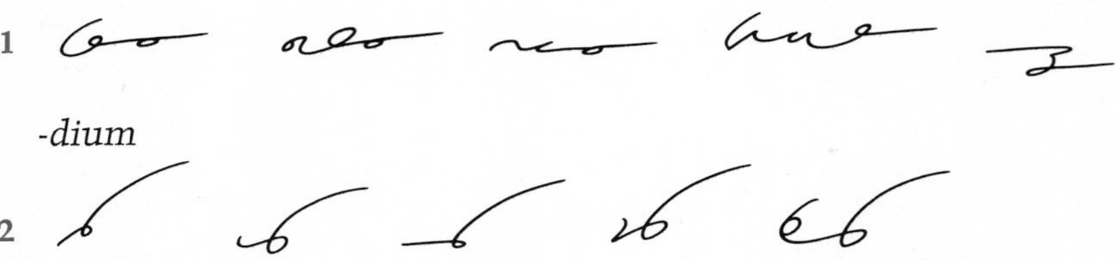

1. *Premium, uranium, chromium, petroleum, museum.*
2. *Tedium, radium, medium, stadium, palladium.*

Building Transcription Skills

655 SIMILAR-WORDS DRILL excess, access

excess That which exceeds or goes beyond; more than the usual amount.

Any excess *equipment must be disposed of before our trip.*

access Approach; admission.

The landowner has granted us access *to the property.*

Reading and Writing Practice

656 Insurance

Everything

[298]

657 LETTERS

ap intro

em·ploy·ees' conj

ne·go·ti·a·tions

pur·chas·ing

intro ac·cess

enu ben·e·fit

if avail·able

ex·cess pre·mi·ums

re·ceive

when

writ·ing

[205]

658

ap·point·ed

po·si·tion

geo

ac·knowl·edged

agen·cy

ser

ca·su·al·ty

if

[129]

Your personal appearance should reflect your personality and should be determined by your features. Let your appearance tell others what a wonderful person you are!

Developing Shorthand Writing Power

659 RECALL DRILL g

In this drill you will review the different uses of the alphabetic stroke g.

G

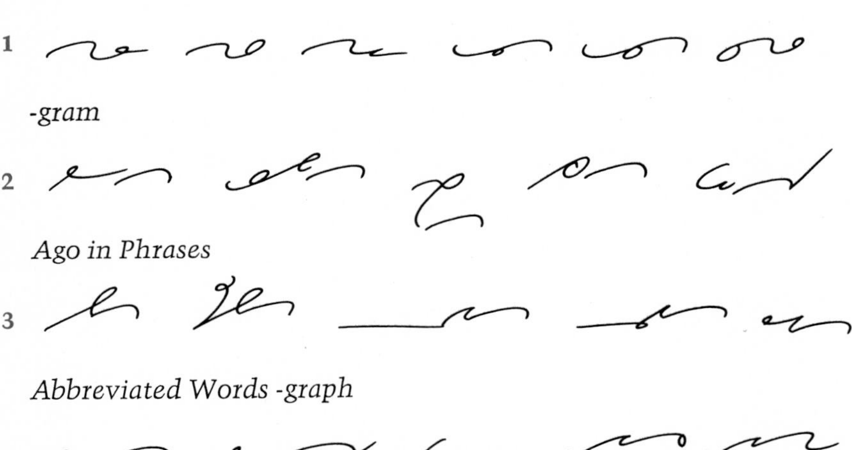

---

1. *Green, gray, grown, leg, lag, agree.*
2. *Telegram, radiogram, cablegram, diagram, programmed.*
3. *Days ago, several days ago, months ago, minutes ago, years ago.*
4. *Telegraph, telegraphed, paragraph, stenography, stenographer.*

Building Transcription Skills

660 ACCURACY PRACTICE

In this drill you will practice additional joinings of the two forms of *s*.

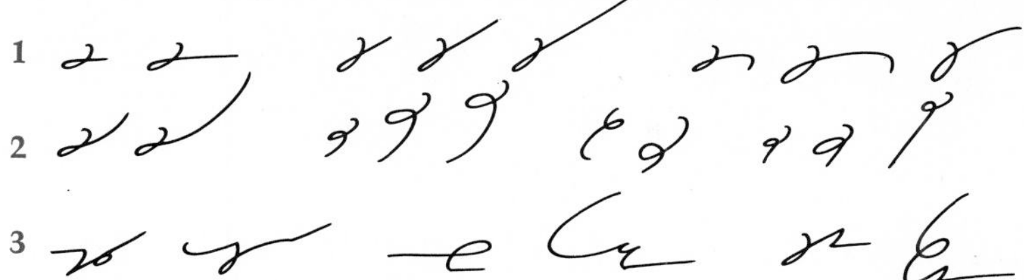

1. *Seen, seem; set, said, seated; seek, sag, sadden.*
2. *Sent, seemed; sees, safe, save; sip, face; session, sash, siege.*
3. *Institute, resident; mason, blossom; citizen, baptism.*

Writing Practice

661 PREVIEW

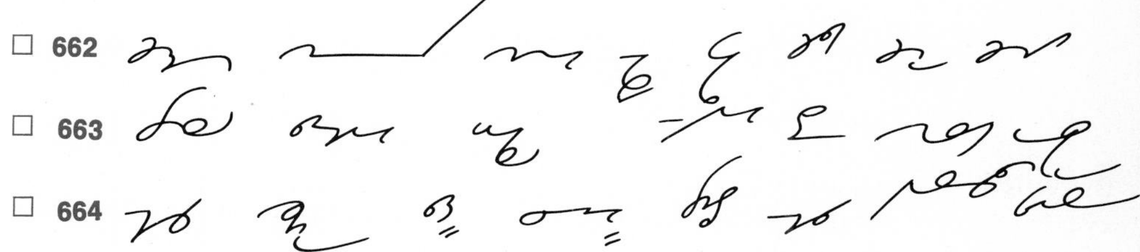

662 *Weeks ago, commented, concurs, in the past, probably, situation, security, week or two.*
663 *Backyard, youngsters, orchard, intruders, assessment, grateful, liability.*
664 *Unfortunate, casualty, United States, Americans, beautifully, institute, dramatic, portrayal.*

LETTERS

662

Dear Tom: A few weeks ago I had dinner with the district manager of a large insurance firm. He commented[1] that few of his customers agree with everything he tells them, but there is one concept on which everyone[2] concurs. That is simply that everyone needs some kind of life insurance protection.

As you know, Tom, I have[3] resisted purchasing insurance in the past. I felt that my life was quite secure and that my small family would[4] probably be well provided for in the event of my death. However, I have discussed our situation[5] with my wife, and we would both like to take a closer look at the possibility of providing ourselves with[6] greater family financial security.

Would you please call me sometime within the next week or two to set[7] up an evening appointment to explain your life insurance programs to my wife and me. Very cordially yours,[8]

663

Gentlemen: Three days ago, two small neighbor boys were playing near my backyard. My wife and I were not at home at the[9] time, and these youngsters decided to climb over my eight-foot fence and try out some fruit in my small orchard. They did[10] not realize that I had a large dog trained to repel intruders on my property. My dog attacked the boys and[11] injured one rather severely.

We have not yet received an assessment of the medical costs involved in the[12] incident, but they will likely be considerable. We have discussed the matter with the parents of both boys,[13] and I am not certain at this time whether they will bring suit against us.

During a crisis like this, I am[14] most grateful to have fine liability insurance. I have just completed a thorough investigation[15] of the terms of my policy, and it appears that I am fully protected.

I will let you know of further[16] developments in this situation; I hope it will be resolved as soon as possible. Very truly yours,[17]

664

Dear Dr. Wilson: It is unfortunate but true that you never really need insurance until it is too[18] late. Whether the discussion centers on life, casualty, liability, or health and accident insurance,[19] that statement remains valid. Fortunately, most people in the United States know that, which is one of the reasons[20] Americans enjoy greater economic security than any other people in the world.

The[21] insurance industry has done a good deal to help individuals like you and me maintain the high standard[22] of living we currently enjoy. The message of insurance is beautifully portrayed in a new 40-minute[23] film entitled *Insurance, Yesterday and Today*, prepared by the American Institute of Insurance.[24]

This is an educational film that we make available to schools, service groups, and professional[25] organizations. If your organization would be interested in seeing this dramatic portrayal of the[26] rise and growth of insurance in America free of charge, write us and reserve a date for the film. Yours truly,[27] [540]

Reading and Writing Practice

665

ar·ti·cles

intro

16

pro·vi·sions

enu

de·duct·ible

per·ils

as·sessed

par

ap·prais·er

50

vic·tim

conj

un·for·tu·nate

anx·ious

sat·is·fac·to·ri·ly

[194]

666

38762

as

its

ad·e·quate

intro

op·tion

ap

rec·om·mend·ing

[166]

667

as

par

10

ap

de·scribe

com·pa·ny's

4

ten·ta·tive

conj

[152]

Developing Shorthand Writing Power

668 WORD FAMILIES

-spect

1

-mination

2

1. *Inspect, aspect, respect, expect, prospect, self-respect, suspect.*
2. *Termination, determination, examination, nomination, elimination.*

669 FREQUENTLY USED NAMES

Last Names

1

Women's First Names

2

1. *Morris, Moses, Nelson, Phillips, Pierce, Powers.*
2. *Nancy, Patsy, Paula, Phyllis, Rachel, Ramona, Rita.*

Building Transcription Skills

670 Business Vocabulary Builder

shortchanged Deprived of something due.

abandoned Gave up; withdrew from.

termination The act of bringing to an end.

Writing Practice

671 PREVIEW

☐ 672

☐ 673

☐ 674

672 *Updated, rapidly, destroyed, current, almost, eager, provide, security.*
673 *Consistently, shortchanged, probably, independent, combination, comprehensive, directory, you want.*
674 *To make, readjust, frequently, inspected, annually, qualified, objective.*

LETTERS

672

Dear Rita: A recent examination of our files revealed that your homeowner's policy has not been[1] updated for over five years.

As you know, costs of real estate have been increasing very rapidly during the[2] past several years. In fact, during the five-year period since we wrote your insurance policy, replacement[3] costs have increased over 50 percent. Presently we would pay you only $15,000 if your home[4] were destroyed, but its current replacement cost is almost $23,000. Recent figures indicate[5] that costs will not level off in the immediate future.

We suggest that you call us soon so we can bring your[6] policy up to date. We are eager to provide you the security of proper coverage. Yours truly,[7]

673

Dear Mr. Moses: If your insurance agent consistently offers you the lowest rates in town on your[8] various insurance plans, you really might be getting shortchanged. Low premiums may be of immediate appeal,[9] but if your insurance company lets you down when you make a claim, you will probably be in real trouble.

We[10] believe you should select insurance on the basis of price, coverage, and service. Independent insurance[11] agents can provide this combination for you because they have the resources of dozens of companies at[12] their disposal. They carefully examine your needs and then recommend a comprehensive program of protection[13] that will do the best possible job. You see, Mr. Moses, independent insurance agents represent[14] you rather than a particular company, and they know every aspect of their business.

The telephone numbers[15] of local independent insurance agents are listed in the yellow pages of your directory[16] under "Insurance." Call one of them when you want helpful answers to questions about your insurance needs. Yours truly,[17]

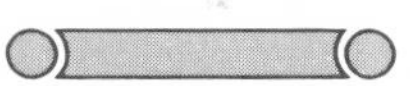

674

Dear Mrs. Nelson: Because of inflation, the replacement value of your property is constantly increasing.[18] Therefore, it is extremely important to make sure that you readjust your insurance frequently to keep[19] pace. Regardless of which company provides your insurance, you should have your coverage inspected annually[20] by a professional independent agent.

Independent insurance brokers and agents are well qualified[21] to advise you. They have no obligation to any one insurance company; consequently, they[22] can give you the kind of objective advice you need.

Speak to an independent insurance expert soon. Updating[23] your present coverage may cost a little more now, but it could save a lot more later. Very truly yours,[24] [480]

• Reading and Writing Practice

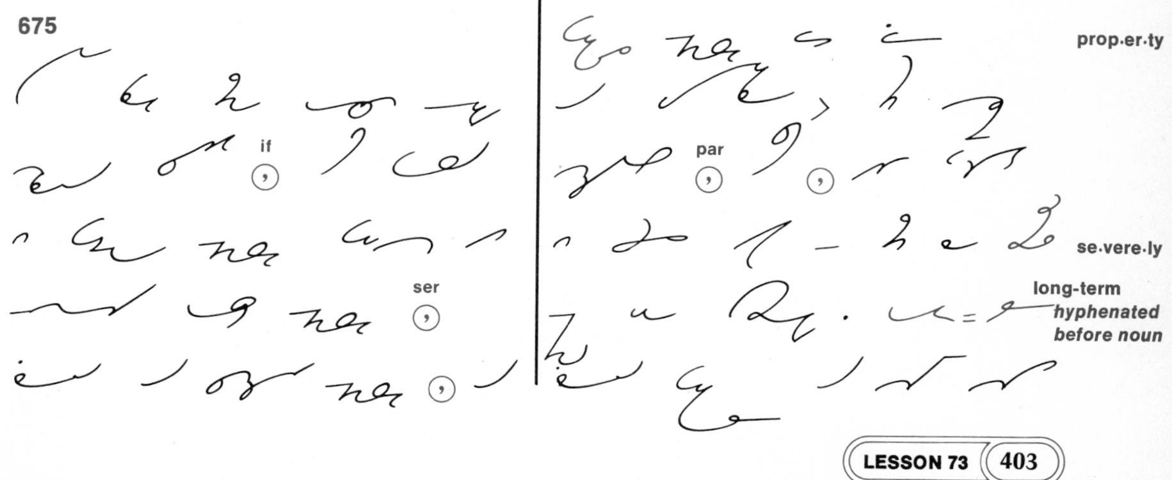

as·sis·tance

long-range *hyphenated before noun*

intro

pos·si·bil·i·ty

pennies

conj

ap·point·ment

[166]

676

received

daugh·ter

ap

pro·cess·ing

25

par

conj

intro

fourth

18

3528

nonr

to·tal

par

pre·mi·ums

un·usu·al·ly

par

semi·an·nu·al

145

55

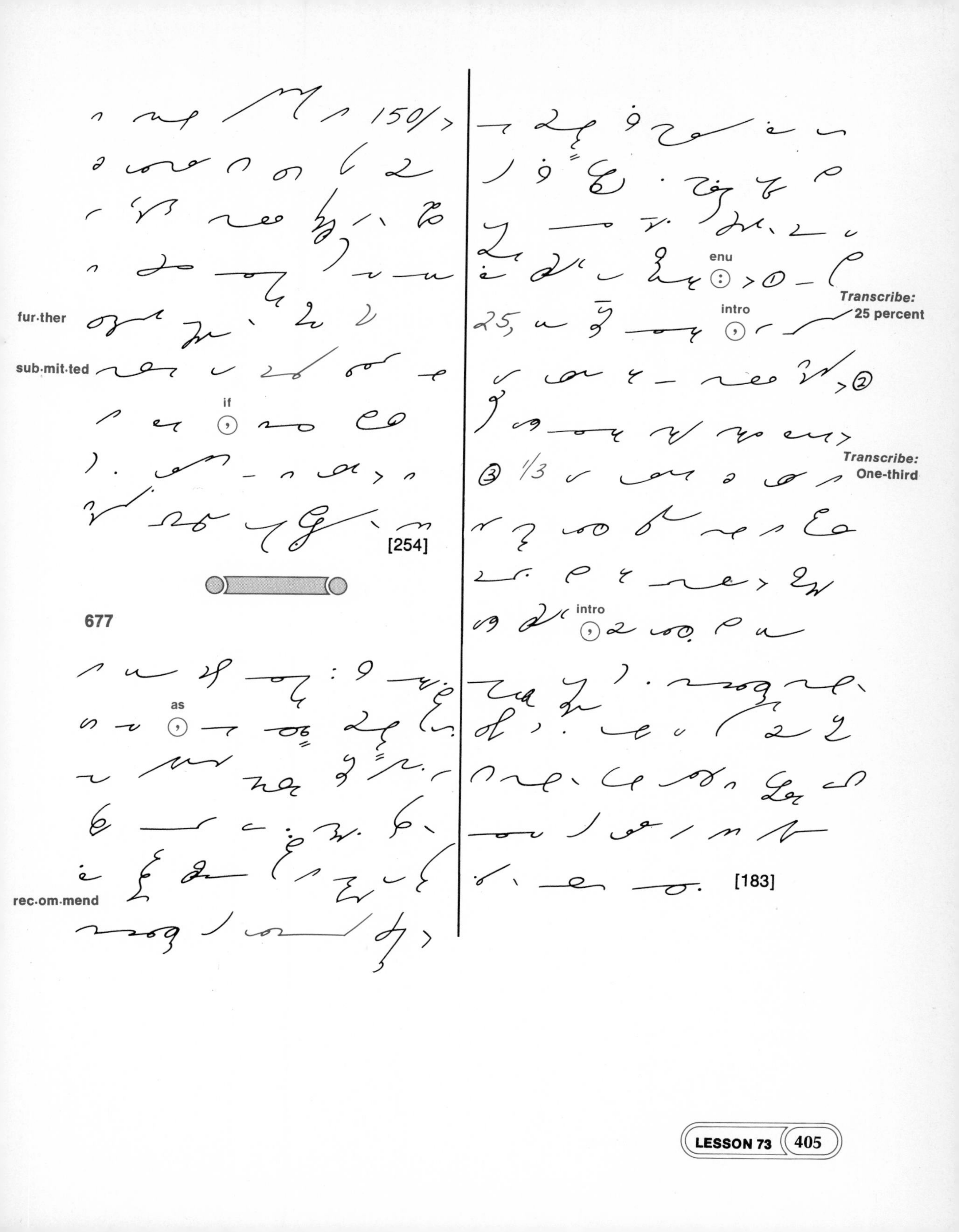

150

further

submitted

if

[254]

677

as

recommend

25

enu

intro

Transcribe: 25 percent

1/3

Transcribe: One-third

intro

[183]

Developing Shorthand Writing Power

678 FREQUENTLY USED PHRASES

Able

Glad

1. *I will be able, I will not be able, we will not be able, I should be able, I might be able, has not been able, to be able.*
2. *I will be glad, he will be glad, I would be glad, glad to say, glad to see.*

679 GEOGRAPHICAL EXPRESSIONS

Major United States Cities

1. *New York, Chicago, Los Angeles, Philadelphia, Houston, Detroit, Seattle.*
2. *Dallas, Baltimore, Washington, San Diego, Phoenix, Atlanta.*

Building Transcription Skills

680 Business Vocabulary Builder

waive To give up voluntarily.

capitalize To profit by; to turn into an advantage.

nonparticipating *(insurance)* Not having the right to share in the profits of a company.

Writing Practice

681 PREVIEW

☐ 682

☐ 683

☐ 684

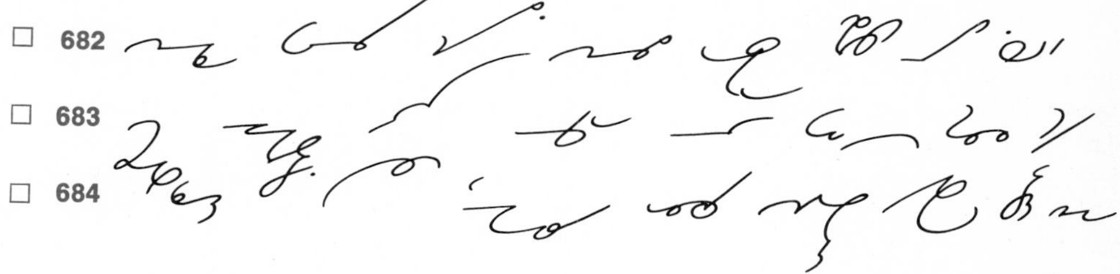

682 *Commissioner, permitted, studying, committee, liability, we hope that this, undue, hardship.*

683 *Conversation, nonparticipating, at the time, maturity, more than, program, frequently, forward.*

684 *Serious, to make, self-employed, required, contributions, disabled, spouse, one of our.*

LETTERS

682

Dear Policyholder: The insurance commissioner recently permitted New York's automobile insurance[1] companies to adjust their rates. Rate increases of up to 20 percent will be allowed under this new[2] ruling, which will become effective July 1.

After carefully studying our own cost factors, our rates[3] adjustments committee has decided to increase liability insurance premiums by 8 percent. This[4] is well below the average increase of the larger New York insurance companies.

We regret having to increase[5] our rates, but our directors find it necessary due to a great increase in our expenses during the[6] past two years. We hope that this modest rise in premiums will not represent an undue hardship to you and that[7] we will be able to continue providing for your total automobile insurance needs. Cordially yours,[8]

683

Dear Al: Recently I was discussing the subject of life insurance costs with Roger Dwyer, a friend of mine.[9] A few interesting facts emerged from our conversation.

In 1975 he purchased a nonparticipating[10] $20,000 ordinary life policy that will be paid up when he retires. At the[11] time of the purchase he was 26 years old, and he claims that the policy will be worth only[12] $13,500 at maturity. His yearly premiums for this policy are $360,[13] which is almost $50 a year more than mine. In addition, my settlement option schedule shows[14] that my policy's cash value will be almost $17,000 when I retire.

Roger lives here in[15] Philadelphia. His telephone number is 555-4787, and he would be glad to have[16] you call him and arrange an appointment to discuss his insurance program. Since Roger travels on business[17] frequently, please contact him on a weekend if possible. He is looking forward to your call. Yours very truly,[18]

684

Dear Mr. Johnson: An accident or a serious illness could keep you away from work for months or even[19] years. That is bad enough, but to make it even worse, if you are self-employed and have an ordinary retirement[20] plan, your plan would simply stop growing because you would not be able to make the required contributions.

A[21] National endowment policy keeps growing even if you are completely disabled. How? You elect in[22] advance to have us waive the premiums if you become totally disabled because of an accident or[23] illness. In addition, a National policy guarantees you and your spouse a monthly income for as long[24] as either of you live.

Before settling on any retirement plan, talk with one of our agents. Sincerely yours,[25] [500]

Reading and Writing Practice

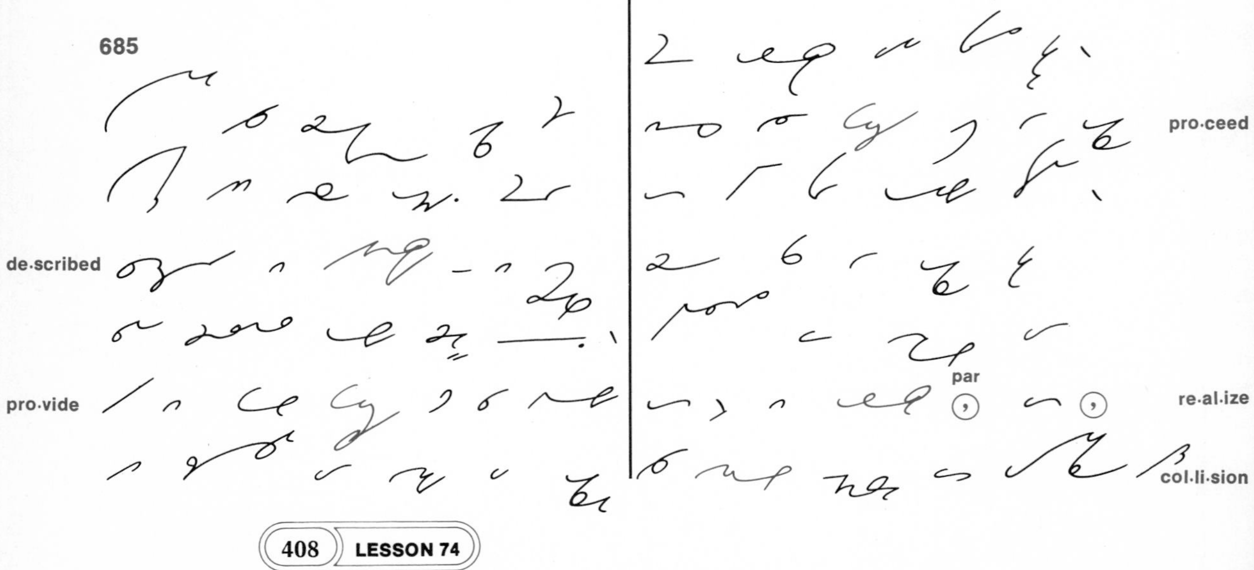

Transcribe: $100

par

arise

if

[142]

686

conj

per·son·al

Feb·ru·ary

mil·lions
wom·en

conj

intro

cap·i·tal·ize

po·ten·tial

for·ward

[173]

seek·ing

687

ap

[46]

Secretarial Tip
The Left-Handed Writer

There are two types of left-handed writers. (1) The "regular" left-hander, who uses basically the same writing position as the right-hander, except that the notebook slants from right to left rather than from left to right. (2) The one who is sometimes facetiously called the "upside down" left-hander; that is, the hand is above the line of writing.

If you belong to the first group, you may find it helpful to start writing in the second column and finish in the first column, as indicated in Figure 1. You may use the same method of turning pages described for the right-hander on page 105 except, of course, it will be your right hand that turns up the corner of the page and eventually turns the page.

If you belong to the second group of left-handers, it may help you to write (in the second column first) from the "bottom" of the page toward the binding as illustrated in Figure 2. This procedure eliminates the irritating contact of your writing hand with the spiral binding of the notebook.

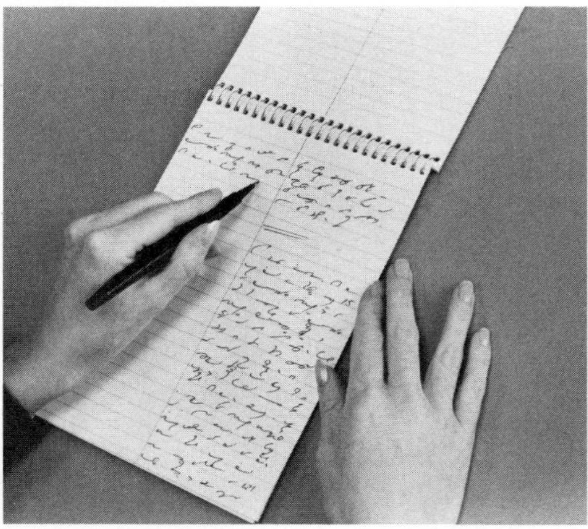

Figure 1: The "regular" left-handed writer may find it helpful to start writing in the second column and finish up in the first column.

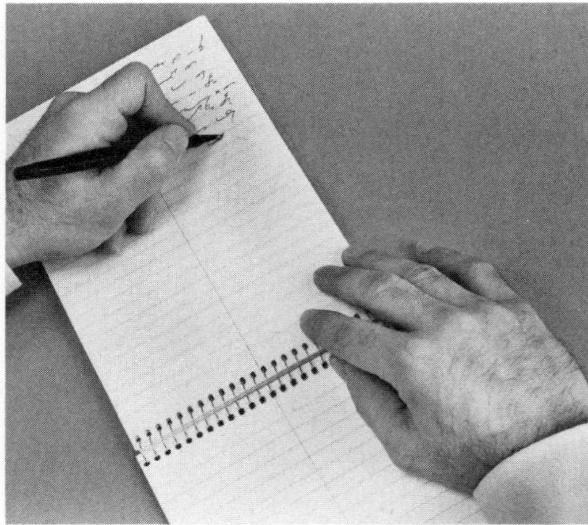

Figure 2: The "upside-down" left-handed writer may find it more comfortable to write (in the second column first) from the "bottom" of the page toward the binding.

Letter of Application

273 North College Avenue
Salida, CA 95368
May 23, 19--

Mr. Ralph Smith, Personnel Manager
Perkins-Nash Engineering Company
Salida, CA 95368

Dear Mr. Smith:

Mrs. Ruth Kent, of the Kent Insurance Agency, has suggested that I apply for a position as stenographer in your company. Mrs. Kent, a friend of my family's for many years, has talked with me on a number of occasions about my future, and she has recommended your company as one of the most desirable in Salida.

Here is a brief summary of my education and experience:

<u>Education</u>: Graduate of Salida High School, June, 19--

Subjects: Typewriting--55 words a minute on straight copy. Able to set up letters, reports, and various kinds of business forms.

Shorthand--120 words a minute. Can transcribe accurately at the rate of approximately 30 words a minute.

English--have made good grades in English throughout high school. Enjoy writing compositions.

Other subjects--Accounting, filing, office machines, business law, secretarial practice.

<u>Experience</u>: One year as part-time secretary at Griffin Department Store on Saturdays and holidays.

Two summers as typist and receptionist for the Salida Real Estate Agency.

<u>References</u>: Miss Agnes Miller, Business Teacher, Salida High School
Mr. Fred Trayton, Manager, Salida Real Estate Agency
Mrs. Ruth Kent, Kent Insurance Agency, 21 Main Street, Salida

May I have an opportunity to come in to talk with you? Since I am in school during the day and cannot be reached by phone until after 4 o'clock, perhaps you would prefer to write me. If you do wish to telephone after 4 o'clock, my number is 476-1042.

Sincerely yours,

Elizabeth Davenport

Elizabeth Davenport

One good way to obtain an interview for that first job is to write an effective letter of application to the firms in which you think you might like to work. Here is an example of a letter that will certainly make a favorable impression on the reader and invite a personal interview.

Developing Shorthand Writing Power

688 WORD BEGINNINGS AND ENDINGS

-ship

1

Mis-

2

For-, Fore-

3

---

1. *Friendship, hardship, steamship, relationship, ownership, partnership, leadership.*
2. *Mistake, misunderstand, mistook, misapprehension, misplace, mystery.*
3. *Afford, fortunately, forget, foreclose, foresight, foregone, unfortunately.*

Building Transcription Skills

689 Business Vocabulary Builder

phenomenal Extraordinary; remarkable.

malpractice The failure to exercise proper professional skill, resulting in injury, loss, or damage.

misfortune Bad luck.

Progressive Speed Builder (120-140)

The letters in this Progressive Speed Builder range from 120 to 140 words a minute. If you can take these letters from dictation and read them back, you need not fear the speed of any dictator, even the most rapid.

Remember, don't stop writing!

690 **PREVIEW**

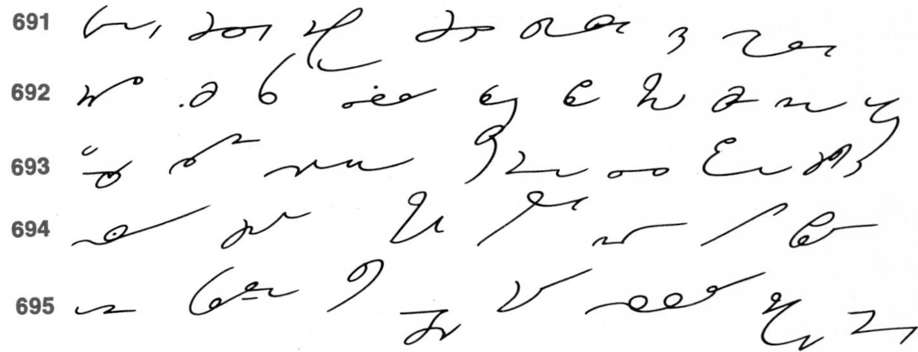

691 *Partnership, financial, stability, family's, outlines, yours, compliments.*
692 *Suddenly, away, be able, inherit, survive, easier, assured, why not, one of our, representatives.*
693 *Overnight, they do not, control, former, immediate, explore, situation.*
694 *Created, sounder, agents, details, one of them, to do, appointment.*
695 *Ruin, breadwinner, however, impact, funded, guaranteed, established, information.*

LETTERS

691

[1 minute at 120]

Dear Mr. Baker: If you have your own business or own a piece of a partnership, we have a booklet that you should read. It explains how you can assure/the financial stability of your business through business life insurance. It suggests ways in which you can cushion your business against the loss of a partner or a//key person. It also describes how you can protect your family's interests. It even outlines a way in which you can provide employees' benefits at very low cost///to your firm.

Would you like to have a copy of this booklet? It is yours with our compliments if you will request one on your company's letterhead. Yours very truly, [1]

692

[1 minute at 125]

Dear Mr. Baker: Have you ever stopped to think what would happen to your business if your partner suddenly passed away? Will you be able to adjust? Who will inherit your/partner's share? How much will the loss of your partner affect your business? Will it survive? The Mutual Life Insurance Company can make it a lot easier for you to answer//these questions. Here is how.

Right now, you and your partner sign a business life insurance agreement with us. If your partner dies, you are assured the right to buy his or her share///of the business. We provide the cash. This plan also protects your family.

Why not call one of our representatives to find out how easy it is. Very sincerely yours, [2]

693

[1 minute at 130]

Dear Mr. Baker: Suppose you are a partner in a good business. Suddenly one day your partner dies, and overnight you find yourself in business with your partner's family. They are/nice people, but they do not know anything about your business. This can cause you many problems.

You can protect yourself against these problems by purchasing our business life insurance.// This insurance helps you keep control of your business and at the same time gives your former partner's family immediate cash for the value of his or her share of the business.

Before///we sell you this insurance, we will explore your situation and develop a plan that will do the best job for you.

Simply call us to arrange for an appointment. Sincerely yours, [3]

694

[1 minute at 135]

Dear Mr. Baker: If you are lucky you may never have to face the difficult problems created by the death of a business partner.

But why trust to luck? There is a much sounder way/to protect your share of a partnership. Take out business life insurance. You and your partner sign an agreement and fund it with National Business Insurance. If your partner dies, your// policy provides you with the cash necessary to purchase his share of the business.

National insurance agents can give you all the details about business life insurance. Why not/// invite one of them to give you these details. All you have to do is indicate on the enclosed card the time our agent may call or arrange an appointment by calling our office. Sincerely yours, [4]

695

[1 minute at 140]

Dear Mr. Baker: In many ways, a business is like a family. The death of a partner or a key person can ruin a company just as the death of a family breadwinner can/make things difficult for a family.

However, you can lessen the impact of the loss of a vital person in your business by buying business life insurance. This insurance makes it possible//for you to get full title to the business upon the death of a partner.

If you should die first, an agreement funded by business life insurance would create a guaranteed market for your///interest at a price you established.

If you would like detailed information on how business life insurance can be made to work for you, invite one of our agents to visit you. Sincerely yours, [5] [650]

Reading and Writing Practice

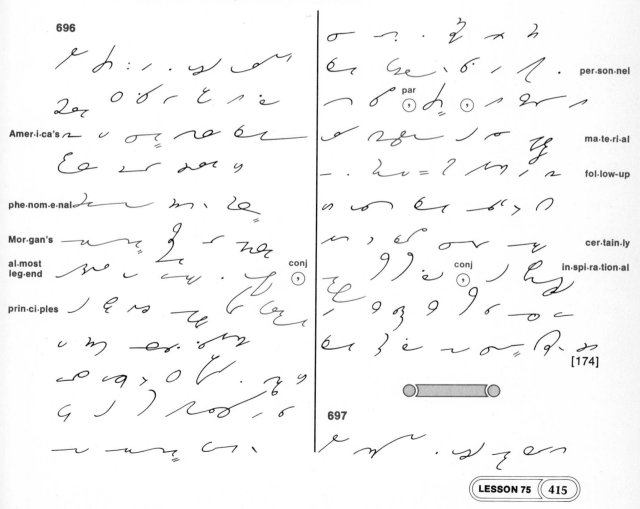

696

Amer·i·ca's

phe·nom·e·nal

Mor·gan's

al·most

leg·end

conj

prin·ci·ples

par

per·son·nel

ma·te·ri·al

fol·low-up

cer·tain·ly

conj

in·spi·ra·tion·al

[174]

697

mal·prac·tice

intro

mir·a·cle

lives

intro

un·sat·is·fied pa·tients

intro

intro

sym·pa·the·tic

juries

Transcribe: 600 percent

intro

par

sim·ply

ris·ing

ev·ery·body's

conj

es·cape

[197]

The person who reads a newspaper every day and who keeps up to date on what is going on in the world can't help but be a more valuable employee as well as a more interesting person.

CHAPTER

16 Food

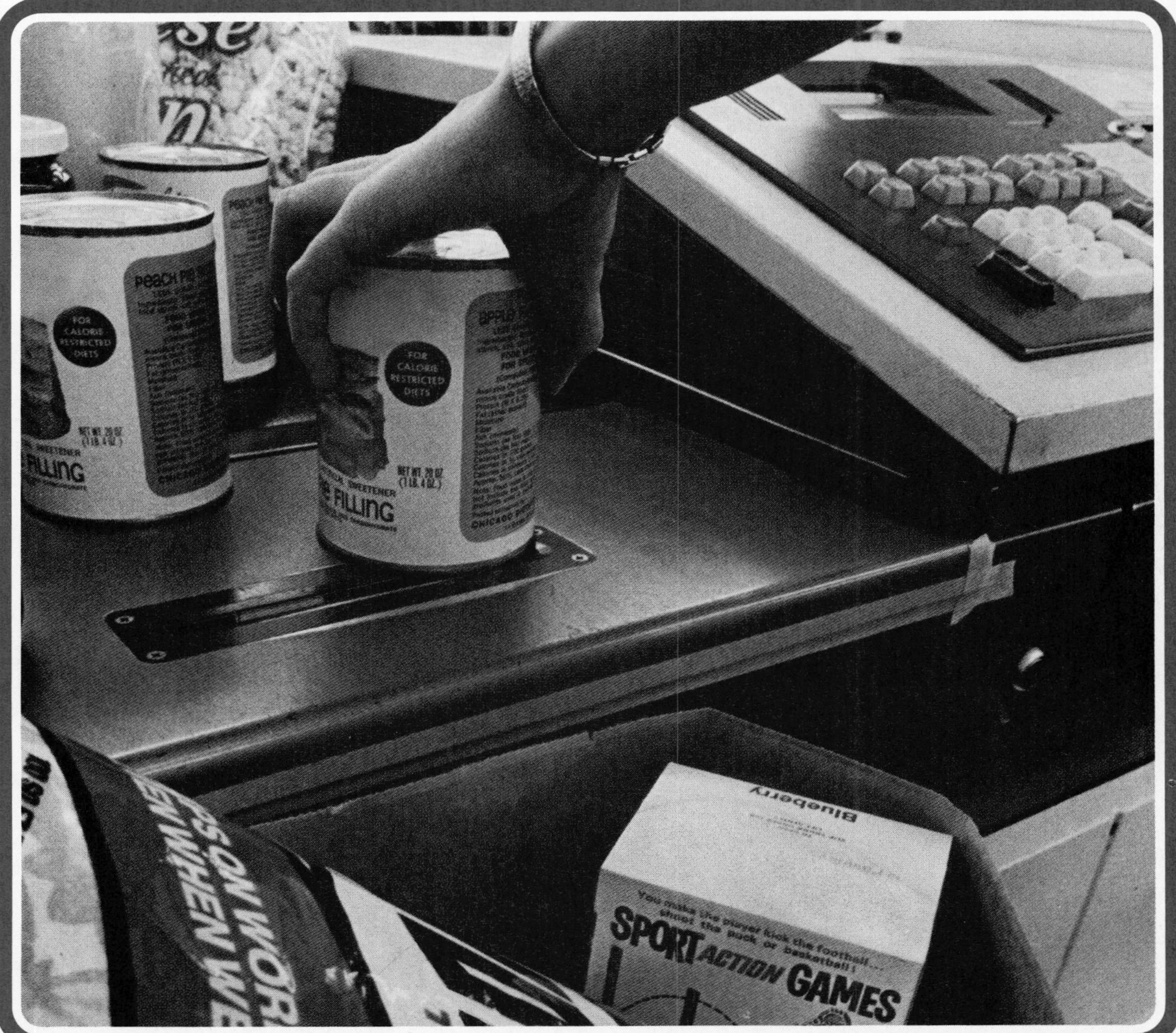

Developing Shorthand Writing Power

698 OUTLINE CONSTRUCTION

Word Endings -uate, -uation, -uity In writing the endings *-uate, -uation, -uity,* we obtain more legible outlines by including the *e* in the diphthong.

1. *Situate, graduate, evaluate, actuate, punctuate.*
2. *Situation, graduation, evaluation, continuity, ingenuity, annuity.*

Building Transcription Skills

699 SIMILAR-WORDS DRILL prominent, permanent

prominent Noted; standing out.

Lee's reputation as a prominent *sports figure is well established.*

permanent Not subject to change; lasting.

They erected a permanent *memorial at the college.*

Reading and Writing Practice

700 Nutrition

The second

[282]

701 LETTERS

its in·spec·tors'

it

en·cour·ag·ing

intro

13

prom·i·nent

min·i·mum

30

26

re·quired

eval·u·ate

as

se·cu·ri·ty

it

man·age·ment

suc·cess

par

[162]

702

ad·van·tages

intro

sum·ma·ry

match

com·pet·i·tors

re·al·ized

conj

fluc·tu·at·ed

par

off·set

ser

board's

[147]

703

al·most

nonr

es·sen·tial

plain

nc

lan·guage

ap

par

and o

when

[113]

Developing Shorthand Writing Power

704 RECALL DRILL nt blend

In this drill you will review the uses of the *nt* blend.

-nt

1

-nd

2

Ind-, Int-

3

End-, Ent-, Ant-

4

Phrases and Amounts

5

---

1. *Print, grant, events, currently, different, slant, plant.*
2. *Spend, expend, brand, ground, mind, defended, refunding.*
3. *Indirect, independent, index, intact, integrity, intellect.*
4. *Endorse, endowment, entail, entitle, anticipate, anticipation.*
5. *He doesn't, I don't, I wouldn't, it wasn't, I couldn't, $600, $900.*

Building Transcription Skills

705 ACCURACY PRACTICE

In this drill you will practice the joining of the diphthongs to the various alphabetic strokes of Gregg Shorthand.

1. *Use, fuse, views; continuation, situation; out, now, loud.*
2. *Toy, oil, voice, loyal, soil, boil.*
3. *Tie, might, iron, pine, dine, sight, silence.*

● Writing Practice

706 PREVIEW

707 *Florida, of course, next year, I have been able, profitable, availability, suitable, unusual.*

708 *Supermarket, consequently, disappointed, further, transparent, lengths, next time.*

709 *Byword, unfortunately, upward, dissatisfaction, as a result, distributing, encouraged, attitudes.*

LETTERS

707

Dear Gary: Because of freezing temperatures experienced in the Florida citrus region this year, it appears[1] that our orange crop will be about 35 percent below last year's harvest. This is bad news for everyone,[2] of course, and consumers will have to anticipate paying higher prices for oranges and orange juice[3] next year.

I have been able to find a local independent processor who still has most of last year's supplies[4] intact. I can purchase almost enough juice to satisfy our usual yearly demand at a cost that is[5] several hundred dollars below current market prices. Considering the certainty of increasing prices,[6] this could be profitable for us.

I am having difficulty, however, trying to find a place to[7] store the juice should we purchase it. Please investigate the availability of suitable storage space in[8] your locality. This is an unusual opportunity we cannot afford to pass up. Yours truly,[9]

708

Dear Mr. Powers: It used to be the policy of the National Supermarket to pack our meat with the[10] better side down. Consequently, you were never disappointed when you got home and unwrapped the package.

Today[11] we have gone one step further; we use transparent trays so that you can see both sides of the meat before you buy it.[12] The trays are made of a special plastic that will not soften, break, or leak.

We go to great lengths to bring our customers[13] what we believe is the best in meat, and this special tray is another step in that direction.

The next time you[14] are in the National Supermarket, stop at the meat department and see our meats packed in these trays. Yours truly,[15]

709

Dear Mr. Wright: A motto that used to be the byword of any retail business is "The customer is always[16] right." Unfortunately, we find that the principles contained in that simple phrase have been hidden away in[17] the back rooms of too many grocery stores in our area.

Customer complaints have increased more than 60[18] percent this year, and our office is concerned with the upward trend in consumer dissatisfaction. As a result,[19] we have prepared a simple booklet that we are distributing to all retail food outlets in the valley.[20] It is entitled *The Customer's Point of View*. I am enclosing enough copies of this publication for[21] your entire staff, and I strongly recommend that your employees be encouraged to read it.

We believe that this[22] one small step can help us restore employee concern for our customers' attitudes and feelings. Cordially yours,[23] [460]

Reading and Writing Practice

710

Eas·ter

ap

conj

too

gra·cious

and o

par

ta·ble

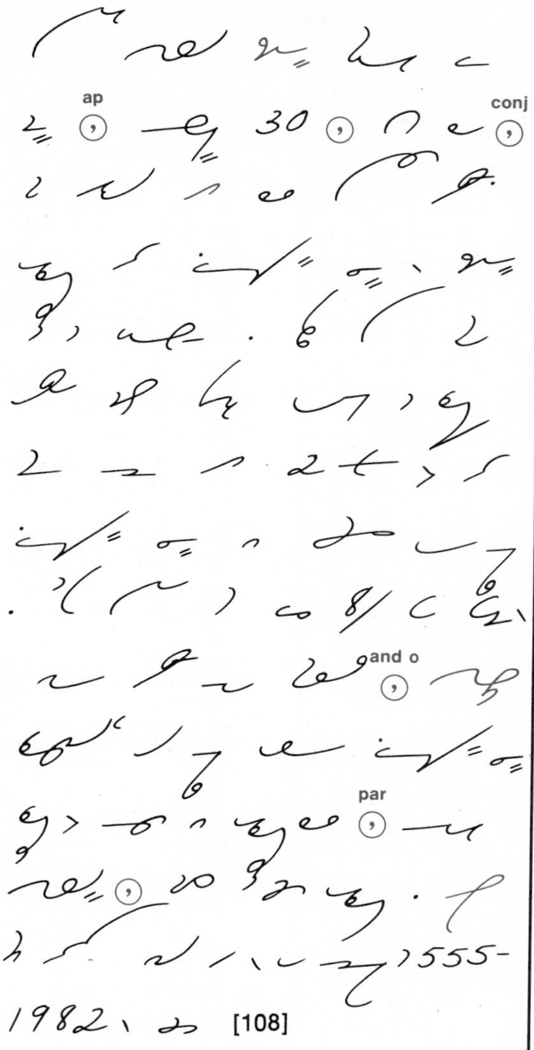

[108]

711

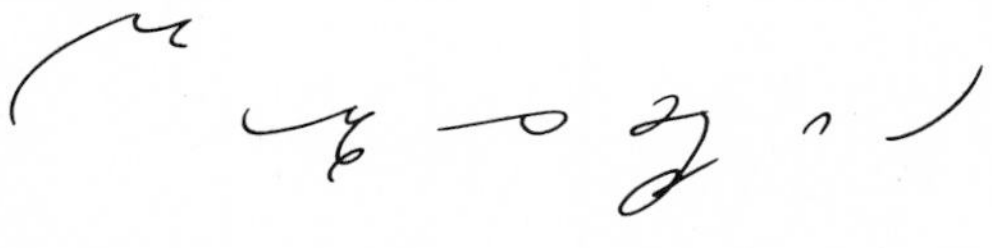

ex·cit·ing

ap

Transcribe: 8 p.m.

as

cur·rent

dried

con·se·quent·ly

intro

di·rec·tor

well-bal·anced *hyphenated before noun*

and o

de·li·cious

ap

for·ward

and o

[138]

en·joy·able

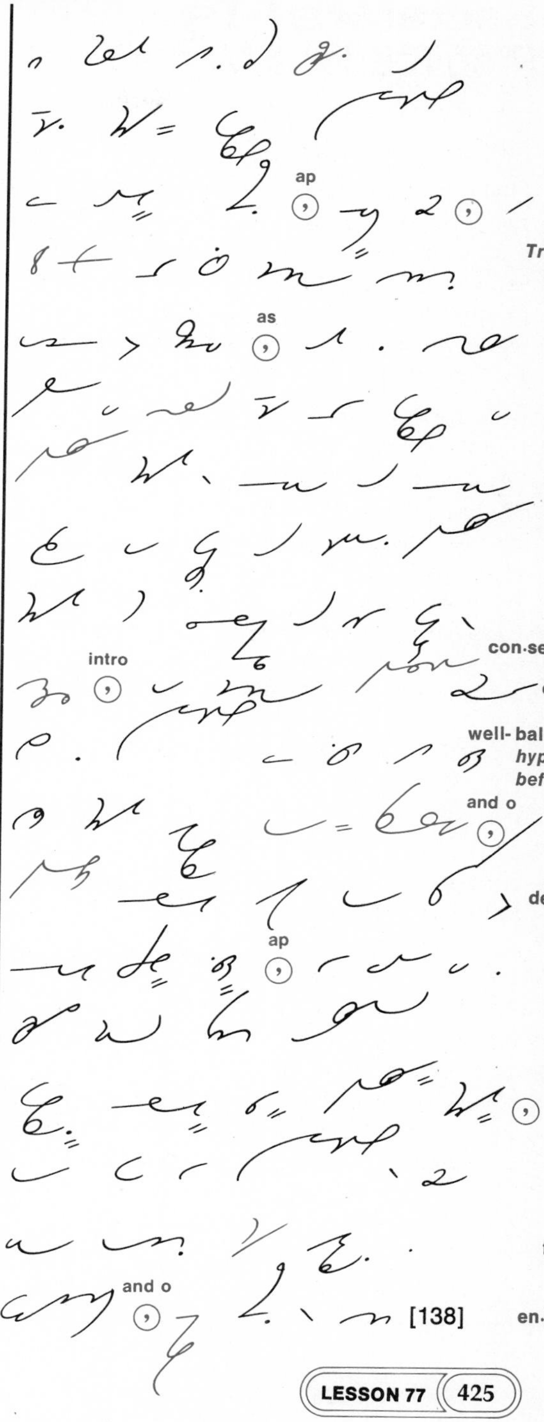

Secretarial Tip
Proofreader's Marks

One of your duties as a secretary may be to type speeches, advertising copy, reports, memorandums, and so on. Usually your employer will ask you to prepare a rough draft to be revised and polished. To save time, proofreader's marks may be used to show some of the changes you are to make. If you are familiar with the meaning of proofreader's marks, you will be able to interpret the changes quickly and accurately when you type the final copy. Here are some of the more frequently used proofreader's marks:

	Mark	*Meaning*	*Example*
^	(caret)	Insert	I will ^ make room for the desk. (, of course,)
^		Insert comma	I will see Alice on Friday ^ March 10.
^		Insert apostrophe	I have Janes book.
ℓ	(delete)	Take out	We cannot come on ~~Monday,~~ January 15.
.....	(stet)	Retain the words that have been crossed out	The booklet will contain about ~~120~~ pages.
¶	(paragraph)	Insert paragraph	The order is incorrect. We will find out who is responsible.
∽	tr	Transpose	The class was told to carefully follow all instructions.
○	sp	Spell out	The film took 6 minutes.
#		Insert space	The value ofthe work was questioned.
lc	(diagonal)	Type lower case	The United States is made up of fifty States.
≡		Capitalize	He lived in the united states.
⁀		Close up	The field trip was worth while.
//		Align	In this study we counted several hundred thousand words of material.
⌒		Run in; no paragraph	The students will be present at the meeting. They will participate in the program.

HOW TO USE NOTES IN REVIEWING

Notes are virtaully indispensable in reviewing and preparing for examinations. An even more permanent value of notes is that they serve as a "memory Storehouse" for you; They are all ways available to refresh your thinking, your recall, your memory.

USING YOUR NOTES IN REVIEWING

Reviewing is a worth-while process in learning. We tend to forget what we learn, and reviewing is an effective means of relearning. In addition through reviewing we often learn things that were not learned--or only partially learned--the first time.

Notes are an invaluable source of material for reviewing, whether they were made from reading a book, from a discussion, or from listening to a lecture.

Review your notes promptly. By reviewing notes promptly, you need less time to relearn and to fix previous learning. Also, notes can be "filled in" if need be, with pertinent bits of information, comments, facts, or ideas that were omitted when the notes were first made. reviewing promptly also givesyou an opportunity to change the content or organization of your notes while they are still fresh in mind. For example, a point made in the latter part of a lecture may have significant bearing on a point made in the early part of the lecture.

Be sure that you organise your notes carefully. One effective system is to make your notesin outline form. Leave lots of space around yournotes so that you can make insertions latter if you have to.

A page of manuscript illustrating the use of proofreader's marks.

LESSON 78

Developing Shorthand Writing Power

712 WORD FAMILIES

-form

1 

-tive

2 

1. *Uniform, inform, conform, perform, reform, performance, information.*
2. *Relative, informative, positive, sensitive, constructive, instructive.*

713 FREQUENTLY USED NAMES

Last Names

1 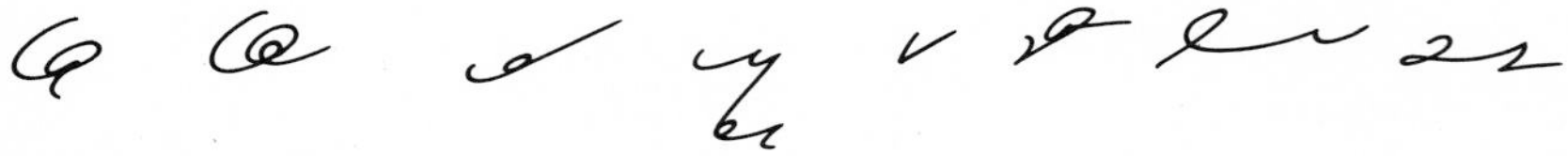

Men's First Names

2 

1. *Price, Prior, Reed, Rogers, Short, Stein, Taylor, Wilson.*
2. *Richard, Robert, Ray, Samuel, Stephen, Thomas, William.*

Building Transcription Skills

714 Business Vocabulary Builder

emporium A store.

forthcoming About to appear; approaching.

elementary Basic; simple.

Writing Practice

715 PREVIEW

☐ 716
☐ 717
☐ 718

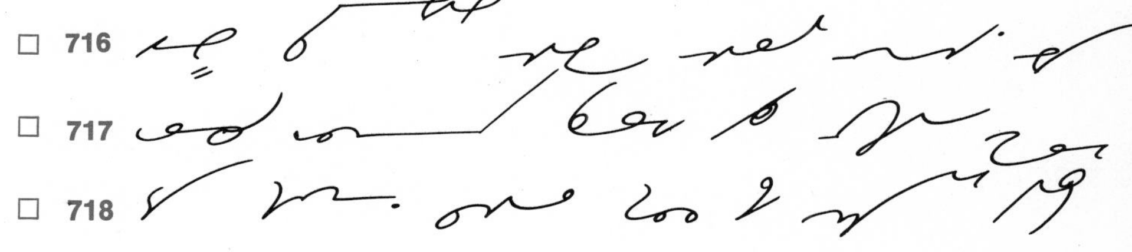

716 *Thomas, administration, nutritional, nutrients, including, next time.*
717 *Remind, recommended, balanced, diet, individual, compliments.*
718 *System, forthcoming, actually, frequently, effort, customers, derive.*

LETTERS

716

Dear Mrs. Thomas: Recently the Food and Drug Administration has encouraged food manufacturers to[1] provide uniform information about the nutritional content of their products. This information can[2] help you to:

1. Become more aware of key nutrients needed for good nutrition and good general health.

2.[3] Recognize the specific nutrients present in a given product.

3. Compare the nutritive values and[4] relative costs of different foods.

We at the Wilson Market are including this nutrition information on[5] many of our private brands. Look for it on our labels the next time you shop at Wilson's. Very cordially yours,[6]

717

Dear Mrs. Stephens: Because next week is National Nutrition Week, we thought this would be a good time to remind[7] our customers of the four basic food groups and the recommended amounts to serve in your daily meal plan. You[8] will find this helpful information in the enclosed publication.

Good nutrition is based on a balanced diet,[9] which, in turn, helps an individual to maintain proper body weight and good general health.

Please accept[10] this informative publication with the compliments of the National Supermarket. Very truly yours,[11]

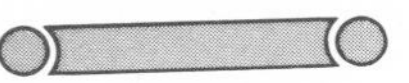

718

Dear Mrs. Stein: At the Taylor Food Market we have a system that warns you of forthcoming price increases. Every[12] week we post a list of any price increases (such as those that we receive from manufacturers) a full[13] seven days before we actually change our prices. You will also find tags on many frequently purchased items[14] showing the exact day on which the price increase will be in effect.

This is another effort on our part[15] to help our customers derive the greatest benefits possible from their food dollars. Very cordially yours,[16] [320]

Reading and Writing Practice

719

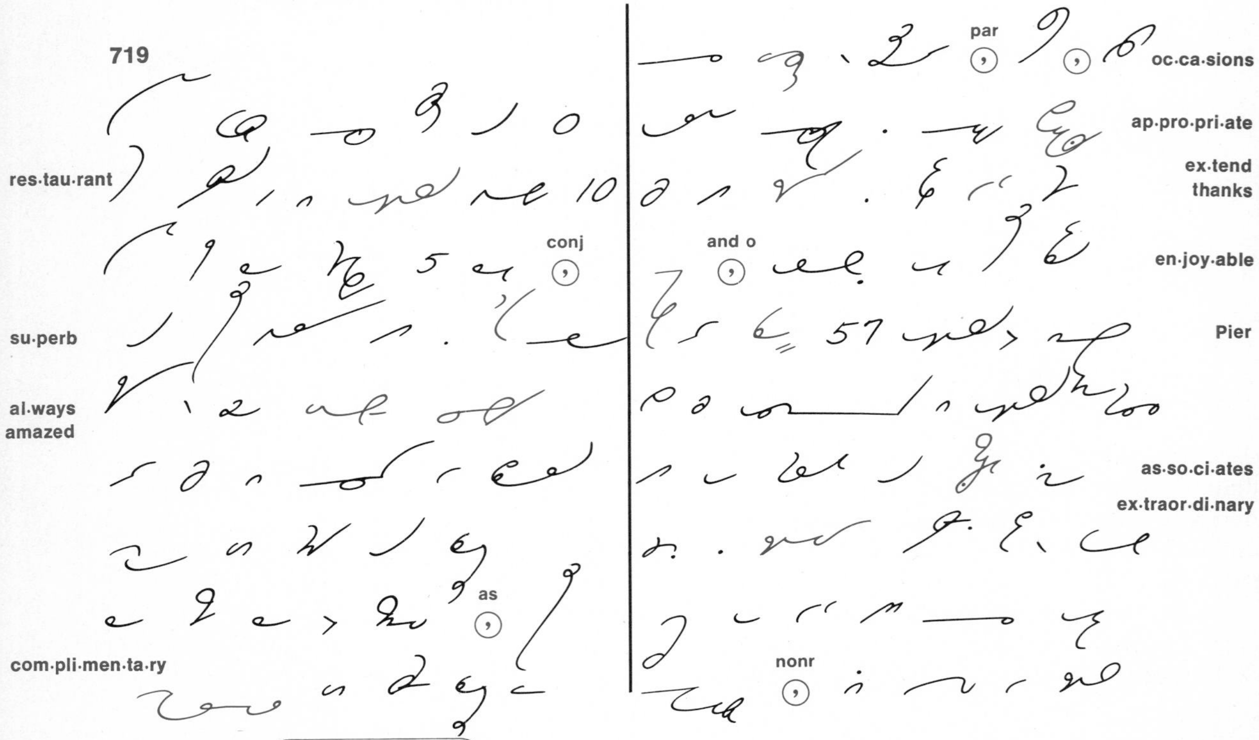

res·tau·rant

conj

su·perb

al·ways

amazed

as

com·pli·men·ta·ry

par

oc·ca·sions

ap·pro·pri·ate

ex·tend

thanks

and o

en·joy·able

Pier

as·so·ci·ates

ex·traor·di·nary

nonr

lev·el

57 [165]

720

when

guar·an·tee

pur·chas·ing

intro

em·po·ri·um

if

month's

over·head

nc

intro

intro

ser

el·e·men·ta·ry

mile·age

week's

re·ac·tion

food-mar·ket·ing *hyphenated before noun*

[187]

721

Transcribe:
35 percent

35,

intro

chil·dren's

el·e·men·ta·ry

conj

cont

intro

as

stress·ing

[181]

722

when

nonr

rushed

pro·duce

if

[87]

Developing Shorthand Writing Power

723 FREQUENTLY USED PHRASES

Many

Some

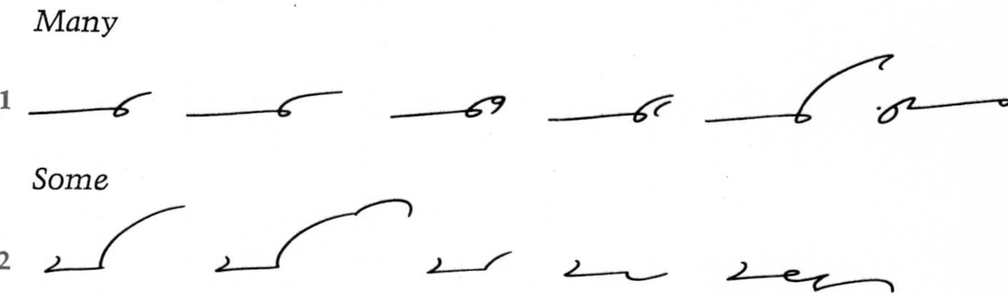

1. *Many of the, many of them, many of these, many things, many times, how many.*
2. *Some time, some time ago, some of the, some of our, some years ago.*

724 GEOGRAPHICAL EXPRESSIONS

Major United States Cities

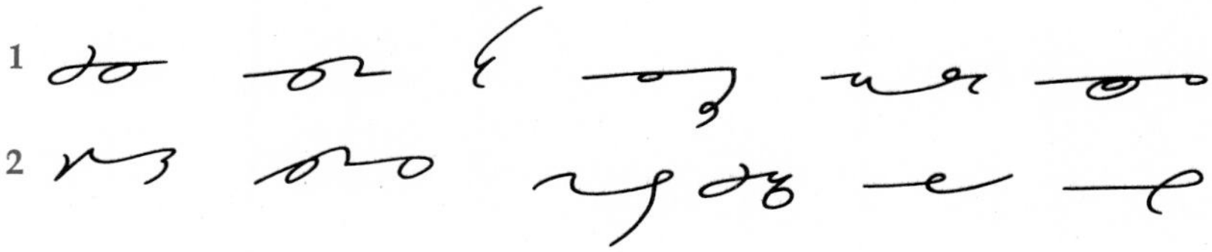

1. *San Antonio, Macon, Boston, Memphis, New Orleans, Miami.*
2. *St. Louis, Tacoma, Cleveland, San Jose, Milwaukee, Minneapolis.*

Building Transcription Skills

725 Business Vocabulary Builder

column A special feature or article appearing regularly in a newspaper.

gimmicks Catchy devices used to promote business (usually in advertising).

elsewhere In another place.

Writing Practice

726 PREVIEW

□ 727

□ 728

□ 729

727 *Advertising, area, coupons, column, tempting, recipes, entertaining, helpful.*
728 *Supermarket, gimmicks, unconditional, elsewhere, reasonable, result, let us have.*
729 *Miami, to celebrate, any one of our, any time, reduction, already, outstanding.*

LETTERS

727

Dear Mrs. Davis: If you are looking for better ways to stretch your food dollars, let the *Minneapolis Times*[1] Food Day pages be your guide.

Every Wednesday these special Food Day pages carry the advertising of many[2] of the large food stores in your area. They offer you a big selection of the best food and plenty of[3] money-saving coupons.

In addition, every Wednesday you will find Mary Wilson's food column, which brings you many[4] tempting recipes as well as interesting stories about food.

So for better shopping, eating, and entertaining[5] every week, take time to read the helpful food pages of the *Minneapolis Times.* Very cordially yours,[6]

728

Dear Mrs. Gates: At the New Orleans Supermarket, we do not believe in gimmicks. We believe in something[7] simple—value. And our unconditional money-back guarantee assures you that you get value.

Our policy[8] has won us many friends over the years. People like to shop in our store. Many of them refuse to shop elsewhere.[9] Our store is always clean. Our food is always fresh. Our prices are always reasonable.

Some of the most important[10] improvements we have made recently have been the result of suggestions made to us by our customers. If[11] you have any suggestions that will make our store an even more pleasant place to shop, please let us have them. As[12] president, I assure you that any suggestions will be acknowledged and acted upon. Very sincerely yours,[13]

729

Dear Neighbor: We are proud to announce that the Save-More Markets are opening two new stores in Miami—one on[14] Fifth Street at Parker Road and the other on the corner of Tenth and Division Streets. The addition of these two[15] new stores makes Save-More the largest grocery chain in Florida, and we are happy about the many friends we[16] have served during our 35 years of operation in this state.

To celebrate the grand opening of our[17] two new stores, we are giving our customers a coupon worth 50 cents on every $10 purchase they make[18] in any one of our stores. These coupons may be used as cash any time during the current year. The discount amounts[19] to a 5 percent reduction on our already low prices.

If you are not among our regular[20] customers, we hope you will take advantage of this outstanding opportunity to save money and learn more about[21] our products and our service. We look forward to having you as a regular customer. Cordially yours,[22] [440]

Reading and Writing Practice

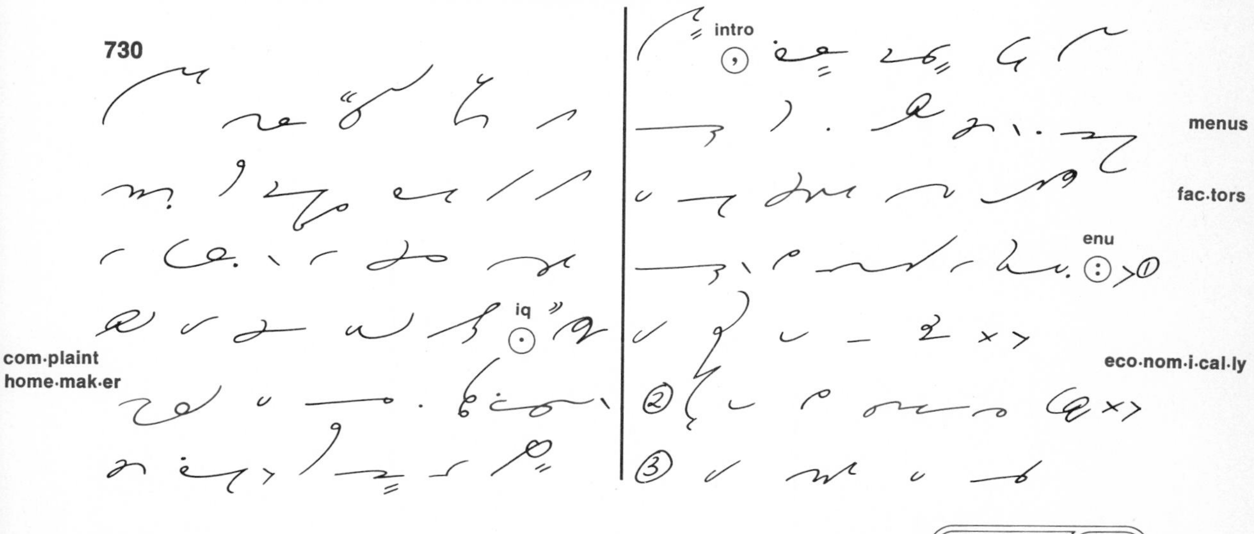

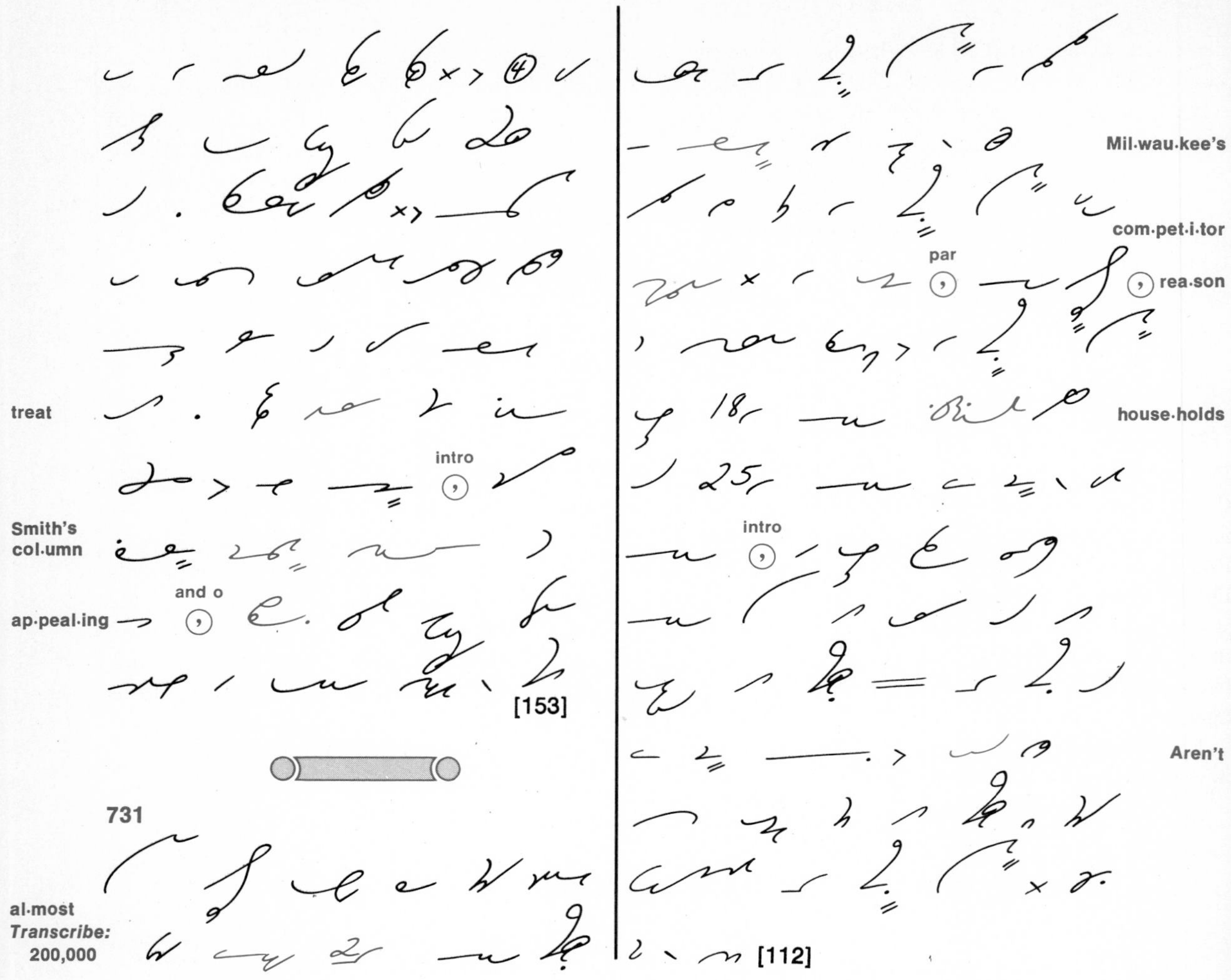

When you can't say anything nice about another person, you will be wise to follow the example of Calvin Coolidge, who said, "I have never been hurt by anything I didn't say."

Developing Shorthand Writing Power

732 WORD BEGINNINGS AND ENDINGS

Electric-, Electr-

Enter-, Entr-

-tial, -cial

1. *Electric, electric wire, electric power, electrode, electronic, electronically, electrotype.*
2. *Entertain, entertainment, entertainingly, enterprise, enterprises, entrance, entrances.*
3. *Partial, initial, social, special, specially, credential, confidential, potential, differential.*

Building Transcription Skills

733 Business Vocabulary Builder

gala A celebration; festivity.

concession A stand that sells products in a given location.

lessees Those who hold property under a lease or rental agreement.

Progressive Speed Builder (120-140)

734 PREVIEW

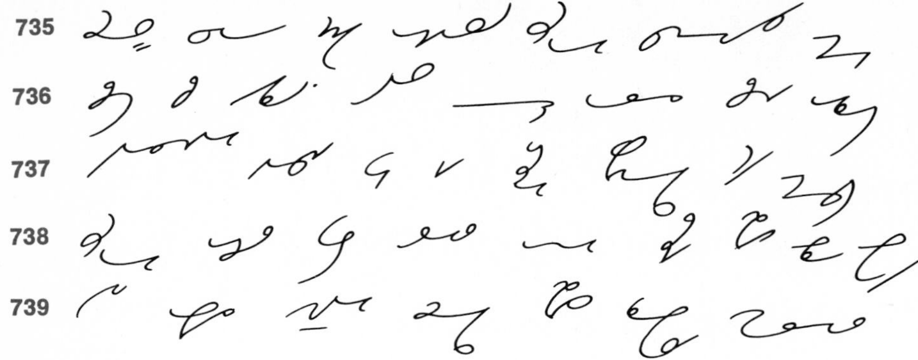

735 *Philadelphia, annual, suitable, restaurant, facilities, accommodate, information.*
736 *Executive, easily, depending, entree, menus, let me, exact, reserve.*
737 *Directors, trout, presentation, short, officers, I hope you will be able, forward, informative.*
738 *Facilities, recently, privilege, thoroughly, workers, efficient, we hope to, next year, neighborhood.*
739 *To know, rapidly, quarters, we will be able, we hope that, celebrate, complimentary.*

LETTERS

735

[1 minute at 120]

Gentlemen: The Philadelphia Garden Club will hold its annual luncheon meeting during the week of May 21, and we are looking for a suitable place/to have it.

Does your restaurant have facilities to take care of a group of 75 to 100 people? We would like to have luncheon served from twelve to one.//From one to two we would like to show some color slides of flower arrangements, and we would need a screen.

If your restaurant can accommodate us, please send me a sample///luncheon menu and give me some idea of what you would charge us per serving. If I could have this information by April 5, I would appreciate it. Yours truly, [1]

736

[1 minute at 125]

Dear Mrs. Drake: It would be a pleasure to take care of the members of the Philadelphia Garden Club at a luncheon during the week of May 21. Our executive/dining room can easily accommodate up to 150 people, and it will be no problem to provide a screen on which you can show your slides.

Our luncheon prices run//from $5 to $8, depending on your choice of entree. I am enclosing several sample menus that will give you an idea of the type of entrees that are available.///

If you will let me know the exact date on which you will hold your garden club meeting, I will reserve the executive dining room for you. Very truly yours, [2]

737

[1 minute at 130]

To All Members: The board of directors of the Philadelphia Garden Club has decided to hold our annual luncheon meeting on Friday, May 25, at the Wilson/Grill at 140 Broad Street. Luncheon will be served from twelve to one, and the price will be $6 a person. Members will have a choice of trout or roast beef.

After the luncheon, Mary Brown//will show some slides of flower arrangements that she took on her trip to Holland last year. Following Mary's presentation, we will have a short business meeting, at which we will///elect officers for next year.

I hope you will be able to be with us on May 25. You may look forward to an interesting and informative meeting. Very truly yours, [3]

738

[1 minute at 135]

Dear Mr. Smith: When you are planning a luncheon or dinner meeting for your staff, come to the Wilson Grill. We have the facilities to take care of as many as 150 people/in our executive dining room. What is more, we serve the finest food and provide the finest service at prices that will please you.

Recently, we had the privilege of serving luncheon to// the Philadelphia Garden Club. After the luncheon, the president wrote us, "We thoroughly enjoyed our luncheon at the Wilson Grill. The food was excellent and your workers were efficient///and polite. We hope to return to the Wilson Grill for our garden club luncheon next year."

Stop in the next time you are in our neighborhood and let us show you our facilities. Sincerely yours, [4]

739

[1 minute at 140]

Dear Mrs. Drake: You will be interested to know that since we had the pleasure of serving luncheon to the Philadelphia Garden Club last May, our business has grown so rapidly that we have/ had to find larger quarters.

On Monday, September 18, we move from our present location at 140 Broad Street to 180 Market Street. In these new quarters we will be able to take//care of more than 500 people at one time. We will have a gala opening of our new quarters on Tuesday, September 19. We hope that you will visit us on that day and help us///celebrate. There will be complimentary refreshments from 5 to 7 p.m. and special prizes for everyone.

Please reserve Tuesday evening for us. We look forward to seeing you. Yours truly, [5] [650]

Reading and Writing Practice

740

con·trol·ling

intro

Acres

busi·ness·es

conj

its

ven·ture

whole·sale
ware·house

intro

de·liv·ery

and o

ef·fi·cient

[124]

741

short-or·der
hyphenated before noun

vis·i·tors
Cove

en·trance

intro

con·ces·sion

tack·le

conj

les·sees

de·vel·op

[142]

Appendix

Addresses For Transcription

CHAPTER 1

1 Mr. Gordon L. Green, 371 Park Avenue, New York, NY 10018
2 Ms. Mary Allen, 5467 State Street, Bridgeport, CT 06604
3 Eastern Plumbing Supply Company, 1800 North Street, Wilmington, DE 19807
4 Mr. James Day, 333 Howard Place, Springfield, MA 01105
5 Mr. L. B. Wellington, 416 Lenox Avenue, Springfield, IL 64353
6 Mrs. Karen Adams, 468 Church Street, Springfield, MA 01107
7 Mr. George A. Miller, Leisure Village, 583 North Cherry Lane, Westport, CT 06813
8 Northern Furniture Corporation, 756 South Liverpool Road, Little Rock, ND 72201
9 Mr. Gerald P. Lyons, Sales Manager, Bailey Construction Company, 589 East Kentucky Street, Chicago, IL 60685
10 Allen Decorators, Inc., 346 Fourth Avenue, Salt Lake City, UT 84001

CHAPTER 2

11 Mr. M. L. Baker, Personnel Director, National Electronics Company, 593 North Ferry Road, Miami, FL 33116
12 Mr. John Jones, President, West Coast Designs, 6581 Cumberland Drive, Fresno, CA 93700
13 Miss Melanie Roberts, District Manager, Master Business Machines, Inc., 489 Fashion Place, Long Beach; CA 90805
14 Mr. Parley N. Sims, Wilson Computer Systems, 428 Parkway Drive, Macon, GA 31204
15 Mrs. Doris Adams, Brown Consulting Company, 543 East State Street, Lynn, MA 01901
16 Mr. James Williams, Baker Brothers' Distributors, 444 West 81 Street, New York, NY 10018
17 Mr. George C. Nelson, Manager, Fire Systems, Inc., 36 Jefferson Street, Muskegon, MI 49440
18 Mr. Ken Flynn, Ohio Electronics, 480 Executive Street, Cincinnati, OH 45225
19 Mr. Richard Glass, Vice President, West Texas Manufacturing Company, 566 Sheffield Avenue, El Paso, TX 79910
20 Ms. Helen Bates, The Harris Corporation, 80 Bradford Street, Baltimore, MD 21205

CHAPTER 3

21 Ms. Carol Taylor, Vice President, Green Advertising Company, 456 South Fortune Street, Montgomery, AL 36107
22 Mr. George Lee, State Highway Department, 118 Fourth Street, Newport, TN 37821
23 Mr. Melvin Holden, President, National Association of Retailers, 445 Pontiac Avenue, Detroit, MI 48207
24 Memorandum from James Shields to Rodney Brown
25 Mr. E. R. Ford, Miller Advertising Agency, 538 Washington Avenue, Seattle, WA 98112
26 Mr. Rex P. Clark, Owens Associates, Inc., 358 Bayonne Drive, Wilkes Barre, PA 18704
27 Mr. Ron O'Brien, 500 Park Place, Boston, MA 02115
28 Ms. Marie R. Smith, Circulation Manager, Reader's Weekly, 621 Peach Blossom Lane, Westport, CT 06813
29 Mr. Robert Bates, Comptroller, Shadow Mountain Industrial Park, 358 West 1200 North, Provo, UT 84601
30 Mr. Ralph Davis, 735 Arapahoe Drive, Phoenix, AZ 85012

CHAPTER 4

31 Ms. Laura R. Parker, 45 Bishop Street, Kansas City, MO 64107
32 Mrs. Wilma Lexington, 400 North Plattsburg Avenue, Elizabeth, NJ 07201
33 Mr. Andrew Young, 356 Ash Avenue, Shelbyville, IN 46176
34 Dr. Michael Brown, 478 Raleigh Street, Burlington, WV 26710
35 Mr. Barry Chandler, 346 Sky View Drive, San Francisco, CA 94108
36 Memorandum from Dennis Lee to George Reynolds
37 Memorandum from Jane Day to Lee Smith
38 Mrs. Eileen Kelley, Nevada State Tax Commission, Carson City, NV 89701
39 Memorandum from Roger Day to Dean James
40 Mr. Theodore L. Harrington, 54 Wilson Avenue, South Bend, IN 46617

CHAPTER 5

41 Mr. Robert Stein, 3101 Rockwell Street South, Chicago, IL 60608
42 Dr. Louis Chan, American College, 455 Becker Boulevard, Camden, NJ 08103
43 Mrs. Reva Smith, 414 Center Street, Orlando, FL 32811
44 Memorandum from Jane Green to Martin Flint
45 Mr. Albert Edwards, 555 Madison Boulevard, Lincoln, NE 68507
46 Mrs. Mary Dwyer, 780 Walnut Drive, Philadelphia, PA 19104
47 Mrs. Millie Swenson, Assistant Principal, Jackson County Junior High School, 222 Sycamore Street, Montgomery, AL 36107
48 Dr. James Jackson, Superintendent, Ridgewood School District, 439 Tollison Avenue, Covington, KY 41011
49 Ms. Eunice Washington, Reliable Business Institute, 302 East 21 Street, New York, NY 10017
50 Miss Nancy Casey, 392 Amsterdam Avenue, New York, NY 10023

CHAPTER 6

51 Memorandum from Alice Turner to Lee Whiting
52 Mr. David L. Franklin, Service Representative, President Services, Inc., 64 West Borego Pass Highway, Houston, TX 77012
53 Smith Luggage Corporation, 579 Blaisdell Street, Denver, CO 80205
54 Mr. Ross Gray, Atlantic Auto Center, 45 Prescott Avenue, Jacksonville, FL 32201
55 Mr. Fred Andrews, International Airlines, 358 Jamestown Avenue, Miami, FL 33116
56 Mr. Edward Smith, Interstate Bus Lines Corporation, 48 Oak Street, Baton Rouge, LA 70815
57 Mr. Dan Wallace, Travel Unlimited, 357 Walcott Avenue, Dover, DE 19901
58 Mr. Maxwell James, 32 Carterville Road, Lake Charles, LA 70604
59 Mr. Joseph King, United Movers, Inc., 366 Hillside Towers, Rochester, MN 55907
60 Memorandum to The Staff from Mary Hardy

CHAPTER 7

61 Miss Cheryl Briggs, Account Manager, Wilson Clothing Manufacturers, 52 Crane Road, Scarsdale, NY 10583
62 Mr. Larry Douglas, 467 McGregor Road, Mount Vernon, OH 43050
63 Memorandum from J. M. Trent to Charles Cummings
64 Mr. Ralph Casey, Casey's Shoe Emporium, 368 Walker Avenue, Winfield, KS 67156
65 Miss Ann Hale, Manager, Nelson's Department Store, 423 South Street, Chicago, IL 60604

66 Mr. Frank L. Frazer, 45 Field Point Road, Greenwich, CT 06830
67 Mr. Richard R. Lester, Wilson Men's Shop, 457 North Kentucky Avenue, Charleston, SC 29401
68 Memorandum to All Sales Representatives from James Best
69 Mrs. Beth Chandler, 468 Northwest Blakely Road, Alexandria, VA 22305
70 Mr. Solomon Briggs, Wilson Men's Shop, 457 North Kentucky Avenue, Charleston, SC 29401

CHAPTER 8

71 Mr. Russell Parker, 346 North Ridge Road, Great Falls, MT 59401
72 Mr. Stanfield Smith, Smith and Company, 355 Madison Avenue, Pittsburgh, PA 15209
73 Mr. Walter Hall, Hall's Repair Shop, 358 Alhambra Drive, Los Angeles, CA 90055
74 Miss Ann Boyle, American Television Reporter, 347 Johnson Avenue, Bowling Green, KY 42101
75 Miss Julia Carter, Advertising Manager, American Home Products, Inc., 116 Commercial Avenue, Trenton, NJ 08608
76 Mrs. Barbara Geoffrey, The American Television Station, 457 Hiawatha Street, Cincinnati, OH 45225
77 Mr. Harold Birmingham, 33 Portal Road, Jacksonville, FL 32201
78 Mr. Leslie Yates, Manager, American Cable Television Service, 45 North Woodcrest Road, Salem, OR 97301
79 Mrs. Amanda Greenburg, Station KWXY, 356 West Street, Great Falls, MT 59401
80 Mr. Herman T. Garcia, Research, Inc., 357 Valley View Drive, Alexandria, VA 22305

CHAPTER 9

81 Mrs. Paul James, Institute for Effective Writing, 13 Jefferson Street, San Diego, CA 92110
82 Mr. Adam Tate, Human Relations Institute, 356 Atlantic Drive, Baltimore, MD 21230
83 Mr. Raymond L. Brown, Western Industries Company, 357 East Canyon Drive, Los Angeles, CA 90034
84 Mr. Louis Allen, Empire Advertising Company, 589 Hallmark Avenue, Cincinnati, OH 45225
85 Miss Georgia Jackson, Publications Director, General Telephone Company, 421 Eastern Parkway, Omaha, NE 68109
86 Mr. William P. Lane, Vice President, Executive Communications Corporation, 36 Kingman Street, Greenfield, MA 01301
87 Memorandum to The Staff from D. J. Edwards
88 Memorandum from C. L. Prince to Dean Adams
89 Mrs. Susan Bateman, President, Consolidated Telephone Systems, 543 Whitney Street, Bisbee, AZ 85603
90 Ms. Alice Christian, Public Relations Department, Eastern Telephone Company, 300 Victor Avenue, Providence, RI 02908

CHAPTER 10

91 Mr. David L. Gordon, 336 Ocean Drive, Deal, NJ 07723
92 Mr. Mark P. Stevens, Suburban Credit Union, 643 North 30 West, Boise, ID 83702
93 Mr. Steven D. Taylor, President, National Trust Company, 357 Mann Street, Laurel, MD 20810
94 Mr. Jesse Masters, 905 First Avenue, Evansville, IN 47700

95 Ms. Paula Katz, 46 Garden Park Drive, Stamford, CT 06901
96 Mr. Raymond Kennedy, Treasurer, Atlantic Oil Development Corporation, 54 Crestview Avenue, Charleston, SC 29401
97 Mr. Glen J. Charles, 32 Hinckley Avenue, Grand Rapids, MI 49528
98 Mr. and Mrs. W. R. Berlin, 750 North Butte Street, San Francisco, CA 94111
99 Mr. Frank Blair, 643 East Fairmont Avenue, Los Angeles, CA 90040
100 Mr. Arthur Bailey, 522 Oxford Avenue, Madison, WI 53705

CHAPTER 11

101 Sam Smith, Esq., Attorney At Law, 925 Sutherland Drive, Grand River, IA 50108
102 Mr. Alvin R. Raymond, 46 Lake Drive, San Angelo, TX 76901
103 Mrs. Angela Davis, 52 West 11 Street, New York, NY 10082
104 Mr. Lynn P. James, 32 Southeast 85 Avenue, Portland, OR 97250
105 Mr. Harvey N. Lewis, 1850 North University Avenue, Denver, CO 80205
106 Miss Lori Lamb, Reader's Press, 345 Park Avenue, New York, NY 10018
107 Ms. Nancy Goldsboro, 64 Briar Avenue, N.W., Chicago, IL 60607
108 Mr. Michael Day, 333 Montgomery Street, Somerset, KY 42501
109 Mrs. Dorothy Mitchell, 53 South Sapphire Drive, Salem, OR 94301
110 Mr. L. J. Young, Olympic Motors, 53 Brookside Road, Brattleboro, VT 05301

CHAPTER 12

111 Mr. Martin O. Allen, Northeast Sales and Service, 468 Taylor Avenue, Rochester, MN 55400
112 Mr. Ray Hall, Computek, Inc., 350 Clarkston Street, Helena, MT 59601
113 Dr. Ralph A. Taylor, 357 Jefferson Avenue, Lincoln, NE 68502
114 Mr. John Gold, Eastern Computer Company, 568 East Williams Avenue, Trenton, NJ 08611
115 Mrs. Paula Lynch, 458 Emery Avenue, Moline, IL 61265
116 Miss Louise Smith, 12 Manchester Road, Savannah, GA 31410
117 Mr. Reed Charles, 2246 Northwest Bonneville Street, Minneapolis, MN 55410
118 Mr. Andrew Davis, 702 Windsor Street, St. Charles, MO 63301
119 Mrs. Mary Thompson, Systems Analyst, Empire Manufacturing Company, 453 42d Avenue, Chicago, IL 60665
120 Memorandum to All Department Heads from Robert Wise, President

CHAPTER 13

121 Mr. Eugene Simms, Director of Purchasing, Great Lakes Airlines, 480 Michigan Avenue, Detroit, MI 48207
122 Mrs. Alma P. James, Personnel Manager, National Surveys Association, 457 Highland Drive, Chicago, IL 60616
123 Mr. Clyde Nelson, Wilmington Air Conditioner Company, 236 Nevada Avenue, Clarksburg, WV 26301
124 Mr. Terry R. Evans, Sunset Supply Company, 346 Sycamore Lane, Los Angeles, CA 90055
125 Mr. Mark R. Freeman, Branden's Men's Shop, 356 Columbia Lane, Bethel, DE 19931
126 Mr. Charles W. James, 157 Madison Avenue, New York, NY 10017
127 Mr. Randy Norris, 456 North Baker Street, Ft. Worth, TX 76104
128 The Honorable Stan S. Johnson, Mayor of Fort Myers, Fort Myers, FL 33907
129 Mr. Dwight Cotton, Treasurer, Masterson Distributors, Inc., 368 Sherwood Hills Drive, Alexandria, VA 22305

130 Quinn Office Equipment Corporation, 2300 Greenfield Avenue, Akron, OH 44305

CHAPTER 14

131 Mr. David Royal, 46 Hamblin Avenue, Imperial, NE 69033
132 Mrs. Nancy Lane, Ogden Nurseries, 465 North 80 East, Ogden, UT 84401
133 Mr. M. H. Jones, 58 Wesley Avenue, West New York, NJ 07093
134 Mr. Wayne J. Taylor, President, Wilson Publishing Company, 46 Starcrest Drive, Shaker Heights, OH 44150
135 Mr. Nick Morgan, Personnel Director, Stewart's Department Store, 579 North Canyon Avenue, Rapid City, SD 57701
136 Mr. Ted P. Milton, 579 42d Street, Baltimore, MD 21260
137 Mr. Keith L. Frank, Editor in Chief, Bond Book Publishers, Inc., 51 North Freemont Street, Houston, TX 77021
138 Mr. Brent R. Bell, Donaldson Printing Corporation, 46 Cypress Drive, Lancaster, PA 17602
139 Outdoor Digest, 360 Wesley Street, St. Paul, MN 55114
140 Children's Press, 346 Church Street, Hartford, CT 06117

CHAPTER 15

141 Mr. Robert R. Winters, All-Risk Life Insurance Company, 358 East Lakeview Drive, Salem, OR 97301
142 Mr. Melvin R. Powell, 346 South Temple Street, Danville, IN 46122
143 Memorandum from Tom Mason to Mary Jackson
144 Mr. Craig Logan, 3800 North Fucia Avenue, Lancaster, SC 29720
145 Mr. George Pierce, 458 South Glen Cove Drive, Gastonia, NC 28052
146 Mr. Ralph R. Morris, General Manager, Independent Insurance Associates, 46 Winfield Street, Wichita, KS 67210
147 Mr. Orson L. Miles, Midland Insurance Associates, 457 East 35 Avenue, Lincoln, NE 68510
148 Ms. Ann Day, 37 North Jackson Street, Philadelphia, PA 19137
149 Mr. James Lister, Sales Manager, Bard Insurance Agency, 457 Fountain Street, Akron, OH 44304
150 Mrs. Lillian Phillips, 457 Cedar Valley Boulevard, Oshkosh, WI 54900

CHAPTER 16

151 Memorandum to All Staff Members from G. S. Evans
152 Memorandum to All Employees from Harry Jones
153 Mrs. Mary Lloyd, Homestead Inn, 258 South Street, Providence, RI 02904
154 Mrs. Janice S. Hughes, 133 West Willow Road, Dunlap, KS 66848
155 Mr. John L. Samuels, 300 North Fredricks Road, Dallas, TX 75214
156 Mrs. Doris Freeman, Market Basket, 235 Burr Street, San Francisco, CA 94108
157 Ms. Kathy Burns, 358 Lovejoy Lane, Muskegon, MI 49440
158 Mrs. Betty Hale, 357 North Barnett Avenue, Milwaukee, WI 53217
159 Mr. David Birmingham, Hidden Acres Rest Home, 357 Dallas Street, Springfield, IL 62708
160 Mr. Lee R. Bell, Commissioner, Montana State Department of Recreation, Helena, MT 59601

Index

The number next to each entry refers to the page in the text in which the entry appears.

Brief Forms of Gregg Shorthand

IN ALPHABETICAL ORDER

	A	B	C	D	E	F	G
1							
2							
3							
4							
5							
6							
7							
8							
9							
10							
11							
12							
13							
14							
15							
16							
17